Process Philosophy and Political Liberalism

To my son, Damien

Process Philosophy and Political Liberalism

Rawls, Whitehead, Hartshorne

Daniel A. Dombrowski

EDINBURGH
University Press

Edinburgh University Press is one of the leading university presses in the UK. We publish academic books and journals in our selected subject areas across the humanities and social sciences, combining cutting-edge scholarship with high editorial and production values to produce academic works of lasting importance. For more information visit our website: edinburghuniversitypress.com

Edinburgh University Press Ltd
The Tun – Holyrood Road, 12(2f) Jackson's Entry, Edinburgh EH8 8PJ

First published in hardback by Edinburgh University Press 2019

Typeset in 10/12 Bembo by
Servis Filmsetting Ltd, Stockport, Cheshire

A CIP record for this book is available from the British Library

ISBN 978 1 4744 5340 0 (hardback)
ISBN 978 1 4744 5341 7 (paperback)
ISBN 978 1 4744 5342 4 (webready PDF)
ISBN 978 1 4744 5343 1 (epub)

Contents

Acknowledgements

Parts of Chapter 3 appeared in 'Gamwell on "The Comprehensive Question": A Rawlsian Critique', *American Journal of Theology & Philosophy*, 38 (2017): 27–48. Likewise, parts of Chapter 4 appeared in the same journal in the article 'Religion, Solitariness, and the Bloodlands', 36 (2015): 226–39.

Preface

The purpose of the present book is to defend the processual character of political liberalism. This defence will bring together the thought of the greatest political liberal, John Rawls, who was also throughout his long career at Harvard the most influential political philosopher of the twentieth century, and the thought of the greatest process philosophers, Alfred North Whitehead and Charles Hartshorne, who spent most of their illustrious careers at Cambridge and Harvard, in Whitehead's case, and at University of Chicago, in Hartshorne's case. It is unfortunate that Rawls is not better known as a process thinker; and it is equally unfortunate that Whitehead and Hartshorne are not better known as political philosophers. My aim is to remedy these defects such that scholars in philosophy, politics, theology and religious studies will be better equipped to defend political liberalism against its illiberal detractors on both the political right and left.

Despite current illiberal tendencies in politics that are obvious, the twenty-first century may very well turn out to be the Rawlsian century. Samuel Freeman is one political philosopher who notes that some of the giants in political theory had their greatest influence in the century after they wrote (see Freeman 2007b: 5, 458, 472). John Locke lived in the seventeenth century, but the American state based on his views did not come into existence until the late eighteenth century; Adam Smith wrote in the late eighteenth century, but invisible hand economics did not spread across the globe until the nineteenth and twentieth centuries; and Karl Marx wrote in the nineteenth century, but the communist revolutions fought in his name did not occur until the twentieth century and in places Marx did not anticipate. I think it is safe to say that pervasive pluralism is here to stay such that either we will find a fair, politically liberal decision-making procedure to deal with such pluralism in the twenty-first century or we will unravel into ethnic or racial or religious warfare, class or gender conflict, and fratricidal/sororal chaos of all sorts. To put the point even more dramatically, in the future we will either continue to advance the politically liberal process of inclusion and toleration of reasonable differences or we will perish. Because it would not be rational to allow the latter option to occur, the *ongoing* process of political justification in a democratic context is our only viable option if we hope to approximate justice.

The book has seven chapters. The first chapter deals with method and hence informs what occurs in the remaining six chapters. Specifically, it deals with the processual method of reflective equilibrium. This method is wider than and includes Rawls's more famous methodological device of deliberating about justice in an original position behind a veil of ignorance. The hope is that the mistaken idea that the Rawlsian method of justification in political philosophy is static will be thoroughly discredited. My primary interlocutor in this chapter will be Nicholas Wolterstorff. The second chapter continues the effort to bring together the twin concepts of 'political liberalism' and 'process' by tracing the origin and history of political liberalism and by detailing the politically liberal views of Whitehead and Hartshorne. The emphasis in these first two chapters is the ongoing character of both political liberalism and the method by which politically liberal principles are justified. In the third chapter I examine the most notable challenge to Rawlsian political liberalism from a thinker who is very well versed in process thought: Franklin Gamwell. Here I will try to sort out the relationship between metaphysics and political philosophy in a way that is conducive to the justification and flourishing of politically liberal institutions.

By the end of the third chapter my own processual defence of political liberalism will be open to view for readers' consideration. The next three chapters deal with alternative views that, each in their own way, are theoretically problematic because they lead us away from reflective equilibrium. In the fourth chapter I examine the historian Timothy Snyder's magisterial book titled *Bloodlands* so as to alert (or remind) readers to the disastrous consequences of illiberal political philosophies of both the right and left. The fourth chapter prepares the way for the fifth, where I examine Martin Heidegger's right-wing, indeed fascist, political philosophy. And in the sixth chapter I will look at some recent defences of 'organic Marxism' by Philip Clayton and Justin Heinzekehr, who argue for a close connection between process thought and Marxism. This contrasts with my own efforts to get political liberals to be more explicit about their implicit processuality and to encourage process thinkers to continue to affirm their historic liberality.

In the seventh chapter I offer a politically liberal defence of both nonhuman animal rights and environmental ethics so as to call into question the assumptions that in order to understand our place within nature we need to travel towards either the green nationalism that often characterizes right-wing political views or a revised version of Marxism that is alleged to steer us away from anthropocentrism. Even in light of the mass killing in the Bloodlands discussed in the fourth chapter and the environmental crisis discussed in the seventh chapter, I think that it makes sense to remain cautiously optimistic regarding the processual effort to asymptotically approach a realistic utopia that is just.

1

Reflective Equilibrium as a Process

Introduction

In the present chapter I will be defending the views that: (1) reflective equilibrium should be seen as the overall method at work in political philosophy; and (2) reflective equilibrium should be seen as an ongoing process. The latter thesis is a novel one that helps to both clarify what reflective equilibrium is and establishes the cogency of the former thesis. It is precisely the processual character of reflective equilibrium that forges a crucial link between liberal political philosophers like John Rawls and liberal process thinkers like Alfred North Whitehead and Charles Hartshorne. In order to establish this link, however, it will be fruitful to first understand Nicholas Wolterstorff's interpretation of Rawls's theory.

Wolterstorff's *Justice: Rights and Wrongs* (2008) was hailed, on its dust jacket, by one notable critic as the most important work on the subject since Rawls's *A Theory of Justice* in 1971. Quite a compliment! Wolterstorff's extremely interesting comments on Rawls raise important questions for how we should interpret Rawls's work. Specifically, Wolterstorff provides a most useful frame for considering Rawls's overall method of reflective equilibrium. He presses Rawls's defenders to account for their belief that human beings are free and equal, a belief that is an integral part of any effort to achieve reflective equilibrium in liberal democratic political theory. Wolterstorff's insistence in this regard (and his own traditional religious account of this belief) helps us develop a richer understanding of the method of reflective equilibrium. Granted,

Wolterstorff is not criticising the idea of reflective equilibrium per se. Rather, he asserts that there is an unacknowledged reliance on natural rights in Rawls. But as a result of his criticisms, we acquire a much better understanding of the method of reflective equilibrium that will be at work throughout the present book.

Wolterstorff's View

Wolterstorff makes the startling, but understandable, claim that Rawls's theory of justice is an inherent natural rights theory (hereafter I will drop 'inherent' and refer simply to natural rights theory), but that Rawls 'does nothing at all to develop an account of such rights. He simply assumes their existence' (Wolterstorff 2008: 15). This is why Wolterstorff largely ignores Rawls; Wolterstorff is concerned with developing an account of natural rights. As he puts it, 'my interlocutors will be those who do not just appeal to such rights but have something to say about them' (Wolterstorff 2008: 15). Because Wolterstorff's claim will shock many readers, we should ask why he claims that Rawls's early theory of justice is a natural rights theory. Wolterstorff's response to this question rests squarely on the work of two scholars, Michael Zuckert and Ronald Dworkin.

Zuckert's thesis is that, whereas John Locke understood rights, and therefore justice, to derive from 'property' (he used the term to include life and liberty), Rawls understood rights, and therefore justice, to derive from fairness. There is no idiosyncratic use of 'rights' here; the term is used in a familiar way to refer to legitimate claims.

It seems that what Wolterstorff likes most about Zuckert's interpretation concerns Rawls's view of the inviolability of the human person. Whereas for Locke justice derives from the inviolability of the human person (i.e. from rights), which in turn is derived from property, Rawls takes almost the reverse stance: justice derives from fairness, and inviolability (i.e. rights) derives from justice. As Zuckert sees things, this stance jars our intuitive or common-sense notion of justice, in that we normally tend to think that justice follows from, and does not ground or serve as the source of, rights. In other words, the Rawlsian account of inviolability is in a state of disequilibrium with our intuitive or common-sense notion of justice.

Zuckert and Wolterstorff are in agreement with Rawls, and against utilitarian thinkers, in thinking that human beings are inviolable. For example, all three thinkers agree that the utilitarian critique of slavery is problematic because it condemns slavery only contingently. Under certain conditions, a utilitarian might have to permit, or even encourage, slavery, as is well known. By contrast, Zuckert and Wolterstorff agree with Rawls that we should condemn slavery as a matter of principle.

The key criticism that Wolterstorff, with the aid of Zuckert, would like to make is that Rawls's defence of the inviolability of the person *should* be based on something like Locke's (and Wolterstorff's) concept of natural rights, a concept that relies on the biblical tradition of seeing a human person as an *imago Dei*, as being made in the image of God. Indeed, Zuckert suggests that Rawls's defence of inviolability is in fact parasitic on Locke's view. In this respect Zuckert and Wolterstorff are articulating the now familiar view, endorsed as well by the process thinker David Ray Griffin and Jürgen Habermas (e.g. Griffin 2007: ch. 7; Habermas 2002), that various 'postreligion' ethicists and political philosophers are living off the capital accumulated during the Judaeo-Christian ages: they conveniently receive a great deal of insurance without having to pay any premiums. Think of the reductionistic biologist who sees human beings as so much protoplasmic stuff, as strictly accidental by-products of blind evolutionary history, but who also belongs to Amnesty International. The issue here is not the theory of evolution per se, which is perfectly compatible with many types of religious belief, but its reductionist materialist interpretation, which is very difficult to reconcile with any sort of belief in the inviolability of the human person. But Rawls muddies the water by speaking as if the inviolability of human persons is not prior to justice as fairness, but is derived from it.

Zuckert is not alleging foul play or subterfuge on Rawls's part. Rather, he thinks that Rawls is led into genuine confusion as a result of his belief that there no more could be justice outside of (democratic) practices than there could be strikeouts outside of the practice of baseball. An athlete could swing a stick in the air three times, but outside of the practice of baseball this would not be a strikeout. Likewise, outside of certain political practices there could be no rights and hence no inviolability of the human person, on Zuckert's interpretation of Rawls, adopted by Wolterstorff. On this interpretation, a Rawlsian would presumably have to admit that 'Hugo would be perfectly in the right to gratuitously kill Samuel if they met on a desert island'. Rawls would be better served, Zuckert thinks, if he considered 'more carefully the preconditions for his own edifice of fairness' (Zuckert 2002: 327).

Now let us consider how Dworkin's thought, as filtered through Wolterstorff, can facilitate an appreciation of Rawls. Several features of Dworkin's liberal critique of Rawls do not figure in Wolterstorff's account. It is Dworkin's treatment of Rawlsian reflective equilibrium that positively influences Wolterstorff, who has complained about the 'inarticulate' nature of Rawls's epistemology, such that interpreters of Rawls have to engage in an inordinate amount of exegetical industry in order to figure out what Rawls means by reasonableness, rationality and reflective equilibrium (see Wolterstorff and Audi 1997: 69, 75, 77–9, 98–9, 109, 111–12, 148). I assume, however, that reasonableness can be understood as the willingness to abide by fair terms of agreement and that rationality can be understood as the ability to follow arguments and the like. Whereas it takes a reasonable person to be willing to enter the Rawlsian original position and to abide by the decisions made there, it takes a rational person to do the deliberating.

Dworkin, however, correctly makes it clear that it is a mistake to assume that there is a direct, one-way argument from the original position to Rawls's famous two (actually three) principles of justice. This is a simplistic (because static) approach that is nonetheless the basis for the pedagogy through which many or most students come into contact with Rawls's thought. Dworkin rightly emphasises that Rawls's more complex processual method consists in seeking reflective equilibrium 'between our ordinary, unreflective moral beliefs and some theoretical structure that might unify and justify these ordinary beliefs' (Dworkin 1977: 155).

On the one hand, the method involves the effort to provide a structure of principles that supports (i.e. that unifies *and* justifies) our ordinary, unreflective moral beliefs. On the other hand, we should also be prepared to alter or even abandon immediate convictions in the face of powerful theory:

> We can expect to proceed back and forth between our immediate judgments and the structure of explanatory principles in this way, tinkering first with one side and then the other, until we arrive at what Rawls calls . . . reflective equilibrium in which we are satisfied, or as much satisfied as we can reasonably expect. (Dworkin 1977: 156)

Dworkin notices, as few critics do, that for Rawls (and for Dworkin himself, if not for Wolterstorff) the conditions that are embodied in the description of the original position are not imposed from without, but are those that we either do in fact accept or could be led to accept as a result of the process of philosophical reflection (Dworkin 1977: 158–9; Rawls 1999c: 19, 514).

Dworkin, along with many commentators, sees reflective equilibrium as part of a coherence theory of morality. But, unlike most commentators, he sees two sorts of coherence. One of these is 'natural', wherein human beings have a moral faculty that enables them to discover eternal and static moral reality, as in the intuition that slavery just *is* wrong. This faculty is analogous to the physical observations in science that are the clues to the existence and nature of physical laws.

The second of these coherence models is processual and 'constructive', in which the practitioner of the type of moral philosophy found in the model does not assume that principles of justice have a fixed, objective existence, as in the natural model. For example, the intuition that slavery is wrong is not a clue regarding the existence of an independent, eternal principle, but a stipulated feature of the general theory to be constructed.

Most commentators do not see the natural model as a type of coherence theory. Rawls would seem to agree with these commentators. Dworkin's classification of the natural model as a type of coherence theory seems to be the result of the analogy he draws with scientific observation. For example, if an astronomer has clear observational data that do not cohere with any existing theory, the astronomer understandably thinks that observational powers have temporarily outstripped explanatory powers and that the task is to try to have the latter catch up with the former so that coherence is eventually reached.

By way of partial contrast, when 'observations' are made by a moral faculty, the situation is a bit more complicated in that it is not automatically assumed that theory has to 'catch up'. This is because in the constructive model the 'observations' regarding justice or injustice are more likely to be contested than in the natural model. There is something gained in the constructive model, however. Coherence is eventually reached owing to the responsibility and persistence of the moral agents who take initial intuitions regarding justice or injustice seriously along with the rational desire to be consistent. The point is not that scientific inquirers are not responsible or persistent. Rather, the idea is that, although these traits may facilitate coherence between observation and theory in science, they are not absolutely essential, as they are in the constructive model. That is, in the constructive model, moral philosophers themselves must take responsibility for the processual drive for coherence.

As before, Rawls's constructivist notion of reflective equilibrium is a two-way process that goes back and forth between adjustments to conviction and adjustments to theory until the most adequate fit is achieved. (On the natural model this might look like 'cooking' the evidence.) Once again, reflective equilibrium is a process notion rather than an algorithm that gives us the right answer once and for all. Although such an algorithm might not be found in the natural model either, it seems fair to claim that scientists at least hope to approximate such algorithmic thinking.

If one's tentative theory of justice does not fit some particular intuition, this should serve as a warning that we should consider whether we really want to hold on to the intuition. Or perhaps it leads us to question the theory. The key point here is that the two-way process of reflective equilibrium is at odds with the natural model, which Dworkin thinks aims at the 'timeless features of some independent moral reality' (Dworkin 1977: 166). It should be noted that, although Wolterstorff relies on Dworkin in his criticism of Rawls, Wolterstorff's own view of natural rights as ultimately resting on a theistic basis (on a traditional theistic basis at that, where God is seen as immutable) would seem to ally him with what

Dworkin calls 'the timeless features' of 'the natural view'. I will argue in due course that (despite the fact that I am a theist, albeit a process one) this gets Wolterstorff into trouble.

What is not in dispute among Dworkin, Wolterstorff and Rawls is that a rights-oriented approach should be defended. For example, Wolterstorff and Rawls would agree with Dworkin that

> there is a difference between the idea that you have a duty not to lie to me because I have a right not to be lied to, and the idea that I have a right that you not lie to me because you have a duty not to tell lies . . . A theory that takes rights as fundamental is a theory of a different character from one that takes duties as fundamental. (Dworkin 1977: 171)

The questions before us are how we should account for rights and how rights fit into the processual method of reflective equilibrium.

Although Dworkin does not give a great deal of evidence of agreeing with the conservative elements in Zuckert's and Wolterstorff's views of justice, he does think, along with them, that Rawls's view is ultimately a natural rights position:

> It must be a theory that is based on the concept . . . of rights that are *natural*, in the sense that they are not the product of any legislation, or convention, or hypothetical contract. I have avoided that phrase because it has, for many people, disqualifying metaphysical associations. They think that natural rights are supposed to be spectral attributes worn by primitive men like amulets, which they carry into civilization to ward off tyranny. (Dworkin 1977: 176)

Dworkin tries to reassure his readers that Rawls's natural rights are not, as perhaps they are in Wolterstorff, parts of a 'metaphysically ambitious' project (Dworkin 1977: 177).

Rather, they are connected to the practical political goal of protecting citizens. Nonetheless, Dworkin admits, to Wolterstorff's delight, that natural rights are *assumed* by Rawls without argument in that they are 'not simply the product of deliberate legislation or explicit social custom, but are independent grounds for judging legislation and custom' (Dworkin 1977: 177). Simply put, Rawls's social contract assumes natural rights even if Rawls himself prefers to think of his view as 'ideal-based' rather than 'right-based', and even if at times he tries to distance himself from any association with natural law (see Rawls 1999a: 400; 1996: 406).

Wolterstorff goes along with Zuckert and Dworkin in admitting that Rawls's presentation of his theory does not *appear* to be a natural rights theory. The argument that it is in fact a natural rights theory is strictly deductive, given other things that Rawls has to say. For example, it is basic to Rawls's theory that there be equal respect for all citizens, or at least for all reasonable/rational agents who *deliberate* in the original position. (More precisely, if the agents who deliberate in the original position are rational but not reasonable, this is because the information constraints they work under 'stand for' reasonableness [Rawls 1999a: 317].) Wolterstorff unfortunately refers to agents who *bargain* in the original position, which confuses the Rawlsian original position with the Hobbesian state of nature (Wolterstorff 2008: 16; Rawls 1999c: 116n10, 120–1). The equal respect that is owed to those deliberating in the original position is due to . . . due to what? The Rawlsian response to this question would seem to involve a natural right to equality of concern and respect, 'a right they possess not by virtue of birth or characteristic or merit or excellence but simply as human beings with a capacity to make plans and give justice' (Dworkin 1977: 182; also see Wolterstorff 2008: 16).

Wolterstorff cites two passages from Rawls himself to support the claim that Rawls's theory of justice in *A Theory of Justice* is built on natural rights. The first is in the main body of the text, where Rawls refers to equality as it applies to the respect that is owed to persons irrespective of their social position. This sort of equality is 'fundamental', according to Rawls. He says that this type of equality 'is defined by the first principle of justice and by such natural duties as that of mutual respect; it is owed to human beings as moral persons. The natural basis of equality explains its deeper significance' (Rawls 1999c: 447; see Wolterstorff 2008: 16).

A second, more explicit, passage is found in a footnote. Its location outside the main body of the text Wolterstorff reads as a sign of Rawls's reluctance to parade the fact that his theory is built on natural rights, perhaps because of the aforementioned fear that he would be interpreted as advancing a metaphysically ambitious project.

No doubt it is this fear that scares away many potential readers of explicitly process philosophers like Whitehead and Hartshorne, both of whom were political liberals who defended the concept of rights, it should be noted (see Morris 1991; Dombrowski 1997c). This is unfortunate given their process contributions to political liberalism, most notably their defence of a version of theism wherein God is not an omnipotent king, the imitation of which gets in the way of democratic virtues, but is rather the ideal being-in-becoming who facilitates the liberal transition from force to persuasion (Whitehead 1967a: ch. 5; Hartshorne 1984c; Dombrowski 2002). This is no small accomplishment given that many or most people in the United States, in particular, and in the world, in general, are religious believers of some sort. Unfortunately, many of them have religious beliefs that contradict democratic virtues. Hence process theism is well positioned to try to persuade religious believers towards a better social world. Process or relational theism fits hand in glove with political liberalism even if it is but one among many reasonable comprehensive doctrines that are compatible with liberal citizenship, including many that are not religious. My hope in the present chapter is to add another process contribution to political theory by explicating the *dynamic* character of reflective equilibrium.

Now back to the second passage, where Rawls says that the fact that the capacity for moral personality is a sufficient condition for being entitled to equal justice 'can be used to interpret the concept of natural rights':

> For one thing, it explains why it is appropriate to call by this name the rights that justice protects. These claims depend solely on certain natural attributes the presence of which can be ascertained by natural reason pursuing common sense methods of inquiry. The existence of these attributes and the claims based on them is established independently from social conventions and legal norms. The propriety of the term 'natural' is that it suggests the contrast between the rights identified by the theory of justice

and the rights defined by law and custom. But more than this, the concept of natural rights includes the idea that these rights are assigned in the first instance to persons, and that they are given a special weight. Claims easily overridden for other values are not natural rights. Now the rights protected by the first principle have both of these features in view of the priority rules. Thus justice as fairness has the characteristic marks of a natural rights theory. Not only does it ground fundamental rights on natural attributes and distinguish their bases from social norms, but it assigns rights to persons by principles of equal justice, these principles having a special force against which other values cannot normally prevail. Although specific rights are not absolute, the system of equal liberties is absolute practically speaking under favorable conditions. (Rawls 1999c: 442–3n30)

It is to Wolterstorff's credit that he highlights this footnote, for philosophers should not be startled to hear about the natural rights dimension of Rawls's early theory. But my purpose in what follows is to interpret this crucial statement in a way that differs somewhat from Dworkin's interpretation and a great deal from Zuckert's and Wolterstorff's static and religiously conservative interpretations.

Finding the best possible interpretation of this quotation is crucial if we are to confront head-on Wolterstorff's claim that the deepest issue in Rawlsian theory is one that is rarely discussed: the fact that the theory is based on natural rights and that these rights must somehow be located within the processual method of reflective equilibrium. From Wolterstorff's point of view, a theory of justice that is based on natural rights *should* give us an account of these rights, and it *should* declare that a society is just to the extent that it honours these rights. In this regard, it is Wolterstorff's view, not Rawls's, that sees political philosophy in static terms amenable to deductive explication. Rawls, Wolterstorff alleges, does something different. He develops a theory of justice that appeals to only one natural right: the right of rational agents (Wolterstorff should say: reasonable/rational agents) to be treated with equal respect. On Wolterstorff's view, Rawls wistfully hopes that if this natural right is honoured, then all of the others will be secured (Wolterstorff 2008: 17).

Critique of Wolterstorff's View

One of the classic debates in moral theory concerns the question of starting points. Should we start with particular moral judgements or with general (or universal) moral principles? We can call those who defend the former approach particularists and those who defend the latter generalists. The debate between the defenders of these two approaches is perhaps due to the fact that these thinkers are primarily interested in different questions. The particularist is primarily interested in responding to the question, which actions are morally right (or wrong)? Whereas the generalist is primarily interested in the question, what are the criteria of right (or wrong) actions?

Both of these views, it should be emphasised, are opposed to moral scepticism. But they combat moral scepticism in quite different ways. Despite the well-known and powerful Kantian arguments against particularism, some philosophers continue to insist that the best way to argue against moral scepticism is to start with particular moral judgements that are widely shared (e.g. that the mass killings at Auschwitz were unjust, that the treatment of Africans on the slave ships in the Middle Passage was immoral) and then try to work out the theoretical criteria for moral (or immoral) action later. Most of the major figures in the history of moral theory have made some contribution to this debate.

I understand Rawls's contribution to lie in his processual method of reflective equilibrium, which in effect asks the question, *why* does one have to choose between particular moral beliefs and general (or universal) moral principles when searching either for starting points in political philosophy (which is only one part of moral philosophy) or for the source of justificatory warrant? Rawls thinks it makes better sense to make use of *both* sorts of belief in the articulation and defence of moral theory. We sometimes begin a conversation in moral philosophy with the statement of a particular judgement; in other conversations we start with an affirmation of a moral principle, as in a statement of the golden rule. There is no good reason to restrict ourselves to only one of these starting points or sources of moral judgement (see DePaul 1988: 72). Or better, given that both particular moral judgements and general (or universal) moral principles are necessary conditions for, and perhaps jointly sufficient conditions for, moral discourse, the burden of proof should be on the person who wishes to crowd out one or the other of these features.

A partial response to Wolterstorff is available at this point. One of the reasons, but not the only one, why Rawls does not talk more about natural rights is that they collectively function only as a *part* of a theory of justice, rather than as its cornerstone, as in Wolterstorff. That is, Wolterstorff needs to manage his expectations regarding the place of natural rights within the Rawlsian processual method of reflective equilibrium. He should not expect natural rights to play as large a role in Rawls's thought as they play in Locke's thought. There are many ways to incorporate the strengths of both particularism and generalism, of course, and reflective equilibrium is only one of them. But by pointing out the hybrid character of the method we can trim Wolterstorff's expectation that if natural rights are in play they must take centre stage. As in process thought in general, reflective equilibrium is thoroughly *relational* in character.

The mereological character of natural rights in Rawls's thought (that is, the fact that it is only one part of the whole theory) is signalled by the fact that he prefers to label his view 'conception-based' or 'ideal-based', rather than 'rights-based', despite the obvious part that rights play. But his view is nonetheless 'right-based', in the singular, so as to signify the Rawlsian commonplace that the right is prior to the good (Rawls 1999a: 400–1; Freeman 2007a: 18–19, 24).

As Samuel Freeman sees the issue, in Rawls's revival of 'the natural rights theory of the social contract' there is a transition to a reflective equilibrium that involves 'separate strands of argument', much like Peircian strands of cable that mutually reinforce one another and unlike the metaphor that a chain of argument is only as strong as its weakest link. That is, the cable metaphor comes closer to what reflective equilibrium is all about than the chain metaphor does – indeed, the chain metaphor has become so familiar that it is usually not even perceived as a metaphor (Freeman 2007b: x, 42).

By considering the many situations in which moral questions arise (i.e. by trying to incorporate the legitimate insights of moral particularists), we are inevitably led, whether explicitly or implicitly, to moral principle and to a region much wider than, but admittedly not at odds with, natural rights. As Michael DePaul puts the point, 'most people have both general and particular initial beliefs' (DePaul 1988: 79), including both general and particular beliefs about natural rights. But the key question is, how are we to bring these disparate beliefs into some sort of consistent whole? Particular beliefs, including particular beliefs about natural rights, can lead to disaster if they are not examined from some sort of reticulative perspective like that taken by the person who aspires to reflective equilibrium or the person who thinks systematically along the lines of Whitehead or Hartshorne. Robert Nozick's version of libertarianism, to cite one example, involves some extremely questionable judgements based on a runaway version of natural rights. Do we really want to privatise both the national park system and the public (state) school system, as seems to be required by his version of libertarian theory?

Although there are clear differences between natural rights and natural duties, an important similarity between the two should not escape our notice. Natural duties are those that all reasonable beings already agree to and thus need not be adjudicated by a fair decision-making procedure. We do not need a social contract to determine that cruelty is wrong. The natural duty not to be cruel holds between persons regardless of their institutional relationships, hence 'the propriety of the adjective "natural"' (Rawls 1999c: 99). No matter what comprehensive doctrine one believes in, if the doctrine is reasonable it includes the belief that we have a duty not to be cruel and a duty not to murder. This latter duty would thus apply even on a desert island, contra Zuckert. In this regard we should notice that Rawls incorporates the best from Thomas Hobbes and Locke regarding the concept of natural duties (Rawls 2007: 37, 43, 118–21, 144–6; also see Freeman 2007b: 418, 422).

Likewise, there is something antecedent about natural rights. These are the rights that are presupposed by the process of reflective equilibrium, as Wolterstorff rightly notes. But this need not be a problem, as Wolterstorff assumes. 'The way in which it is rational for a person to resolve a conflict between beliefs will not be determined by which of those beliefs is general and which is particular, but by which belief seems most likely to be true to the person after thoroughly considering the matter' (DePaul 1988: 80).

Once again, appeal to particular natural rights is only a part of the process of developing a defensible theory of justice. That the original position, or some other device used to develop a fair decision-making procedure, is needed indicates that the critic who alleges that reflective equilibrium leans more in the direction of generalism than particularism is on to something. But the method is hardly an attempt to run roughshod over particular moral beliefs. It is quite possible for theory as well as intuition to be overridden. The process of reflective equilibrium here looks similar to Whitehead's famous metaphor in *Process and Reality*. Theory is like a plane that takes off from the ground (of particular intuitions) so as to develop an abstract account of the phenomena in question, making sure eventually to touch ground again (Whitehead 1978: 5).

The place of natural rights in Rawlsian political theory is further contextualised when a distinction is made between narrow reflective equilibrium, as I have described it thus far in political liberalism, and the effort to find wide equilibrium between political principles and non-political principles in philosophy of mind, science and so on (see Daniels 1979). In both endeavours there is an understandable reluctance to give up on a seemingly well-established belief (e.g. that cruelty is wrong) when challenged by an untested one. And in both there is the requirement of intellectual honesty, such that an inconsistent or poorly supported belief is relinquished in the face of a more powerful one that is internally consistent. Further, reflective equilibrium in its widest sense also involves the effort to reach coherence between one's view of justice and one's comprehensive doctrine, which will be the topic of Chapter 3 of the present book (see Daniels 2015).

The starting points in the process of reflective equilibrium can be seen as shared notions latent in common sense (Rawls 1999a: 327), but this does not mean that they are self-evident. Both Rawls and Wolterstorff are understandably opposed to the idea of self-evident starting points (see Rawls 1999c: 18–19, 42–5). Or at least self-evident starting points, if such things exist, would have to be analysed critically along with other proposed starting points (Rawls 1999a: 288–91). Wolterstorff even goes so far as to claim that the appeal to self-evident rights in the US Declaration of Independence is 'a piece of epistemological bluster' (Wolterstorff 2008: 319n). In

Rawlsian language, to say that our starting points have some basis in our common democratic heritage is obviously not to say that they are metaphysically basic moral truths. In fact, they are clearly open to revision (Ebertz 1993: 196–7, 200, 212). (Nonetheless, some starting points – e.g. that cruelty is wrong – when revised put all of our other moral beliefs into a dangerous disequilibrium.) As Whitehead put a related point, the deadly foe of morality is not change, but stagnation (Whitehead 1967a: 269).

It is often noticed that behind the initial beliefs that get the process of reflective equilibrium started lies a Rawlsian view of the human person. At times Rawls distinguishes between *conceptions* of the human person and *ideals* of the human person (Rawls 1999a: 321–2, 352). The former are connected, once again, to issues in philosophy of mind regarding, say, personal identity over time, whereas the latter are connected to issues in moral philosophy regarding how a human person ought to act and what a human person ought to be. It should be emphasised that, although there may well be useful connections between conceptions of and ideals of the human person, conceptions of the human person under-determine moral theory. Even if Rawls himself seems to believe in a Kantian conception of the human person (as free, equal, reasonable and rational), which pushes strongly in the direction of human rights, he is well aware that competing conceptions of the human person must be considered in a politically liberal society.

Granted, there are only a finite number of conceptions of the human person that see human persons as reasonable. And granted, each conception of the human person makes some moral theories more probable than others (Brink 1987: 81–6). But even if one grants these points, one is still able to defend the thesis that conceptions of the human person underdetermine moral theory. For example, to grant that a human person is made in the image of God still leaves unresolved many of the most important issues in political philosophy. Among Catholics, say, who believe in the *imago Dei* hypothesis, we find liberation thinkers who are heavily influenced by Marxist thought, Opus Dei members who consort with fascism, and political liberals, broadly construed. Luckily, this last group is now the largest of the three.

The treatment thus far of the problem that the process of

reflective equilibrium is meant to solve makes it possible both to better situate the place of natural rights in Rawls's view and to better understand the place of starting points within the process of reflective equilibrium.

But one of the difficulties that any interpreter of Rawls must confront is how to navigate among three different methods or types of justification in his thought: (1) the processual method of reflective equilibrium; (2) the original position, which can be understood as that part of reflective equilibrium wherein particular beliefs or intuitions regarding justice are put to the test of objective rationality; and (3) public reason, which is more restrictive than reflective equilibrium in general because it concerns only those values that can be affirmed by all reasonable beings regardless of the comprehensive doctrines that they affirm. Regarding (3) it can be said that not all considered judgements meet the publicity criterion (e.g. those that concern many religious beliefs). Like the original position, public reason can profitably be seen as part of the process of reflective equilibrium, the part that deals with concepts that constitute an overlapping consensus with other reasonable citizens on the subject of justice (Rawls 1996; Dombrowski 2001a). The original position is admittedly, in a way, deductive and non-processual, but reflective equilibrium as a whole is a process.

However these three methods or types of justification are related, it is requisite that we understand reflective equilibrium itself as including three moments: identifying initial beliefs or intuitions about justice, trying to account for these from some objective point of view, and trying to reach equilibrium when the previous two moments diverge. Equilibrium, it should be noted, is a goal or an ideal rather than an accomplished fact. Thus, we should be wary of having our starting points do too much work for us, as Thomas Scanlon emphasises (Scanlon 2003: 139–41).

Scanlon is also helpful in distinguishing between descriptive and deliberative understandings of reflective equilibrium. Whereas the former enables us to better understand the implications of what we already believe, the latter enables us to better understand what we ought to believe. Once again, the former provides some reason for a conservative understanding of reflective equilibrium, and the latter does the same for a radical understanding of it, as when Norman

Daniels has us notice that a society that conformed to Rawls's three principles of justice (the first principle – the equal liberty principle – plus the two parts of the second principle, the equality of opportunity principle and the difference principle) would be more egalitarian than any existing society, including the social welfare states! (Daniels 2003: 243; Rawls 2001: 135–40, 158–62). Although there is no compulsion to steer the method of reflective equilibrium into the descriptive mode, it must be admitted that the method does require that we account for those judgements concerning which we are most confident, including judgements regarding natural rights (Scanlon 2003: 142–4).

The Rawlsian *original position* (a decision-making procedure that helps us to achieve a certain degree of objectivity regarding the concept of justice) requires that we deliberate about justice behind a *veil of ignorance* regarding the particularities of our existence such that we should decide what a just society would look like if we did not know, for example, what our race would be in such a society. In this decision-making procedure, reasonable/rational agents would universally agree that basic goods (whether material or formal) would be distributed equally to everyone in society, and all of the goods beyond what it would take to fund the basic goods could be distributed unequally, but only if such unequal distribution was in principle open to all and to everyone's advantage, especially the least advantaged. This is the radical understanding of reflective equilibrium towards which Rawls's theory of justice points.

One of the most common mistakes that interpreters of Rawls make is to assume that Rawlsian justification occurs only within the deliberation in the original position. But Rawls is quite clear that 'justification is a matter of mutual support of many considerations' (Rawls 1999c: 507). That is, reflective equilibrium is both thoroughly processual *and* thoroughly relational in that all of the elements can be revised in light of the others.

If there are no good grounds for doubting our beliefs, it is reasonable to grant them initial credibility and a fallible authority. It is not merely *that* we believe them that counts, but that they are credible, as Wolterstorff would otherwise admit as a reformed epistemologist. The stance of reformed epistemology involves an innocent-until-proven-guilty quality: we should be free to believe whatever we wish until the belief is shown to be inconsistent, contradicted by the facts, and so on. Rawls is rightly most famous, however, for the deliberations that occur in the original position, so it makes sense for Scanlon to say that, if we had to choose between the descriptive and the deliberative understandings of the processual method of reflective equilibrium, the latter deserves the nod. At least in principle, our initial judgements can change significantly over the course of time in that reflective equilibrium is not only a process, but a 'Socratic' process. It is because this method is self-correcting that Scanlon says that it is 'the best way of making up one's mind about moral matters and about many other subjects. Indeed, it is the only defensible method' (Scanlon 2003: 149).

This is a remarkable claim. But I do not think that Scanlon hyperbolises here, for the process of reflective equilibrium is exactly what is required if we are to avoid the twin evils of reifying either particular moral judgements or general (or universal) moral principles. Reflective equilibrium is process ethics at its best. Further, the results of other proposed philosophical methods (e.g. the transcendental method) are subject to the dialectical criticisms that other thinkers typically offer.

It must be admitted that at times Rawls gives the impression that principles of justice are *given* to us by practical reason, but because it is *our* practical reason that does the giving, I assume that there is no big problem with this impression, in that human actions are shaped by self-examination and criticism. And it is this criticism that prevents contractarianism from degenerating into conventionalism. Reflective equilibrium is an ideal, it will be remembered, rather than an already accomplished fact; the process of modifying ideas and rejecting recalcitrant ones is ongoing. This asymptotic effort is complicated considerably in the later Rawls by the fact that one must also bring into equilibrium the principles of justice operative in politics with one's own comprehensive doctrine. The complications are especially noteworthy if the comprehensive doctrine in question does not have an obvious place for human autonomy (Freeman 2007a: 6, 27, 38, 40, 240; Rawls 1996: 385).

To say that the method of reflective equilibrium is processual is to say that one always begins one's thinking about justice in the middle of things. One 'starts' with intuitive considerations, but one does not exactly ground them, as Wolterstorff hopes to do in spite of his reformed epistemology. One 'then' moves to the original position, but the rational deliberations found there are framed by the reasonable, which includes the *desire* to abide by fair terms of agreement, a desire that is implied in the willingness to deliberate under the constraints imposed by the veil of ignorance. As Burton Dreben emphasises regarding the process of reflective equilibrium (Dreben is almost alone among scholars in explicitly referring to reflective equilibrium as a *process*), the key phrases in Rawls, which have hardly been noticed, are 'working through' or 'working out'. Rawls spent an entire career working through the fund of implicitly shared ideas in liberal democracies. His working out of the concept of justice as fairness gave him more than enough to do; he ended up contributing more to political philosophy than any other twentieth-century philosopher. Further, he ended up a more consistent critic of foundationalism than Wolterstorff, once again despite the latter's reformed epistemology. Or again, Rawls himself speaks not so much of 'analysing' the idea of a just society as of 'unfolding' it, as Freeman rightly emphasises (Freeman 2007b: 337–8; Rawls 1996: 27).

Because one begins in the middle of things, the preliminary tasks in political philosophy consist not so much in refuting defenders of fascism like Heidegger (although we will see that this effort is needed nonetheless) or various defenders of Marxism (although Dreben does not mention that Rawls carefully examines Marx as a political philosopher – Rawls 2007: 319–72; 2001: 176–9). Rather, one tries to explicate both the benefits of living in a liberal democracy and the conceptual details of what such a society would look like. 'A basic task of political philosophy is to work out the best terms of what would be fair' (Dreben 2003: 336). This involves the search for a liberal constitutional democracy that is stable, but stable for the right reasons. This search, in turn, involves dialectic, as Rawls himself admits when he compares reflective equilibrium to Aristotle's dialectical procedure in the *Nicomachean Ethics*. In Aristotle there are starting points (*archai*), received opinions (*endoxa*), commonplaces (*topoi*) and, of course, habits ('ethics' is derived from the Greek word for habit, *ethos*) that enable us eventually to move dialectically *to* principle. But it is also possible to move *from* principle deductively. Both dialectic and deduction are required (see Hardie 1968: ch. 3; Rawls 1999c: 45).

Dreben confuses matters a bit when he compares the back-and-forth dialectical character of the process of reflective equilibrium with circular reasoning, which does not bother him. But because circular reasoning *does* bother most philosophers, it is better to stick with the claim that reflective equilibrium involves the give-and-take movement of dialectic at its best, wherein conceptual snags are untangled and inconsistencies exposed (Dreben 2003: 338). By contrast, Dreben is insightful when he says, 'You cannot do substantial political or moral philosophy in any Cartesian-framed manner' (Dreben 2003: 343), which is precisely (and ironically, given his reformed epistemology) what Wolterstorff tries to do when he attempts to ground natural rights in the *imago Dei* hypothesis and then judge society's practice against the standard provided by such rights.

I would like to emphasise that Wolterstorff is to be commended for defending theistic philosophy with a capital 'P'. But I am not convinced that (1) theism has to be defended in the traditional, static terms Wolterstorff uses (see Dombrowski 2004a; 2005; 2006), or that (2) philosophy with a capital 'P' is appropriate in political thought, where the goal is to articulate fair terms of agreement among reasonable people with different, sometimes uncompromisingly different, comprehensive doctrines, including both religious and non-religious ones (Rawls 1996). That is, Rawlsian political philosophy is no less important or difficult because it is done with a lowercase 'p', as we will see (Dreben 2003: 346). As Hartshorne puts a related point, a liberal is one who knows that he or she is not God (Hartshorne 1984a: 9).

To those who fear that the process of reflective equilibrium is relativistic, I would respond that although coherence is a necessary condition for justification in political philosophy, it is not sufficient. Common presuppositions in liberal democracies (e.g. that slavery and cruelty are wrong) and considered moral judgements in liberal democracies (e.g. that deviations from equality require justification) provide stable points that enable us to stave off the horrors of relativism. Roger Ebertz even goes so far as to refer to these stable points as 'modest foundations' (Ebertz 1993: 206–7), such that the process of reflective equilibrium can profitably be seen not so much as an opposition to foundationalism per se as to strong foundationalism. We should both allow the defender of slavery to state the case for slavery *and* insist that the extremely heavy burden of proof is on him, not his opponent. As Abraham Lincoln observed, 'If slavery is not wrong, nothing is wrong' (quoted in Rawls 2001: 29; also see Mandle 2009: 40–1, 170–8).

Further, the method under consideration here is not equilibrium at any cost, which would indeed be relativistic. Rather, it is a method that involves a reflective, dialectically responsible process. Theories of justice should be viewed historically (i.e. processually) as involving concepts that are gradually purified in the fire of reasonable/rational criticism, with the best available concepts (considered judgements) providing preliminary standards for further dialectical criticism.

The provisional fixed points mentioned above (e.g. Lincoln's claim that if slavery is not wrong, nothing is wrong, which Rawls cites many times – see Lehning 2009: 34) are sufficient to hold the wolf of relativism at bay. This is consistent with the claim that the content of public reason is not fixed, particularly if it is an expression of an especially dynamic society. Think, say, of how attitudes towards class, race and gender have changed in liberal democracies over the past several decades. But even in the swift stream of contemporary history, the goal should remain to reach equilibrium between our real beliefs and what would be chosen in the original position behind a veil of ignorance. Overlapping consensus among reasonable beings is at least partially in place already, so this goal is not utopian in the pejorative sense of the term. Society's political conception should be publicly, though never finally, justified, as Rawls himself urges (Rawls 1996: 388–9; also see Lehning 2009: 115, 122–5).

Or, more precisely, the realistic goal is that reasonable people would come to agree on a family of politically liberal views, of which Rawlsian justice as fairness is but one representative, albeit the most egalitarian member of the family. The Rawlsian hope for justice as fairness, in particular, is that other politically liberal views would cluster around it for comparison and contrast. It can be seen as a carefully defended 'center of the focal class', as Lehning puts it, in the process of political justification (Lehning 2009: 136, 144; also see Daniels 1996).

It is to be hoped that the processual character of the method of reflective equilibrium will become better known to both political philosophers, in general, and to process thinkers who are political liberals, in particular, such that these two groups could help to further 'work out' the concept of justice, which is, as Rawls emphasises (Rawls 1999c: 3), the first virtue of social institutions, just as truth is the first virtue of systems of thought.

It *is* well known that from the time of his doctoral dissertation and his first publication, Rawls was very much interested in a procedure that would correct our considered moral beliefs against a set of moral principles, a procedure that came to be known as reflective equilibrium. I have argued in this chapter, however, for a feature of reflective equilibrium that is not well known: that such equilibrium is not really a permanent state but a process (see Rawls 1999a: ch. 1; Pogge 2007: 15, 165; Tebbe 2017: part I). This realisation changes things significantly, I think. For example, the familiar charge that Rawls's method is ahistorical and hence irrelevant to the flux of historical events begins to look inaccurate in the extreme.

In this regard it is worthwhile to consider the way that Rawls's views in *A Theory of Justice* were later clarified in *Political Liberalism*. As a result of the aftermath of the wars of religion, some defended a liberal, Enlightenment, comprehensive doctrine in an effort to replace religious comprehensive doctrines. In turn, this *comprehensive* liberalism is replaced by Rawlsian *political* liberalism, which is meant to be congenial to both religious comprehensive doctrines and sceptical comprehensive doctrines. For this reason, Rawls's explicit flirtation with natural rights (and with their implicit religiosity) in *A Theory of Justice* ends at the level of public, political discourse in *Political Liberalism*, even if the affair can nonetheless continue in the non-public realm of associational freedom.

2

Political Liberalism and Process Thought

Introduction

It is precisely the inescapability of religious, aesthetic, moral (and hence political) questions that provides the transition to the present chapter. How can people live together in a free yet peaceful manner in a condition of pervasive pluralism of religious and moral comprehensive doctrines? It is precisely this question that is the focus of the present chapter. However, the purpose of this chapter is not to develop an entire political philosophy on the basis of process theism, which would be an enormous undertaking. Rather, my goal is to indicate the ramifications of *a* version of political theory based on process theism for one of the themes of the present book: the transition from force to persuasion that characterises a just society. This theme is closely related to conviviality or living together in a peaceful and fair way with both those who share one's own religious beliefs (or lack thereof) as well as those who do not share them. Although it would be hubristic to claim to have *the* process view of politics, the politically liberal stance I will defend nonetheless deserves serious consideration if only because the two greatest figures in process theism – Whitehead and Hartshorne – were themselves 'political liberals', as I will define this term. In fact, the theme of force to persuasion lies precisely in the area where political liberalism has achieved its greatest success: in ending both theoretically and practically the wars of religion that plagued Europe in the early modern period.

The hope is that politically liberal conviviality will continue to spread across the globe in peaceful ways as a result of a willingness of citizens of various states in a condition of pervasive pluralism to show respect for fellow citizens, no matter what their religious beliefs (or lack thereof), so long as they are 'reasonable', as this semi-technical term has been defined. Throughout the chapter I will be arguing for a conception of political liberalism very similar to that found in Rawls, whose views help to illuminate the political liberalisms of Whitehead and Hartshorne. I will also indicate how Whitehead and Hartshorne can offer metaphysical support for political liberalism. To be clear, process philosophy is but one among many comprehensive doctrines that are compatible with politically liberal justice. It has the advantage of not only being compatible with political liberalism but actually facilitating the goals of political liberalism in a manner that is superior to rival comprehensive doctrines that are theistic. Imitation of the omnipotent tyrant found in classical theism, often criticised by Whitehead and Hartshorne, is ill-suited to the development of democratic virtues. Imitation of the persuasive God of neoclassical or process theism, by contrast, *is* conducive to such development.

Before Liberalism

Pre-liberal political philosophy or political theology concentrated on two major tasks: (1) to figure out the characteristics of *the* good (the definite article is crucial here); and (2) to figure out how to get those who understood the good into power and to make sure that they were succeeded by rulers who were equally knowledgeable. This characterisation of pre-liberal political thought applies equally to thinkers who are otherwise quite different: Plato, Aristotle, St Augustine, St Thomas Aquinas, Martin Luther, John Calvin and so on. They may have differed in their accounts of the good, but they agreed that one of the main tasks of political thought was to come to grips with it intellectually. And they may have differed regarding how many individuals were equipped to understand the good, how difficult it would be to get them into power, and how best to solve the problem of succession, but they agreed that the overall goal was to get those who understood the good into power and to keep them there.

One very interesting feature of pre-liberal political thought was that in these views toleration was not seen as a virtue. Indeed, it was a vice. The reason why pre-liberal political theorists wanted those who understood the good to be in power was to guard against those who did not understand it. To cite just three examples, think of Plato's expulsion of the poets from the ideal city (e.g. *Republic* 605b); Thomas Aquinas's willingness to have recalcitrant heretics put to death (*Summa Theologiae* 2a2ae. q. 11. a. 3); and Calvin's willingness to kill Servetus, which was noticed more than once by Hartshorne (see Dombrowski 2001a: ch. 1; Hartshorne 1997: 70, 79). An admirable ruler, in pre-liberal political thought, guarded the populace against heresy or against anything else that would lead them away from the good. In fact, not to do so would be to fail to do one's duty as a just ruler in that their very success as rulers was measured in terms of the degree to which they could lead the populace toward an approximation of the good. In sum, pre-liberal political thought was characterised more by force than by persuasion.

Before moving to liberal political philosophy, it will be helpful to consider in more detail Rawls's view of two prominent pre-liberal political philosophers: Aristotle and Thomas Aquinas. In at least five different ways Rawls's thought is indebted to Aristotle's. First, Rawls's overall method of reflective equilibrium goes back to Aristotle's dialectic in *Nicomachean Ethics*, as interpreted by W. F. R. Hardie (Rawls 1999c: 45). Second, his theory of primary goods (much like Martha Nussbaum's capabilities approach) relies heavily on Aristotle (Rawls 1999c: 79, 351). Third, Aristotle's belief that the fact that human beings possess a sense of justice is what makes possible a *polis* is analogous to Rawls's belief that humanity's common understanding of fairness is what makes possible a constitutional democracy (Rawls 1999c: 214). Fourth, Rawls relies on Aristotle in thinking that justice consists in refraining from *pleonexia* – that is, unfairly gaining at the expense of others (Rawls 1999c: 9–10). And fifth, Rawls relies on Aristotle's idea that no one should tailor the canons of legitimate complaint to fit his or her own special conditions (Rawls 1999a: 200–1).

The chief point of conflict between Rawls's views and Aristotle's lies in the latter's perfectionism, as Rawls interprets Aristotle (Rawls

1999c: 22, 286). He notes that Aristotle was interpreted as a tele-ological and metaphysical perfectionist at least until the time of Immanuel Kant (Rawls 1999a: 343). Because perfectionism is a type of teleological doctrine, it comes under the sway of Rawls's critique of teleological doctrines, in general, which is one of the main aims of *A Theory of Justice*.

Aristotle's eudaemonistic perfectionism (along with Thomas Aquinas's) is connected to his commitment to the common good. This commitment is compatible with political liberalism as long as it is expressed in terms of *political* values, rather than in terms of a particular comprehensive doctrine. In the latter case it is subject to the restrictions on comprehensive doctrines, in general, that are required in a condition of reasonable pluralism (Rawls 1999a: 583; 1999b: 142). Nevertheless, Rawls acknowledges that Aristotle's treatment of happiness as an inclusive end for a human life (rather than as a dominant end) is the most influential in the history of philosophy (Rawls 1999c: 481), and even influences Rawls's own treatment of a rational plan of life.

Aristotle's perfectionism led him to affirm only one reasonable and rational good, on Rawls's interpretation. Institutions were jus-tifiable to the extent that they promoted this good (Rawls 1996: 134); and intoleration of those who did not promote this good was permissible. Aristotle thus set the tone in at least two ways for clas-sical moral philosophy: human beings by nature desired to know, and knowledge in ethics centred on the idea of the highest good in the pursuit of true happiness (Rawls 2000: 4, 47). Rawls uses these features of classical moral philosophy to better understand Kant and G. W. F. Hegel. For Kant, contra Aristotle, the religious or the holy in some fashion transcends happiness. And for Hegel, along with Aristotle, the highest good is desired for its own sake and is self-sufficient (Rawls 2000: 160, 371).

The rational intuitionism of Aristotle, wherein moral concepts are not analysable in terms of non-moral concepts and first princi-ples of morality are self-evident propositions, is not Rawls's view. This 'self-evidence', if there is such, is subject to the constraints of reflective equilibrium, in general. Rawls would hold this view even if W. D. Ross is correct in claiming that moral decisions almost always rely on intuitions regarding a balance of reasons (Rawls

1999a: 343, 350). In fact, such a balance is very close to what Rawls means by reflective equilibrium.

There are at least two different types of contemporary political philosophy that are heavily influenced by Aristotle and concerning which Rawls's view can be contrasted. *Classical republicanism* (or civic republicanism) in the tradition of Aristotle affirms the priority of ancient liberties to modern ones, such that we should encourage active participation in public life in order to preserve basic rights and liberties. Rawls's thought is consistent with this view, at least when classical republicanism is balanced by a commitment to modern liberties. However, political liberalism is much more likely to be at odds with *civic humanism*. This latter view is a type of essentialist Aristotelianism wherein a human being's nature is most fully achieved in participation in political life. Because civic humanists like Hannah Arendt see politics as a privileged locus for our complete good, such that without vigorous participation in politics one's *telos* cannot be achieved, it is itself a comprehensive doctrine that must be held in check along with other comprehensive doctrines in a condition of reasonable pluralism (Rawls 1996: 205–6, 410; 2001: 142–3).

Rawls is also affected by Aristotle's treatment of particular vices, like envy, which implies badness of character from the start in that it does not admit of a mean (Rawls 1999c: 466). In a way, spite is the flip side of envy in that, if envy consists in negative feelings towards the good fortune of others, spite consists in the pleasure brought about by the bad fortune of others (Rawls 1999c: 468). Rawls, along with Aristotle, thinks it is virtuous, however, to prefer a short yet noble life to a long life of vice or to many years of 'humdrum existence'. In this regard he uses Aristotle in his critique of hedonism as a dominant end (Rawls 1999c: 488).

It should also be noted that in Rawls's undergraduate thesis he exhibited a very negative attitude towards Aristotle in many different passages. We should stop 'kow-towing' to him, Rawls thought, in that 'an ounce of the Bible is worth a pound (possibly a ton) of Aristotle'. He was mainly critical of Aristotle's 'naturalism', by which he did not mean 'materialism'. Rather, naturalism in ethics refers to turning desire to its proper object, the good. According to the very early Rawls, this misses the spiritual or personal element in ethics. In effect, Aristotle turned God into the good, he thought. Rawls feared that this depersonalising tendency in Aristotle would eventually lead to egoism and to the destruction of community (see Rawls 2009: especially 107, 114, 227 et al.).

Now let us consider another major pre-modern political theorist, Thomas Aquinas. The mature Rawls viewed Thomas Aquinas's *Summa Theologiae* as a 'magnificent' achievement. Just as Gottfried Leibniz rendered the scientific discoveries of the seventeenth century compatible with Christian orthodoxy, Thomas Aquinas confronted the new Aristotelianism of the thirteenth century so as to restate Christian theology in Aristotelian terms (Rawls 2000: 12, 106). Both the very early Rawls and the 1997 Rawls of 'On My Religion' opposed the predeterminism of Thomas Aquinas (alleged to be every bit as severe as that of Calvin) as well as Thomas Aquinas's effort to offer rational proofs for God's existence. Throughout his life Rawls seemed to remain a fideist (Rawls 2009: 224, 247, 263–4).

Rawls thinks that his own view that justice is a complex of three ideas – liberty, equality and reward for services contributing to the common good (once primary goods are fulfilled regardless of contribution) – is compatible with Thomas Aquinas's political philosophy. But Thomas Aquinas failed to draw out the implicit egalitarianism of these three ideas. What is needed is not merely the announcement of these ideas, but also their interpretation and application (Rawls 1999a: 193).

Rawls's view is compatible with Thomas Aquinas's stance regarding the common good and solidarity *when it is expressed in terms of a political value*, rather than in terms of a value associated with a particular comprehensive doctrine. It can thus be said that Rawls's view is that of a (political) common good of (various comprehensive and sometimes conflicting) common goods. In this regard Rawls's view is also compatible with the stances of Thomists like Jacques Maritain and John Finnis (Rawls 1999a: 582–3; 1999b: 142).

In a similar vein, Rawls's view is compatible with Thomas Aquinas's stance regarding the dignity of the human person *when it is expressed as a political conception* of the person, rather than in terms of a conception of the person peculiar to a particular comprehensive doctrine. Regarding the latter, Thomists tend to say that all human beings desire, even if unknown to themselves, the vision of God, just as Platonists tend to say that all human beings desire a vision of the good. Political liberalism sets aside comprehensive accounts of human nature such as these, although it should also be noted that it permits them as long as they are reasonable (Rawls 1999b: 172).

Rawls's view is especially at odds with Thomas Aquinas's (along with Plato's, Aristotle's, Augustine's and the Protestant reformers') stance that there is only one reasonable and rational good such that political institutions are justifiable to the extent that they promote this good. On this basis, intoleration of those who impede this good is justifiable. This sort of intoleration, which is based on (very often dogmatic) confidence in one's own comprehensive doctrine, is different from (very often reluctant) intoleration based on a concern for justice in a politically liberal society. Decision making in the original position favours equal liberty of conscience that can be limited only when it interferes with public order and the liberty of others. Or again, liberty can be constrained only by liberty itself (Rawls 1999c: 189–90; 1996: 34).

A dramatic example of the difference between Thomas Aquinas and Rawls on the basis of intoleration is provided by Thomas Aquinas's defence of the death penalty for heretics on the ground that corrupting the soul is worse than counterfeiting money – the latter of which was a capital crime in the thirteenth century (see *Summa Theologiae* 2a2ae. q. 11. a. 3). The view that intoleration of heretics is necessary for the safety of souls is only apparently reasonable, according to Rawls, in that it relies on one comprehensive doctrine that is forced on everyone else (Rawls, 1999c: 189–90; 1999a: 91).

Likewise, in Rawls's later works comprehensive liberalism, in contrast to political liberalism, is utopian in the pejorative sense and is no better than the comprehensive religious views of Thomas Aquinas or Luther when these are imposed on others (Rawls 1999a: 490; 2001: 188). But Rawls anticipated this point even in *A Theory of Justice* in his rejection of the 'omnicompetent laicist state' (Rawls 1999c: 186).

Rawls agrees with Thomas Aquinas on the good when simpler cases are involved, concerning which reasonable people do not disagree (e.g. that cruelty is wrong). Here he is also in agreement with philosophers who have been positively influenced by Thomas Aquinas like Philippa Foot (Rawls 1999c: 350–1). And he also agrees with Thomas Aquinas that play and amusement are crucial in the effort to moderate one's pursuit of a dominant end in life, otherwise such a pursuit, according to Rawls, tends to lead to fanaticism or irrationality (Rawls 1999c: 484–5).

The importance of natural duty in Rawls (Rawls 1999c: 293–301) also indicates overlap with Thomas Aquinas's view of natural duty. But because the compatibility between Rawls and Thomas Aquinas lies at the level of *political values*, rather than at the level of comprehensive doctrine, there is no overlap between Rawls and Thomas Aquinas regarding the latter's belief that eternal law is the basis of ethics and politics, regardless of whether eternal law is defended in terms of divine command theory or natural law theory. That is, natural duty in Rawls is affirmed without a metaphysical account of its underlying basis. Such a basis, if there is such, is left for those who adhere to any one of a number of different comprehensive doctrines (Rawls 2000: 7; 1999c: 293–301). Nonetheless Rawls appreciates the monumental contributions to a politically liberal society made by Martin Luther King, who held the Thomistic view that unjust laws were those that violated eternal law, including natural law, as in Jim Crow laws that denigrated blacks (Rawls 1996: 250).

Liberal Political Theory

In the early modern period in Europe something of a crisis occurred in political theory. (Outside of Europe there were historically pockets of religious toleration, as in Asoka's leadership in India, even if such commendable toleration did not at the time receive much by way of theoretical justification.) What are we to do when two competing conceptions of the good (in Rawlsian terms, competing comprehensive doctrines) each claim to have *the* truth (once again, the definite article is crucial here) on their side and each claim absolute political authority, such that as a result society is ripped apart in religious warfare? Locke's rightly famous 'A Letter Concerning Toleration' is an initial attempt to deal with this crisis.

Either one could wait until one of the competing comprehensive doctrines eventually got the upper hand and dominated the other *or* one could develop a political theory that would allow adherents to competing comprehensive doctrines to coexist in peace. Political liberalism is the disciplined effort to think through carefully and to justify the latter approach. In contrast to pre-liberal political thinkers, political liberals see toleration not as a vice but as a virtue. Indeed, it is usually seen by political liberals as the key virtue that is necessary for people not only to survive but to flourish in a state with a plurality of comprehensive doctrines. In other words, in order for politically liberal states to flourish, there has to be a certain victory of persuasion over force.

In order to bring about justice in a condition of a plurality of competing comprehensive doctrines, however, questions regarding the good have to be largely taken off the table *in politics*, although it makes sense to debate them elsewhere. That is, politics is not the place to debate *ultimate* questions regarding the purpose of human life, the meaning of death, the existence of God, or the theodicy problem. Rather, political questions are *penultimate* and concern the conditions under which defenders of different comprehensive doctrines can nonetheless get along with each other in a peaceful and fair manner. In short, political liberals concentrate in politics on justice or fairness in contrast to *the* good or *the* truth of any comprehensive doctrine, whether religious or non-religious.

It must be admitted that, according to Whitehead, despite the contributions of liberal democracies to the humanitarian ideal, the long-term prospects are not good *if* political liberalism entails a loss of intellectual justification (Whitehead 1967a: 36). (I have Franklin Gamwell to thank for this important reference.) But to rightly claim that political liberalism requires *some* sort of intellectual justification is not to claim that there is only one such justification. The Rawlsian view I defend is that such a justification could be provided by a defender of any reasonable comprehensive doctrine. For example, it makes sense to assume that there is a rather formidable overlapping consensus among theistic defences of political liberalism and secular defences of the same. All that is needed is sufficient overlap on the assumptions that in politics human beings are free, equal, reasonable and rational, and that they are not means only.

The fact that there are many ways to do this is indicative of the fact that we can meet Whitehead's (and Gamwell's) understandable concern for intellectual justification in terms of many different, yet in some respects compatible, intellectual justifications. That is, political liberalism is a module that in different ways fits into, and can be supported by, various reasonable comprehensive doctrines (see Rawls 1996: 144–5; also see Gamwell 2005).

Two Kinds of Peacefulness

At this point in my argument it is possible to distinguish between two sorts of peacefulness: peacefulness-L and peacefulness-C. The former, liberal peacefulness, refers to literal conviviality or 'living with' others who are committed to comprehensive doctrines different from one's own, sometimes uncompromisingly so. Peacefulness-L is found when citizens in a democracy get along with each other in a peaceful and fair manner despite the fact of religious pluralism, indeed despite the fact that many citizens in liberal democracies defend non-religious comprehensive doctrines. In this regard political liberalism should be seen as one of the great achievements of human civilisation! No longer do we believe in principle that everyone has to share the same comprehensive beliefs about what is important in life in order to get along in a peaceful and fair manner.

Peacefulness-C, or communitarian peacefulness, generally refers to the more intimate sort of conviviality present when one banquets with those who share one's own comprehensive doctrine. Think of the Christian Eucharist, the Jewish Passover or the Muslim post-Ramadan feast. Or again, think of a Thanksgiving meal with family members or sharing beers after a game with one's intramural basketball teammates.

Some Objections

The warmth associated with peacefulness-C leads some to speak disparagingly about the 'mere toleration' associated with peacefulness-L, but political liberals think that this indicates a misunderstanding of peacefulness-L. That is, the two sorts of conviviality are perfectly compatible with each other in that, in the context of liberal pluralism, peacefulness-L is the generic sort of conviviality that can include many different types of peacefulness-C. The politically liberal hope is that one would have both peaceful-L relations with all reasonable persons in a democratic state and peaceful-C relations with those with whom one shares comprehensive beliefs, family ties or joyful activities. To be precise, to expect that we would have peaceful-C relations with *everyone* in the state is both unrealistic (given the fact of pervasive pluralism) and dangerous (in that it runs the risk of encouraging some enthusiastic defenders of certain comprehensive doctrines to ram their views down the throats of those who do not share these comprehensive doctrines or at least to proselytise others in disrespectful ways).

In addition to the allegation that peacefulness-L is too tepid, it is also common to hear something like the following criticism: the price one has to pay for peacefulness-L is too costly in that one must 'privatise' one's religious beliefs. According to those who offer this criticism, it is unfair to demand that one sequester that which is most dear. One is forced, it is alleged, to segment one's life in peacefulness-L between the religious and the political, thus violating the whole cloth of what should be an integrated life.

To be honest, I think that this criticism is telling against some political liberalisms, but not all. The issue is quite complicated and has elicited an internecine dispute among political liberals themselves. Some political liberals like Richard Rorty think that in a liberal democracy religious beliefs do in fact have to be privatised in order to maintain an approximation to justice or even to maintain public order. At the other extreme from a pure exclusivist view like Rorty's is a pure inclusivist stance that suggests that one should be able to include one's comprehensive (religious or non-religious) beliefs into what one says and does in the public square because to prohibit them would be to violate citizens' rights in a democracy. Pure inclusivists are thus not to be confused with pre-liberal political theorists whose commitment was to the good more than it was to justice in a condition of pluralism in the midst of competing conceptions of the good. That is, the pure exclusivism/pure inclusivism debate occurs within political liberalism itself. It should also be noted that among the pure inclusivists can be found both conservative-leaning liberals like Wolterstorff and progressive liberals like Gamwell, who is also a process theist.

My own Rawlsian view on this matter is, I contend, a moderate one between these two positions. I think that one can legitimately bring one's comprehensive doctrine into the public square *as long as* one is willing to translate it into terms that any reasonable citizen could understand and possibly accept. Not being willing to engage in such translation efforts (*a la* pure inclusivism) could be seen as disrespectful of fellow citizens who are not committed to one's comprehensive doctrine, or who might not even understand the terms of that doctrine; and not being willing to have *any* introduction of comprehensive doctrine into the public square (à la pure exclusivism) does in fact violate the basic (first amendment to the United States constitution) right of a citizen to free exercise of religion. I am proposing this Rawlsian translation proviso as a moral, if not constitutional, essential in a just state.

Think of the success Martin Luther King had in translating his explicitly Christian view into the terms of public reason, the latter of which became codified in United States law. Even atheists and agnostics who were reasonable agreed wholeheartedly with him. By 'reasonable' I once again mean a willingness to abide by fair terms of agreement, in partial contrast to being 'rational' in terms of the abilities to follow a logical argument, weigh evidence and so on. To put the point in Rawlsian terms, it takes a *reasonable* person to be willing to enter the original position, but it takes a *rational* person to deliberate there. Full moral agency requires both reasonableness and rationality, even if moral patiency status is far less demanding and requires only sentiency.

Not Comprehensive Liberalism

The upshot of my responses to the above two criticisms is that, first, various peacefulnesses-C can flourish in a peaceful-L state, and second, reasonable religious believers (along with reasonable religious sceptics) can bring their comprehensive doctrines to bear in the public square as long as they do so in terms of the translation proviso, which is meant to show peaceful-L respect for persons who do not share one's own comprehensive doctrine.

These responses are part of *political* liberalism, not *comprehensive* liberalism. The latter is the view (exemplified by Kant, John Stuart Mill and John Dewey) that, as a consequence of the Enlightenment, as people converted to reason they would and should leave behind the religious ages and move towards liberalism interpreted in terms of agnosticism or atheism or merely pragmatic theism. The problem is that this view is just one more comprehensive doctrine that has to compete with others in the pluralist world that we live in. It makes sense to see politically liberal democracies as not only post-religious, but also as post-secular, with 'secular' here referring to the hubristic hopes of comprehensive liberals. (I have benefitted greatly from Thomas Schmidt regarding the concept of liberalism as post-secular.) Political liberalism does not privilege comprehensive liberalism in that it is now clear both that religion is not going away and that reasonable religious believers can and should be brought within the sphere of peacefulness-L. Presumably, religious believers always engaged in peaceful-C relations, but now they can and should be seen as fully fledged members of the peaceful-L society. John Courtney Murray is one of several theologians who have carefully examined the consequences of this view. That is, one's peaceful-C relations with co-religionists can coexist with one's peaceful-L relations with everyone else in the state who is reasonable. In stronger terms, in order to ensure the long-term flourishing of peaceful-C relations with likeminded people it is crucial for all of us to foster peaceful-L relations. Murray helps to clear up a long-standing ambiguity wherein religious believers argue for freedom of religion when they are in the minority and for intolerance of others when they are in the majority.

In the remaining sections of this chapter I would like to explore the political liberalisms of Whitehead and Hartshorne so as to benefit from the light they shed on these two sorts of peacefulness. Their contributions to political theory lie primarily in the metaphysical background they supply for both types of peacefulness. Political liberalism and toleration can be seen as parts of what Whitehead refers to as the transition from force to persuasion. This transition, in turn, is part of the upward adventure of the cosmos itself; indeed, the very meaning of life *is* adventure. Or, in Hartshornian terms, the best hope for politically liberal democracies is if religions themselves grow up and accentuate worship of Love (*Deus est caritas*) or of a God who omnibenevolently cooperates with others (see Whitehead 1967a: 50, 69–86; 1954: 254; Hartshorne 1997: 72–3).

Metaphysical Background

Although neither Whitehead nor Hartshorne developed a systematic political theory, they did explicitly identify themselves as liberals in politics. Whitehead worked tirelessly on the issues of egalitarian educational reform and women's suffrage, causes that led him to be pelted with rotten eggs and oranges. His overall sympathies were with the Labour Party in England. And Hartshorne was one of the founders of the Liberal Club at Harvard, although we will see a certain tension in his political thought: his idealism pushed him towards socialism and his defence of freedom pushed him towards some version of free enterprise. Further, his social background (this is probably true of Whitehead as well) gave him a certain sense of noblesse oblige (e.g. Whitehead 1941: 13; 1947: 13; 1954: 358; Hartshorne 1935; 1990: 69–70, 155, 168). By 'liberalism' here I do not mean the laissez faire version of liberalism popular in the nineteenth century, which Whitehead thought had given to us a remarkably unconvivial industrial slavery at the base of the state (Whitehead 1967a: 34). This type of classical liberalism relies on a view of human persons as independent substances that are unrelated to the rest of nature and to each other, a view that is opposed to Whitehead's and Hartshorne's metaphysical commitments to events (rather than substances) as the *res verae* and to a relational worldview (rather than to a worldview that emphasises independent existents). So, although Whitehead and Hartshorne were political liberals at least in part due to their theism (as in Whitehead's religious beliefs as they developed from the 1920s on), they were not classical liberals if this means a commitment to laissez faire economics. In Whitehead's case, at least, his own label for his overall view, philosophy of organism, applies not only to his view of nature, but also *in a way* to his view of the state as quasi-organic and relational.

For Whitehead and Hartshorne, to be is to have the dynamic power to be affected by others and the dynamic power to affect others, in however slight a degree (see Dombrowski 2005: ch. 2).

In different terms, to be is to be causally implicated in the lives of others. One result of this view is that, although it enshrines freedom or creativity in every event, it is also at odds with the laissez faire fetish for *absolute* freedom or independence. The past actual world both supplies the possibilities for creative advance *and* limits the degree to which this freedom can be exercised. Freedom is always canalised and social. By metaphysically excluding both absolute determinism and absolute freedom, Whitehead and Hartshorne provide the context within which we can better understand the peacefulness-L that characterises social relations with others in a democratic state. Or again, Whitehead and Hartshorne share an aesthetic theory wherein both the uniformity and monotony of collectivist states, on the one hand, and the diversity bordering on chaos in laissez faire and some other states, on the other, are deviations from beauty that are extreme. It is the intensity of the experience of unity in the midst of diversity that is the ideal (see Dombrowski 2004a: ch. 2; Hartshorne 1970: 97).

Hartshorne agrees with Whitehead that if one were to alter the data from the past that are prehended by a present event, then one would alter the subject of the experience. Thus, both thinkers subscribe to a view that could be described as either partial freedom or partial determinism. In this view God establishes optimal limits within which this partial freedom (and peacefulness-L) can be exercised, although political rulers are nonetheless needed to protect this freedom when it is threatened. Both thinkers reject the idea of a God as a tyrant who decides on all of the details. In fact, political power should ideally be modelled after divine power in being persuasive and peaceful-L rather than coercive, although less than ideal circumstances sometimes threaten to overwhelm this ideal. Too little government control (as in the minimal laissez faire state) flirts with anarchy, whereas too much government control dampens creativity. The optimal limits for the exercise of partial freedom in human beings that are set by God ensure that political arrangements are local exemplifications of cosmic variables (see Loomer 2013). In different terms, as Whitehead sees things, 'morality of outlook is inseparably conjoined with generality of outlook' (Whitehead 1978: 15).

Although both Whitehead and Hartshorne abhorred the

mechanistic view of the state, they nonetheless thought that con-
nectedness was in the order of things, specifically the internal relations between a present event and its past causal influences. Both
saw time as asymmetrical in that a present event is *not* internally
related to 'its' future (if there be such) in that until future determinables are rendered determinate by some decision they cannot be
prehended and hence they cannot be internalised. The state is the
result of several present lines of inheritance being shaped by the
same or by significantly overlapping causal influences from the past.

We have seen that neither Whitehead nor Hartshorne developed a systematic political philosophy. Although they are more
famous for their cosmological or metaphysical views, it should not
escape our notice that the most important function of metaphysics,
on Hartshorne's view, is to help in any way possible to enlighten
us and to encourage us in our agonising struggles in religion *and
politics*. In the mid-decades of the twentieth century this meant
that the tenuous status of the state as a quasi-organism, as found
in Whitehead and to a lesser extent in Hartshorne, to be discussed
momentarily, made both communism and fascism as metaphysically
indefensible as the near absolute freedom that is required for the
laissez faire state. A metaphysics that makes intelligible the claim
Deus est caritas (God is love) is efficacious in relieving this agony, a
relief that is not given in the classical view of God as strictly permanent and immune to human and other influence. Neoclassical or
process metaphysics has us take very seriously the historical struggles of creatures as well as the history of divine reception/response
to these struggles. In fact, because of scientific and metaphysical
problems with simultaneity, even perception is historical in the
sense that it takes a finite amount of time to receive the information
that we see and hear in everyday perceptions, as becomes clear to
us when we perceive really distant events, as in the epistemically
present perception of a star that burned out light years ago. In
effect, history should be our cognitive paradigm, not mathematics
(Hartshorne 1970: 55–6, 119).

The ultimate roots of political freedom can be seen as lying in the
very nature of things, on the process view; hence it is important in
both religion and politics to develop institutions that are compatible
with this fact. As before, the freedom in question does not refer to

the absence of influence from others. Although Hartshorne admits that, as a result of entangling influences, political questions are much harder than metaphysical ones, he is nonetheless convinced that mistakes at the metaphysical level ensure that political disasters will follow (Hartshorne 2011: ch. 13; 2001: 93). Equally disastrous, it seems, would be an unreflective fetishising of either absolute unity or sheer diversity.

Different Emphases

It must be admitted that there are differences in emphasis in the political liberalisms of Whitehead and Hartshorne and that these differences could have an effect on how we might interpret peacefulness-L. Whitehead is more likely than Hartshorne to subscribe to the view of the state as a quasi-organic whole. Although Hartshorne has a view of organic wholes that is similar to Whitehead's (in that both see them as being compounded out of organic, feeling micro-constituents, in contrast to a mere aggregate of microscopic feeling as found in a plant or a rock), he is reticent to talk of states as organic wholes. For Hartshorne, political democracies (and other forms of government) are also metaphysical democracies in that they lack a presiding actual occasion that would make them metaphysical monarchies or true 'ones'. A cell is a true one or a centre of experience, an animal with a central nervous system is a true one or a centre of experience, and God as the soul for the whole body of the world is a true one (the Truest One) or a centre of experience, hence all of these are metaphysical 'monarchies'. But a state is a metaphysical 'democracy', no matter what form of government is in place and despite the fact that such a state is composed of various metaphysical monarchies. Although we whimsically personify the state in the United States in terms of 'Uncle Sam', there really is no organic centre of experience in this state. It is a collection of parts, some of which are metaphysical monarchies and some of which are metaphysical democracies. It must be admitted, however, that Whitehead was aware of the fact that a national hero like George Washington could become a symbol that could metaphorically animate the activities of the state (Whitehead 1985: 77). To put the point in terms of political theory, Hartshorne could be seen as having a bit more in common with classical liberals than Whitehead does. Whitehead could be seen as leaning more in the direction of a modern liberal view, as Randall Morris insightfully argues.

The differences between the two can be easily overstated, however. This is due in part to the fact that even in Whitehead the state is only a quasi-organic whole and is not to be literally identified as a super-organism like 'Mother Russia' or the Heideggerian 'Fatherland'. That is, in both Whitehead and Hartshorne there is opposition not only to anarchic and substantialist individualism, but also to collectivism. These oppositions lead us to realise that political moderation is metaphysically grounded. Both Whitehead and Hartshorne were very familiar with (having lived and suffered through the early and mid-decades of the twentieth century), and both were decidedly opposed to, the remarkably unconvivial relations among people found in those states, both communist and fascist, that had totalitarian aspirations based on their aggressively organic view of the state. Although both had severe criticisms of fascism, Whitehead thought that the Soviet system might have been a slight improvement over political relations in Russia under the czars; and Hartshorne was thankful for the role the Soviet Union played in making an asymptotic approach to the political ideal possible by defeating the Nazis, even if the Soviet Union itself did not closely approximate the ideal: the synthesis of order *and* freedom (Whitehead 1954: 128, 220, 294; Hartshorne 1948: xvi, 150; 1987: 44–7; 2011: 143).

However, the differences between the two can also be easily overstated at Hartshorne's end. His greater reticence to view the state as an organism in its own right could be interpreted, as Morris does, as a tip of the hat to the grain of truth (if the mixed metaphor be permitted) found in defenders of free enterprise. But it could also be interpreted as further evidence of his theocentrism, which is by all accounts somewhat more pronounced than Whitehead's. Hartshorne is a bit more insistent than Whitehead (although the point may well be implicit in Whitehead, too) that we are more citizens of the cosmos than we are citizens of any quasi-organic (at best) state. Once again, the cosmos as a whole is an organism, according to Hartshorne, that is animated by a panentheistic God. In addition to the two aforementioned peacefulnesses, Hartshorne points us towards peacefulness-W, world-inclusive conviviality, where the transition from force to persuasion has relevance for, say, our current environmental crisis.

In effect, Whitehead sometimes tempts us in a communitarian way to have peaceful-C values seep into our appreciation for peacefulness-L, whereas there is less of a temptation to do this in Hartshorne. On my own Hartshornian view, peacefulness-L should remain somewhat abstract due not only to the desire to be fair to others in a condition of pervasive pluralism of comprehensive doctrines, but also to remind us of the more concrete sorts of organic reality found in peacefulness-C and peacefulness-W. Nonetheless, Hartshorne is as much a political liberal as Whitehead, with a 'liberal' once again being defined as one who knows he or she is not God (Hartshorne 1984a: 9). Further, Hartshorne is insightful in pointing out that most political incompatibilities involve a conflict of good with good; it is the mark of unconvivial dogmatism to think that the major source of discord is the conflict between good and evil (Hartshorne 1953b: 99). The noticeable unconviviality evidenced in recent United States politics seems to be due to a failure to acknowledge Hartshorne's point here. The problem, as political liberals have long noticed, is the unmitigated intensity with which religious and political beliefs are often held. Hartshorne tellingly admires Jews and Christians who are friends without the (especially Christian) temptation to convert the other (Hartshorne 1997: 67, 77).

In both thinkers there is, on the one hand, an affirmation of the partial freedom of the *individual* and, on the other, an affirmation of what Hartshorne calls reality as *social* process. And in both thinkers there is an admiration for a mixed economy that includes both individual initiative and socialised industry and projects (like universal health care). Like Whitehead, Hartshorne saw contemporary capitalism as ugly. The mixed economy need not be seen as a lukewarm compromise, but could be seen as a use of bold contrasts in an overall aesthetic harmony (e.g. Hartshorne 1953b: 47). It is interesting to note that in Rawls, too, there is an admiration for a mixed economy in that the demands of the two (three) principles of justice could be met by *either* some version of a market economy, but not laissez faire capitalism, *or* some version of socialism, but not a centralised command economy, *or both* (Rawls 1999c: 239–40). For both Whitehead and Hartshorne there is an attempt to avoid the twin evils of abstract individualism and abstract or mythically organic collectivism. There is never a vacuum of power in that, when the gods leave, the half-gods arrive. Among these half-gods are state worship, Nazi power worship, Lenin or Mao worship, but also self-worship or despair (Hartshorne 1948: 148; 1953b: 68).

The differences in emphasis in the two thinkers are thus not as striking as their similarities, on my view. No mere state is a subject because it does not experience. (Nor do corporations experience, hence they ought not be seen as persons.) To say that a state *does* experience is shorthand for saying that the state's members do. Likewise, states are real and important because their members are real and important. The intrinsic value in the world is to be found in experiencing individuals (i.e. metaphysical monarchies) in that only they enjoy or suffer. If Whitehead and Hartshorne are panpsychists, as I think they are, this is not to be taken to mean that literally *everything* feels or experiences. To be a panpsychist is to hold that all concrete singulars feel or experience, but not abstractions or abstract aggregates of concrete singulars. Animals (including human ones) are distinctive in the ways that they can take the feelings of concrete singulars like cells and then gather them together and transmute them at the multicellular level such that, as Hartshorne emphasises, if you hurt my cells you can hurt *me*. But states are only metaphorically sentient. Any whole that has less unity than its most unified parts is not a sentient organism in any morally relevant sense (Hartshorne 1970: 111, 141; 1962: 192). In this regard Peirce's synechism might make sense wherein there is a continuum of unity from a pile of leaves, say, at the low end, and truly organic unity, on the other, with varying degrees of unity in between.

Hartshorne bridges whatever gap there might be between his view and Whitehead's when he devotes an entire chapter to the elements of truth in the group mind concept. The key idea here is that the characters of individuals vary in light of the characters of groups they belong to (Hartshorne 1953b: ch. 3). But a state cannot love us, as God can. Hence extreme organicism should be avoided. We need to resist the absolutisation and personification of the state or the party, just as we should resist the selfishness that is permitted (despite Adam Smith's distinction between rational self-interest and selfishness) in capitalist countries (Hartshorne 1937: 33–4). The process metaphysics of democracy, for both Whitehead and Hartshorne, also involves a critique of the classical theistic God, who functions as a despot and who provides a model for various political dictators. That is, the worship of sheer omnipotence is not unconnected to a hierarchical and undemocratic view of ecclesial or other polity. By contrast, the model provided by the neoclassical, process God is that of a divinity who is not only influenced by the creatures, but who is omnibenevolently *most* influenced by them. It is a poor ruler (or dialectical partner) who only speaks and does not listen (Hartshorne 1948: 50–1, 111; 1953a: 20; 1970: 232).

It should be noted that strictly speaking in process thought the most concrete realities are neither states *nor individuals*, but sequences of events that are characterised by a high level of symbolic functioning and a certain degree of creative freedom. Both Whitehead and Hartshorne militate against the dominant Western tradition of taking individualism as ultimate. This tradition prevented many people in the West during the Cold War from seeing the ignoble side of individualism in addition to the noble (human rights) side. This failure is not unrelated to metaphysical confusion regarding the relation of events to enduring things (which are called 'societies' by Whitehead and Hartshorne). Event pluralism 'cuts the nerve' of even subtle forms of self-interest theory in politics (Hartshorne 1970: 190–1, 198; 1997: ch. 12, titled 'Beyond Enlightened Self-Interest: The Illusions of Egoism'). Process thought involves a social conception of the universe that Hartshorne even calls 'societism'. The divine attributes themselves are types of social relationship (e.g. being affected by the object known or the person loved). And our own feeling is really a feeling *of* feeling at the cellular level, hence human experience itself is inherently social: the individual freedom of action found in an event is conditioned by its partial passivity to the influence of preceding others. We have seen that this power to receive influence from others and to creatively respond to it is spread throughout the universe on the process view (Hartshorne 1934: 193–5; 1948: 134, 156; 1953b: 24).

Need for Ideology Critique?

Hartshorne has argued that there are metaphysical reasons for optimism. On the basis of traditional metaphysics, causes were seen as more exalted than effects, such that the transition from one to the other meant a descent from better to worse. This etiolatry (worship of causes) makes pessimism a metaphysical axiom. On the neoclassical or process view, however, God both causally influences all *and* is influenced by all, so it is just as true to say that God is first effect as it is to say that God is first cause. In fact, effects are more inclusive than causes in that effects both assimilate the influence from causes and creatively advance beyond them (Hartshorne 1970: 108, 127, 157).

The inherent optimism of the process view is in contrast, say, to Martin Heidegger's version of Romanticism, as we will see, which is inherently pessimistic in that, if philosophy and hence culture have been deteriorating ever since the time of the Pre-Socratics, our best or perhaps only hope comes from recovering or unearthing something from the past. Whitehead goes so far as to claim that 'the pure conservative is fighting against the essence of the universe' (Whitehead 1967a: 274). And Hartshorne thinks that unmitigated conservativism is doomed (Hartshorne 1953b: 51). Despite the dominant progressive tendency in both Whitehead and Hartshorne, their politics is ironically just as likely to be criticised from the left as from the right. This is odd when it is considered that Hartshorne thought that politics requires *mutual* sympathy and that he commended a book by Martin Weitzman with the title *The Share Economy*; this citation provides a counterbalance to his treatment of the Chicago economist Henry Simons (Hartshorne 1997: 20, 69; also 1935).

For example, Morris thinks that the political thought of Whitehead and especially Hartshorne is in dire need of ideology critique because it is alleged that their cosmological or metaphysical positions are masks for underlying bourgeois ideals like 'freedom' and 'individuality' (Morris 1991: 221). Because Morris has offered one of the most insightful commentaries on the political thought of Whitehead and Hartshorne to date (and who, Hartshorne thought, surely got some things right regarding process political philosophy

– see Hartshorne 2001: 92), his position here deserves criticism on at least two points, both of which are related to the theme of conviviality and the transition from force to persuasion.

First, even in Hartshorne, and especially in Whitehead, there is not only familiarity with, but also agreement with, the traditional Marxist criticism that market freedoms *as found in* laissez faire arrangements are merely formal. That is, peaceful-L freedoms of religion or the press do not amount to much for people who are starving or who do not have the material basis on which to exercise such freedoms. Consider Hartshorne's comment that 'without a substantial measure of economic equality genuine political equality cannot be achieved' (Hartshorne 1984a: 235). The fact that the measure of economic equality called for is 'substantial' gives Hartshorne's view a family resemblance to the Rawlsian view, with its three principles of justice (the first principle – the equal liberty principle – plus the two parts of the second principle – the equality of opportunity principle and the difference principle). If this politically liberal, rather than libertarian, view were enacted in practice we have seen that it would lead to a state that was more egalitarian than any existing one, including the Scandinavian social welfare states (see Daniels 2003). My claim here is that if we unmask process metaphysics what we find underneath is not something concerning which we should be ashamed but, by contrast, a nuanced and defensible view of what a just state would look like with all three peacefulnesses or convivialities flourishing: L, C and W (regarding peacefulness-W, see Hartshorne 1937: 238–9).

Second, 'freedom' and 'individual', as these terms are used in Whitehead and Hartshorne, strike me as quite unlike the bourgeois uses of these terms that Morris rightly disparages. We have seen above that in process thought freedom is always canalised by historical circumstances (and hence is opposed to classical liberalism's myth regarding absolute freedom) and is inherently social and relational (and hence is opposed to classical liberalism's and modern philosophy's myth regarding non-relational independent substances). Thus, the uses of 'freedom' in Whitehead and Hartshorne are thoroughly consistent with, and actually foster, all three sorts of peacefulness mentioned above.

Likewise, 'individuals' in process thought are identified in terms of their ability to be centres of feeling. Reasonable people can disagree, for example, regarding whether or not plants can feel as 'ones' in addition to the feelings that occur in the cellular parts of plants. Whitehead and Hartshorne think that they cannot; hence plants are metaphysical democracies, on their view. Or again, neither Whitehead nor (especially) Hartshorne think that contemporary political states are really metaphysical 'ones', but this does not commit them to individualism as construed by defenders of laissez faire. Human individuals have only partial freedom and are subject to all of the constraints present in a relational, event-pluralist worldview as such is defended by Whitehead and Hartshorne. The quite different types of real conviviality, I allege, are to be found within such constraints. Granted, some human rights claims are argued *against* the state, as in the right not to be lied to or tortured by the government, but others are argued *through* the state, as in the right to health care (Hartshorne 1937: 32).

Although their contributions to political theory lie primarily in the metaphysical backing they provide for Rawlsian politically liberal attitudes and institutions, at times Whitehead and Hartshorne can be quite perceptive about very particular social realities. For example, Whitehead argues that, because of the relative paucity of class barriers in the United States, those who have, through talent or luck or both, risen through economic strata have tended to leave behind those with whom they were previously connected; deracination is the rule. By contrast, the thicker class barriers in England have encouraged talented people from the lower classes to stick with their class, as in the historically energetic labour movement in that country that cannot be ignored by those who are in power. The result, Whitehead insightfully observes, is that in England the aristocracy is being forced to bring into existence a more genuine sort of democracy than in the United States; and in the latter country there is a real danger that democracy could evolve into an economic aristocracy (Whitehead 1954: 44, 86). Whether Whitehead is correct in this nuanced observation is less important than the fact that he provides ample evidence that he is anything but naive about political and economic realities. The political beliefs of Whitehead and Hartshorne are in the open and available for criticism; there is no need to unmask them or to disentangle them from metaphysical abstractions.

Process thinkers can agree not merely with the idea *that* there is a need to have sufficient material goods in order for formal rights to have any meaning, but also with the idea that highlights *how* people meet their needs for food, shelter, health care and so on, which can affect religious, philosophical and political beliefs. But process thinkers are, like Rawls, typically skittish about the claim that this material underpinning to ideation is all-determining or absolute. In different terms, it is one thing to admit that people tend to think positively about the political system under which they live as long as it provides a satisfying life, but it is another to push beyond this to claim, as Morris does, that process metaphysics is a mask for Whiteheadian or Hartshornian material contentedness. For example, there are independent reasons to agree with Hartshorne in his critique of the Soviet system, where 'orders are not given gently or rarely' (Hartshorne 1983: 220). It now seems that the tyranny and cruelty that Hartshorne noticed in the Soviet Union were even worse than they seemed, as we will see (see Snyder 2010; also see Hartshorne 1987: 139). Hartshorne readily granted that the relatively mixed economy of the United States had been good to him, but this is not sufficient warrant for the idea that we should adopt a hermeneutics of suspicion with respect to either his political or metaphysical views.

'Our vast inequalities in economic status are no cause for complacency insofar as they mean near helplessness for many to achieve decent, healthy, and intelligent participation in social and political life' (Hartshorne 1983: 222). With these words we realise why Hartshorne, like Whitehead, opposed the unconvivial character of laissez faire economics, or, if he did sometimes speak favourably of the laissez faire idea, it was an odd version of the idea that included consumer cooperatives, limitations on advertising, and measures that would be conducive to all three ideals of the French Revolution: not merely liberty, but also equality (as long as it is not absolutised) and fraternity/sorority. In this regard, process thinkers are like Rawls is moving beyond libertarian fascination with only the first of these three ideals. Pervasive belief in the brotherhood/sisterhood of all human beings is especially conducive to peacefulness-L as well as to various peacefulnesses-C (Hartshorne 1983: 226–7; 1970: 221; 1997: 67 as well as ch. 14; Rawls 1999b: 90–1).

Process Liberalism

As Thomas Nagel emphasises, the term 'liberal' can mean many different things to many different people (Nagel 2003: 62). In Europe and Latin America, it tends to be used (along with 'neoliberal') by those on the left to castigate the right, whereas in the United States it tends to be used by those on the right to castigate the left. It is therefore just as important to be clear regarding what one does not mean by 'liberalism' as by what one means. Four points should be made.

First, I am not defending, nor were Whitehead or Hartshorne or Rawls defending, *comprehensive* liberalism as a non-religious worldview meant to replace the one that dominated in the religious ages. My goal (as well as Whitehead's and Hartshorne's and Rawls's goal) is the more modest one of defending *political* liberalism, which in Whitehead and Hartshorne involves the search for metaphysical principles that facilitate the articulation of principles of justice whereby citizens who adhere to quite different comprehensive doctrines can nonetheless live together in a peaceful and fair manner. I do not detect even the slightest bit of evidence in Whitehead or Hartshorne in favour of the view that one would have to be 'converted' to a process worldview or to theism in order to be a fully fledged and equal member of a democratic state. In this regard Whitehead and Hartshorne contribute to peacefulness-L by encouraging religious believers to emulate the neoclassical God as persuasive rather than the traditional God as coercive, indeed as omnipotent tyrant, who is even compared by Whitehead to Adolf Hitler (Whitehead 1954: 176)!

Second, I am not defending what can variously be called classical liberalism or neoliberalism or libertarianism or a laissez faire state. In fact, the Rawlsian view of liberalism I defend is at odds with these views, as the sharp debate between the libertarian Robert Nozick and Rawlsians indicates (see Nozick 1974: ch. 7). Whitehead clearly saw problems with laissez faire versions of liberalism, as is indicated in his aforementioned nasty language regarding industrial slavery and the ugliness of contemporary capitalism. Further, I would like to emphasise that even Hartshorne, who admittedly has an attitude towards markets and economic competition that is a bit more friendly than Whitehead's, defends a stance 'between present-day capitalism and socialism', in which 'the ideal of complete socialization is illiberal', yet also in which the notion that private agencies could manage all business is 'calamitous'. That is, Hartshorne is well aware of the facts, as we all should be, that both unbridled competition and unchecked government bureaucracy (as ridiculed by Franz Kafka) can be unconvivial. In fact, they can be unjust to individuals. Neither of these are fool-proof and neither should be fetishised (Hartshorne 1935; 2001: 14; also 1997, ch. 4).

Hartshorne is also clear that unthinking attachment to Smith's invisible hand unwittingly commits one to a sort of Stoic determinism. (In fact, Smith borrowed the invisible hand metaphor from the Stoics.) But this implied determinism is at odds with process metaphysics, wherein each concrete singular exhibits at least *some* degree of creative response to what it has received. In different terms, all determinists are theologians in the sense that they are positing, whether explicitly or implicitly, the sort of knowledge of the future, with absolute assurance and in minute detail, that was claimed for the classical theistic God. But this is to turn the indeterminateness of the future into the determinateness of the past and it is to trivialise the power of creative agents to render future determinables determinate in the clutch of vivid immediacy in the present. Further, as we have seen, neither selfishness nor an ethics based on self-interest make sense metaphysically if, as process theists maintain, one's purpose is not merely to serve oneself, but to serve others and to serve God, who is here seen as an analogy between a thinking animal and the cosmos conceived as animate. As before, the political consequences of metaphysical blunders can be catastrophic, it seems (Hartshorne 1937: 151; 1948: 133; 1953b: 108; 1970: 220).

Third, just as peacefulness-L acts as an umbrella for various peacefulnesses-C, analogously peacefulness-W shelters various peacefulnesses-L and *a fortiori* peacefulnesses-C. Whitehead's way of articulating peacefulness-W is in terms of his triadic theory of value, wherein intrinsic (i.e. not merely instrumental) value is found in sentient individuals, others *and the whole* − God (e.g. Whitehead 1968: 117; also see Henning 2005) and in terms of what he calls the 'solidarity of the universe' (Whitehead 1978: 56). And Hartshorne's way of understanding peacefulness-W is in terms of his belief that God is the mind or soul who animates not this or that particular body, but the whole embodied cosmos (see Dombrowski 2005: ch. 1). It is no accident that the very first philosophical dissertation in environmental ethics was written from the point of view of process thought (Armstrong 1976) and that environmentalism has flourished in process circles in various publications. The reticulative vision encouraged by Whitehead and Hartshorne facilitates not only environmental justice, but also liberal international justice. The problems here are largely conceptual: crises in international justice and environmental justice are very often the result of a failure to even imagine, much less to explicate and defend, an organic reality greater than the state.

And fourth, it is no accident that both Whitehead and Hartshorne were political liberals in that the overall method that is operative in political liberalism (reflective equilibrium) is itself thoroughly processual and fallibilist, as we have seen. The Rawlsian method of reflective equilibrium is an attempt to move away from the proof paradigm in political philosophy, wherein the goal is to search for absolutely certain starting points and then to deduce secure political conclusions from them. Period. By contrast, we have also seen that reflective equilibrium is similar to Aristotelian dialectic, wherein one starts from intuition or habit or prevailing opinion, but then these starting points are put to the test by theory and empirical investigation and counterexamples (see Rawls 1999b: 45). If disequilibrium occurs between, say, intuition and theory, then further inquiry is required in order to more closely approximate equilibrium between the two. Nothing is held to be fixed in advance in that intuition or public opinion may change and theory may be criticised in the *ongoing process* of dialectical exchange. That is, the method of reflective equilibrium is a self-correcting procedure in the continuing effort to live together in a peaceful and fair manner in a peaceful-L state (see Dombrowski 2011: ch. 1; also see Malone-France 2012: ch. 6). When the transition from force to persuasion or peacefulness-L breaks down, the tendency of political liberals like Whitehead, Hartshorne, Rawls and me is to urge that further civil discourse and rational inquiry are required.

From a methodological point of view, political liberalism is not so much a political programme as it is a *process* for both adjudication of disputes and facilitation of convivialities when and where these exist.

3

Gamwell on 'The Comprehensive Question': A Rawlsian Critique

Introduction

We have seen that Rawls is widely acknowledged to be the most influential political philosopher of the twentieth century. But the implications of his views for both religious belief and religious believers are hotly contested. Some think that he is largely on the right track, indeed that he solves many of the traditional (and bloody) problems regarding the relationship between politics and religion (see Dombrowski 2001a; 2011; Freeman 2007b; Pogge 2007). Others are critical of his approach (see Weithman 2002; 2011; Wolterstorff 2008; Eberle 2002). Perhaps the most insightful of these critics of Rawls, who argues from the perspective of a process metaphysical view or a comprehensive neoclassical religious doctrine, is Franklin Gamwell. It will be the purpose of the present chapter to both order Gamwell's criticisms of Rawls, which are spread across seven books that span thirty-two years, and to offer a Rawlsian response to Gamwell's criticisms.

Some terminological issues should be treated at the outset. By 'comprehensive doctrine' Rawls means an overall view of what is valuable in life and that covers all recognised values and virtues in a rather precisely articulated system. One reason he uses this label rather than 'religion' is to make it clear that, in addition to religious comprehensive doctrines, there are also non-religious, or at least non-theistic, comprehensive doctrines affirmed by many reasonable citizens in contemporary democratic societies.

Rawls's 'comprehensive doctrine' has at least a family resemblance to Gamwell's 'comprehensive question' or the 'comprehensive order of reflection', where human beings question and reflect on what the meaning to human life is in the context of the wider cosmos. Rawls's 'comprehensive doctrine' is also similar to what Gamwell calls a 'metaphysical view', but this latter designation also has a more precise meaning in Gamwell. To be specific, metaphysics is the critical study of what must be the case regarding *everything* that exists. Gamwell's metaphysics is transcendental in the sense that it studies what is the case in *every* experience of the real, rather than concerning itself with what is outside of or beyond experience.

Thus, it makes sense from a Rawlsian point of view to say that Gamwell's process metaphysics is but one among many comprehensive doctrines in a contemporary liberal democracy. Gamwell does not accept this characterisation of his position, but not because of any religious intolerance on his part. This is why his thought is so very interesting and poses a challenge to Rawlsian theory.

That is, Gamwell defends a view of metaphysics that purports to stand above the conflicting comprehensive doctrines in contemporary democratic societies; hence he implies an exemption from the restrictions Rawls places on comprehensive doctrines. In effect, there are two different senses of 'metaphysics' that have to be distinguished. Metaphysics-1 refers to any general worldview that orders values and virtues and is roughly synonymous with Rawls's 'comprehensive doctrine', whereas metaphysics-2 refers to the study of the really abstract and ubiquitous features of *all* reality. Or again, metaphysics-2 refers to the discipline that discovers and articulates the general ideas that are indispensable to the analysis of *everything* that happens. Gamwell uses 'metaphysics' in both senses, although his primary interest is metaphysics-2, the type of metaphysics that is the subject of the above-mentioned exemption. While metaphysics-1 roughly corresponds to Rawls's 'comprehensive doctrine', it is only metaphysics-2 that is *truly* comprehensive, as Gamwell insightfully sees things.

Readers of Gamwell's books have to come to terms with two main areas: first, his view, derived from Charles Hartshorne, that if a metaphysical-2 claim is true, it is true about everything; and second, his view that there is a tight connection between metaphysics-2 and political philosophy. I will pull these two areas apart.

Enthusiastic (Hartshornian) support for Gamwell as a metaphysician does not necessarily mean the same for Gamwell's thesis that a response to 'the comprehensive question' is integral to any effort to theoretically understand what a just society would be like. My (Rawlsian) critique of Gamwell as a democratic political philosopher is nonetheless compatible with the belief that he is the most insightful thinker to date of those who think that it is fitting that one unqualifiedly bring one's comprehensive doctrine to bear on political questions, even in a condition of pervasive pluralism. That is, the real comprehensiveness of what Gamwell calls 'the comprehensive question' both counts in favour of his metaphysics-2 and creates problems for his political philosophy.

My procedure will be to lay out eight criticisms that I detect in Gamwell's profound reading of Rawls (five of which are explicitly directed at Rawls and three of which point the way towards Gamwell's own view), then to offer a spirited Rawlsian response to these eight criticisms.

Gamwell on Separation

Rawls is well known for his distinction between the concept of justice (or the right), on the one hand, and the concept of the good, on the other. These two must be separated, he thinks, because of the plurality of opposed concepts of the good that reasonable people defend, sometimes uncompromisingly so. But such opposition, he thinks, need not be a political problem if we can nonetheless agree on democratic principles and procedures that will enable us to live in peace and prosperity and in a fair manner. That is, Rawls thinks that although we cannot agree (or at least that we do not in fact agree) regarding the comprehensive *good* – some are Catholics, some are Jews, some are Buddhists, some are agnostics, and so on – we can (and largely do, in democratic societies) agree regarding the procedures that should be followed in a *just* society.

For at least five nuanced reasons Gamwell is not convinced. First, Rawls's separation of justice from the comprehensive good violates those who defend such a comprehensive doctrine, at least if it is truly comprehensive or metaphysical (metaphysics-2).

Relatively early in his career Gamwell indicated that he saw political liberalism, or at least certain versions of political liberalism, as 'seriously flawed'. This criticism of political liberalism was due to his desire to return to 'the religious character of the comprehensive religious variable'. By this variable he meant that in terms of which all possible existents are understood and evaluated. On this view, the public world only becomes a meaningful concept when diverse and fragmentary human communications are part of a divine, comprehensive unity-in-diversity. That is, a maximal public ideal finds its justification in God (see Gamwell 1984: ix, 151).

Later Gamwell indicated, and no doubt he always realised, that liberalism in general arose as a specific kind of political theory that was meant to deal with the insistence and persistence of religious diversity, both between religious communities and within them. The religious wars of the early modern period were, as Gamwell notes, ruinous. So in addition to the need for comprehensiveness there is also the fact of diversity, the latter of which must in some fashion be tolerated if politics is to avoid both anarchy and coerced uniformity. The distinctive task of liberal theory has been to define the terms on which religious plurality can be civilised (Gamwell 2002: 238). To put the point in interrogative fashion, how can toleration be given reasonable grounds (Gamwell 1995: 9)?

The Rawlsian, politically liberal response to this question, Gamwell thinks, violates popular sovereignty by offering a freestanding view that is independent of, or separated from, ideas of the comprehensive good. The violation presumably occurs with respect to those like Gamwell (and myself) who defend comprehensive doctrines that really are comprehensive (i.e. constitute a metaphysics-2 view), in contrast to those who hold 'comprehensive' doctrines that are only nominally so. Although the Rawlsian freestanding view is very abstract, it nonetheless fails to be 'self-democratising' in light of the above alleged violation (Gamwell 2005: 41). Here Gamwell enlists Jürgen Habermas's support in his criticism of Rawls: practical discourse is compromised if the state teaches that *only its* liberal conception of justice can be redeemed (Gamwell 2002: 248; also see Habermas 2002; finally, see Gamwell 2015: especially 68–71, 94–6, 105–9).

Granted, 'liberalism' can mean many different things to many different thinkers. On one use of the term, any form of democracy where there is government by the people is liberal; on another use the term refers to the view that politics is instrumental to diverse ends; on still another it refers to maximal want-satisfaction. When Gamwell criticises political liberalism, what he has in mind is the idea that there should be a separation of principles of justice from the comprehensive good, a separation that is unfair to those who defend truly comprehensive doctrines because the very idea of the separation of justice from the good militates against comprehensiveness; the concept of a freestanding concept of the just does the same.

Second, Rawls's refusal to consider comprehensive doctrines in politics amounts to a denial that any such doctrine could be true.

Gamwell's critique is rooted in a concern voiced by Whitehead in the 1930s: that democracy without metaphysics loses its intellectual justification (Whitehead 1967a: 36). We will see that the issue here is whether 'without metaphysics' necessarily means 'anti-metaphysics' and whether 'without comprehensive religious backing' means 'anti-religious'. Gamwell thinks that the Rawlsian view *is* anti-metaphysical and anti-religious; indeed, it is a type of secularism (Gamwell 2011: essay 2, part 1).

In this regard Rawls is, as Gamwell sees things, in the lineage of Kantian thinkers who assert that rights are independent of any inclusive *telos* (end or purpose), thus democratic rights are solely the creatures of historical context. As Gamwell sees things, however, the moral status of human beings cannot even be articulated, much less defended, in a non-teleological way. Thus, the Kantian–Rawlsian project is self-destructive because religious comprehensive doctrines give to their adherents the very terms for political evaluation.

By seeking neither to assert nor to deny any particular comprehensive doctrine, Rawls ends up simply refusing (or more forcefully, denying) the comprehensive order of reflection. For Gamwell, there is no relevant distinction between refusing to consider comprehensive doctrines and denying their legitimacy.

Although I think that there *is* an important distinction here, it should not escape our notice that in the effort to conflate refusal and denial Gamwell sheds light on the complex development of Rawls's thought. Gamwell insightfully wonders about the transition from Rawls's early essay 'Two Concepts of Rules' (1955), to *A Theory of Justice* (1971), to *Political Liberalism* (1993). In the early essay Rawls defends the idea that the justification of a practice, in contrast to the justification of a particular action falling under it, appeals to utilitarian principles (see Rawls, 'Two Concepts of Rules', in 1999a; also see 1999c; 1996). Yet by the time of *A Theory of Justice* non-teleological principles are highlighted. Why? Gamwell floats the hypothesis that Rawls was spellbound by the Kantian conviction that political theory must be independent of a metaphysical *telos*. Although he left the impression that he was a comprehensive liberal in *A Theory of Justice* (as before, with comprehensive liberalism, in contrast to political liberalism, consisting in an overall view that competes with other comprehensive doctrines for our allegiance), the fact that he was uneasy about this impression, along with the fact that he altered his view in *Political Liberalism*, highlights this Kantian conviction, which is the ultimate object of Gamwell's criticisms (Gamwell 2002: 185–7, 304–5).

Third, Rawlsian separation of the just from the good means that individuals' conceptions of the good are privatised and hence relativised.

The separation that leads to privatisation is a problem, according to Gamwell, because religious conviction involves a self-understanding that should be exemplified without duplicity in *all* human activity, including political activity. (This is why Gamwell opts for metaphysics-2 and for a comprehensive doctrine that is truly so.) Indeed, Gamwell labels Rawls's stance, by contrast, as 'the privatist view'.

Because Rawls denies the comprehensive order of reflection, he implicitly asserts that political activity is always, even in the condemnation of slavery, relative to given historical and cultural conditions. In anticipation of the fifth criticism below, Gamwell thinks that relativism itself is ironically a comprehensive doctrine to the extent that it asserts a moral comparison of human activities: *all* of these activities are historically and culturally specific. We will see that Gamwell thinks that all such responses to the comprehensive question are self-refuting.

To sum up the criticisms thus far: privatist, putative refusal to consider the comprehensive order of reflection *is* a denial, Gamwell thinks, and such a denial oddly leads to comprehensive, oppressive relativism: 'To assert that one's choice of a purpose is never bound by a norm is also to assert a norm . . . namely, that human authenticity as such is always and in all respects particular or relative to the activity in question' (Gamwell 1995: 141, also 139–43).

Fourth, as a result of the privatisation and relativisation of the good, the most that one can hope for on a Rawlsian basis is a mere *modus vivendi* (or a Hobbesian truce that is temporary because there is no genuine meeting of minds). That is, a stronger overlapping consensus (where those with differing comprehensive doctrines nonetheless agree on the concept of justice) is not possible.

To be precise, Gamwell admits that Rawls's view is compatible with some 'comprehensive' doctrines, but only those that are not truly comprehensive. That is, his political liberalism is incompatible with comprehensive doctrines that have a universalist conception of justice. Democracy implies a truly comprehensive purpose, on Gamwell's interpretation, hence the title of one of his books alludes to democracy *on purpose*. The strongest terms he uses are the following ones: a 'nonteleological theory of justice' is as self-refuting as a 'nontheoretical theory of justice' (Gamwell 2002: 277–9). Without a *telos* justice is purely (Gamwell might say 'merely') procedural; hence the best we could hope for under a non-teleological theory of justice would be a *modus vivendi*, contra Rawls's obvious intent to be arguing for something more than a *modus vivendi* in terms of an overlapping consensus (Gamwell 2005: 42).

Without metaphysical backing, justice as fairness has to remain a type of *modus vivendi*, Gamwell thinks, and cannot rise to the level of overlapping consensus. If we get along with each other on a Rawlsian basis, it has to be due to a contingent and fortunate convergence of interests rather than to an adherence to commonly held and necessarily true principles (Gamwell 1995: 66–7).

As a result, Gamwell thinks that no defender of a really comprehensive doctrine could ever accept an explicitly freestanding and implicitly *modus vivendi* conception of justice. On Gamwell's view, it is the comprehensive doctrine that justifies the political principles rather than the other way around. In fact, it is *only* a true comprehensive doctrine that could justify political principles. Gamwell puts the point directly and controversially as follows:

'there is simply no such thing as a reasonable religious conviction or reasonable answer to the comprehensive question' (Gamwell 1995: 66–7). Here he is assuming the aforementioned Rawlsian distinction between the reasonable and the rational. The former refers to a willingness to abide by fair terms of agreement, and the latter refers to the ability to follow arguments and to adjust means to ends. Simply put, it takes a reasonable person to willingly enter the Rawlsian original position (the place where the hypothetical decision making procedure takes place in the effort to find the abstract principles that would obtain in a just society) and a rational person to deliberate there.

But even with this distinction in mind it is easy to misunderstand Gamwell's point. The quotation in the previous paragraph could easily be taken to mean that Gamwell is opposed to toleration of religious beliefs (or non-beliefs) different from his own. Nothing could be further from the truth. I think that what Gamwell means is that when doing metaphysics-2 one is dealing with those most abstract features of all reality and of our experiences of it, such that when doing metaphysics-2 there is simply no need to reasonably adjudicate disputes regarding more concrete and more contentious aspects of comprehensive doctrines found at the level of metaphysics-1.

It is true that there are also differences of opinion regarding metaphysics-2 claims (e.g. regarding whether becoming should take precedence over being), but Gamwell thinks that *these* differences are not the sort that people literally fight over or that destroy the basis for a just society. These differences of opinion concern questions as to whether 'Something exists' or 'God exists' are necessarily true. I agree with Gamwell's affirmative responses to both of these questions (see Dombrowski 2006), although we will see that I am a bit skittish as to whether the latter question is as politically innocuous as Gamwell thinks.

Fifth, nonetheless, despite what has been said in the above four criticisms, Rawls's view of justice does, in spite of itself, involve a comprehensive doctrine; in fact, it amounts to an established religion.

Because of the counter-intuitiveness of this criticism, it will be worthwhile to try to understand Gamwell's point. The major problem, and an unnoticed one, with Rawls's theory, he thinks, is that any proposed separation of justice and the good implies a concept of justice that involves *its own* concept of the good, hence any such proposed separation involves a performative self-contradiction (Gamwell 2005: 119; also see David Ray Griffin 2001). That is, the separation of justice from concepts of the comprehensive good nonetheless itself involves the creation of another such concept, Gamwell thinks, hence such a separation cannot unify politically a diversity of such concepts (Gamwell 2011: essay 5).

Gamwell thinks that the very statement that no universal concept is valid is itself a statement of what is universally the case (Gamwell 2002: 272–4). The attempt to avoid metaphysics is futile, Gamwell thinks, because the denial of all universalist concepts is contradicted by the confident assertion of a supposedly non-universalist one. Here Gamwell pushes Rorty and Rawls together in a joint denial of the claim that comprehensive doctrines that are truly comprehensive are reasonable. The problem with this view, on Gamwell's grounds, is that democratic discourse itself requires a substantive principle that is universal; in Rawlsian language, it requires a comprehensive doctrine (Gamwell 2002: 275–6; 1995: 136; also see Rorty 2008).

All of Rawls's talk of separation is merely on the surface in that Gamwell thinks that, by refusing or denying the comprehensive question, Rawls ironically ends up with a metaphysical position: that no metaphysics is ever required for the purposes of politics (Gamwell 1995: 47–58). 'Irony' may be too weak a word here because Gamwell thinks that the Rawlsian project is plagued with 'internal incoherence' (Gamwell 1995: 68, 136–7).

Gamwell detects in Rawls an awareness of the criticism being levelled against him (Rawls 1996: 29). The Rawlsian distinction between the reasonable and the rationally discoverable true must itself be true for Rawlsian political philosophy to make sense. That is, Rawls cannot consistently deny metaphysical commitments. And, as before, metaphysics-2 is conceived by Gamwell not as the articulation of just any general view but, in Hartshornian fashion, as the articulation of the a priori or necessary conditions of human (and other) activity. On this basis he is willing to grant to Rawls that no *particular* metaphysical view has to be affirmed if some of the traditional metaphysical views are kept in mind (e.g. Cartesian vs Leibnizian), but regarding the most comprehensive aspects of comprehensive views Rawls cannot remain neutral (Gamwell 1995: 58–9).

Of course, some religious adherents are reasonable and some are not, despite the language above regarding the claim that there is no such thing as a reasonable answer to the comprehensive question. The former, on Gamwell's account, are those who believe that comprehensive convictions can be publicly assessed and the latter are those who are not prepared to defend their comprehensive doctrines in a public forum. On this account it is Rawls himself who is unreasonable in that he is not willing to admit that justice as fairness *is* (at least implicitly) a comprehensive doctrine, hence *a fortiori* he is not willing to defend it in public as such. 'The turn in Rawls's thought from *A Theory of Justice* to *Political Liberalism* has failed to achieve its principal purpose, namely, to propose a political theory that is not itself part of a comprehensive doctrine' (Gamwell 1995: 74). Part of this failure lies in the tendency of the privatist view to assert that *none* of the religious convictions in the community are important in politics (Gamwell 1995: 119).

These five criticisms are aimed directly at Rawls's view and they prepare the way for three more that illuminate Gamwell's own positive alternative to Rawlsian separation, or better, 'separation'.

Sixth, every moral claim at least implicitly includes its metaethical grounding.

This claim is crucial for Gamwell's view and applies to all moral claims, including not only those in one's personal morality, but also those in political philosophy. He calls this stance the 'compound character of justice' in that the democratic principles enshrined in the constitution, say, must rest on something more basic. In Gamwell's terms, justice is both formative and substantive and these two aspects of justice cannot be separated (Gamwell 2002: 232). To put Gamwell's point in Rawlsian language, a concept of justice cannot be freestanding because it must involve a concept of the comprehensive good.

Seventh, Gamwell goes even further. Only a true comprehensive doctrine can redeem political prescriptions, although this does not mean an established religion.

Not only does Gamwell claim that the separation of justice and the good in effect slips in through the back door an implicit concept of the good, it also slips in what amounts to an established religion: the religion of separation. Gamwell does not discuss in detail, although he does notice, that the Rawlsian view is *pro tanto* (to be discussed later) and that, because Rawls's political liberalism is not meant to be universalist, it is a poor candidate for status as a comprehensive doctrine. Only a view that is universalist, in the sense that adherents to the view think that it *alone* can redeem political prescriptions, can be really comprehensive. That is, on Gamwell's view an authentic comprehensive doctrine is incompatible with the Rawlsian *translation proviso*, wherein one's own comprehensive doctrine can be brought into the public sphere only if its terms can be translated in such a way that any reasonable-rational citizen could understand and possibly accept such terms (Gamwell 2002: 266–71).

Gamwell insists that opposition to Rawlsian separation does not itself imply religious establishment, but rather only implies that *some* universal principle or principles could be redeemed in political discourse. Such redemption would, if it were successful, reduce the need for the Rawlsian method of reflective equilibrium among various factors that would have to be balanced within public reason. We have also seen that this method works on the assumption that there are no convenient algorithms available for determining what a just society would be like. Rather, one must work hard, on the basis of this method, to think through how all of the relevant factors are to be brought into harmony with each other. That is, if one factor is overemphasised we are put into an uncomfortable disequilibrium. Or again, on Gamwell's view, in contrast to Rawlsian reflective equilibrium, a zero-sum game is involved in political philosophy: if political liberalism is defensible, then every universalist theory or truly comprehensive doctrine is invalid.

And eighth, religious convictions can be rationally defended and hence are amenable to public debate.

One of the most distinctive of Gamwell's challenging theses is the claim that religious convictions are rationally defensible. In this regard he is commendably militating against the commonly held view that religious convictions are based on personal preferences and are thus not legitimate parts of our common moral (including political) enterprise. But religious convictions, he argues, have no wider comprehensive scope than Rawls's principles of justice. That is, Rawls's refusal to consider (or denial of) comprehensive claims is universal, and if there is a true concept of human authenticity, as Gamwell thinks there is, it would likewise be true under all conditions (Gamwell 1995: 135–45).

Gamwell grants that the critique of traditional metaphysics that began with Kant led many thinkers to discredit normative ethics as well. He thinks that Rawls is one of the heroes in the effort to reclaim a central place for normative ethics and politics in philosophy. But Gamwell thinks that Rawls's achievement is attenuated because of his refusal to consider, or denial of, rationally intelligible metaphysical claims regarding the comprehensive good (Gamwell 2011: preface).

The truncated Rawlsian approach has nonetheless had a profound effect on Gamwell's theory of distributive justice, which is formulated in Hartshornian process terms: maximise the general conditions of creativity to which all have equal access. All three principles in Rawls – the principle of equal basic liberties, the principle of fair equality of opportunity with respect to any inequalities in the distribution of goods, and the difference principle wherein any inequalities or differences in the distribution of goods will work to everyone's advantage (especially the least advantaged) – inform Gamwell's view, especially the idea at the core of the difference principle that undeserved talents won in the natural and social lotteries are justified only if they advantage the least advantaged. Although there are also obvious dissimilarities between Rawls's view and Gamwell's theory regarding the general conditions of emancipation, the significant overlap regarding their theories of distributive justice deserves mention. That is, on Gamwell's view there is much that is accomplished on the attenuated basis of Rawlsian political philosophy (Gamwell 1990: 201–2; 2005: 91–2; 2002: 294, 310).

Nor is Gamwell necessarily opposed to the overall method at work in Rawls that was discussed in detail above: reflective equilibrium. Particular convictions that we have no reason to question (commitment to democracy, opposition to racism, and so on) are easier to bring into equilibrium than those convictions that are readily criticised. But this method, once again, is attenuated because, although it works well as moral philosophy, it does not work as moral Philosophy (Gamwell's capitalisation) in terms of 'a foundation or grounding for the moral theory reached in reflective equilibrium' (Gamwell 1990: 116). Because there is no transcendental grounding offered for reflective equilibrium, its results are always tinged with arbitrariness, hence the charge of relativism articulated above (Gamwell 1990: 123–4). This eighth criticism therefore deals not so much with the lack of rationality in Rawls as the lack of Rationality.

In Defence of Separation

Regarding the first criticism, that political liberalism violates those who defend truly comprehensive doctrines, the following can be said in reply. Gamwell is well aware of the problem created by the pluralism of comprehensive doctrines that citizens affirm, very often uncompromisingly. To put the question in his terms: how can religious plurality be civilised? But his response to this question is quite different from the response that is given by political liberals like myself.

Gamwell thinks that religious toleration can be given reasonable grounds by requiring religious believers (at least some of them, if I understand correctly) to give a public defence of the comprehensive doctrine that they affirm. If such a defence is truly public, it will require civil discourse, which in turn requires toleration. The politically liberal response to the question at issue, by way of contrast, is to take the truth or falsity of comprehensive doctrines off the table in politics for at least two reasons. Either defenders of comprehensive doctrines themselves might not be willing to give a rational articulation of their view (after all, fideism, or the idea that religious belief is based on faith rather than reason, has had the upper hand in both philosophy of religion and religious circles at least since the time of Kant), or, if they are willing to offer a rational, publicly articulated version of their view, it might be hopelessly at odds with conflicting articulations.

It should be noted that Gamwell is not only encouraging religious believers to develop rationally (i.e. publicly) defensible versions of their beliefs, but he is also basing the continued existence of civil society on the ability of religious believers to develop such publicly defensible versions of their beliefs. One wonders what would happen if most religious believers remained steadfast in their fideism and did not see the need for, or even the appropriateness of, rationalised religion. I would like to make it clear that I personally see a strong role for reason in religion (see Dombrowski 2004a; 2005; 2006; 2016; 2017), but I am also painfully aware of the fact that there is no swarming multitude in addition to Gamwell that agrees with me in this regard.

There is a certain irony in the fact that, despite the fortunate circumstance that Gamwell and I share roughly the same (Hartshornian) metaphysical-2 view, he thinks any defenders of a truly comprehensive view are treated unfairly in political liberalism. However, I would not think that I would be treated unfairly if my comprehensive doctrine did not provide *the* meta-ethical support for liberal toleration. As Hartshorne himself put the point, a liberal is a thinker who knows that he or she is not God, as we have seen (Hartshorne 1984a: 9). It should also be remembered that Whitehead, like Hartshorne, was a liberal in politics (see Morris 1991), such that his view could be interpreted as saying, as Rawls's view could be interpreted as saying, that liberal political beliefs require the backing provided by *some* comprehensive doctrine, but which one?

It makes sense to distinguish between toleration of reasonable comprehensive doctrines and toleration of different conceptions of justice. Gamwell's aforementioned citation of Habermas seems to indicate that he thinks that Rawls is intolerant in the latter case. Another way to look at the matter, however, is to suggest that Rawls is very tolerant of different concepts of justice *within the politically liberal family*, which includes a large number of well-known political philosophers. Non-liberal concepts of justice (e.g. as defended by Straussians, Marxists and others) are not so much the victims of intoleration as they are rejected in a fair decision-making procedure, such as that found in the original position behind a veil of ignorance (Rawls discusses Marx's own views in detail – see Rawls 2007: 319–72).

I think that we should commend Rawls in this regard. The argument for such rejection, which should not be seen as flippant, relates to reflective equilibrium. That is, if we adopted the Straussian or Marxist stances, which in their different ways actually denigrate justice as either a convenient foil for the unwise or as a bourgeois fetish, respectively, we would put into disequilibrium most of the important beliefs held by reflective citizens in contemporary democracies. Among these beliefs are that in politics citizens should be viewed as ends-in-themselves who are free and equal, reasonable and rational. If these beliefs were false, then admittedly non-liberal concepts of justice would look more attractive. But as it stands, with these beliefs assumed as relatively stable, one would pay far too great a price by adopting a non-liberal concept of justice. We should be concerned if debates in democratic politics appear to citizens to be trivial in that there *is* much at stake in these debates.

Regarding the second criticism, that Rawls's refusal to consider comprehensive doctrines in politics amounts to a denial of them, several different responses are in order. Gamwell moves too quickly, I think, from politically liberal principles that do not rely on any particular version of metaphysical support to the concept that such principles are anti-metaphysical. Likewise, he moves too quickly from the idea that politically liberal principles can be articulated without comprehensive religious backing to the idea that such principles are anti-religious. These 'offsides' infractions by Gamwell (if the American football metaphor be permitted) are prompted by his assumption that Rawlsian political philosophy is a variety of secularism.

This assumption deserves scrutiny. Granted, modern liberal thinkers like Kant, Mill and Dewey seemed to think that, as citizens became more enlightened, and hence less attracted to traditional religious understandings of politics, a secular utopia could be approximated. But the later Rawls clearly tries to distance himself from these varieties of *comprehensive* liberalism, which were meant as replacements for what was thought to be the outmoded wisdom of the Judaeo-Christian ages. We have seen that Rawls thinks of comprehensive liberalism as just one more comprehensive doctrine that must be brought within the sweep of *politically* liberal institutions. Indeed, Rawls thinks that comprehensive liberalism can, and historically has, led to messianic and imperialistic forays that were actually at odds with liberal political principles. Or again, it might be more accurate to view Rawlsian political philosophy as post-secular rather than as secular. The very fact that Rawls uses the label 'comprehensive doctrine' rather than 'religion' indicates, as we have seen, that he thinks that *both* religious believers and non-believers have to submit to reasonable criteria developed in fair decision-making procedures, such as those found in the Rawlsian original positions at both the domestic and international levels.

Or again, Gamwell thinks that political liberalism, in addition to being anti-metaphysical and anti-religious, is also anti-teleological. There is a grain of truth in his position here, but I think that a more accurate way to put the point would be to say that no single *telos* can be isolated that captures the various (and at times conflicting) ends that reasonable citizens affirm in contemporary democracies: the greater glory of God, pleasure, sexual liberation, artistic excellence, wealth and so on. In fact, it is not too much of a stretch to say that, rather than being anti-teleological, political liberalism is hyper-teleological in that it permits as many ends as are compatible with justice. Likewise, political liberalism can be seen as hyper-metaphysical and hyper-religious.

Although it is correct, as Gamwell notices, that Rawls rejects what Gamwell calls the 'comprehensive order of reflection' *in politics*, the point of such rejection is to make the conceptual world safe for the comprehensive order of reflection in other areas: the academy, churches, the arts, responsible journalism and so on. If the comprehensive order of reflection yielded only one concept of *the* good (as we have seen Plato, Aristotle, Augustine, Thomas Aquinas, Luther and Calvin thought), then political matters would be much simpler than they are in the polyglot conceptual world that we inhabit at present and for the foreseeable future.

The third criticism, that Rawlsian separation of the just from the good both privatises and relativises the good, is problematic for several reasons. The contrasting term to 'public' in Rawls is 'non-public' rather than 'private'. This last term is etymologically related to the negativity associated with privation or lack or deficiency. There is nothing in political liberalism, however, that associates religious or metaphysical belief with privation. People just happen to believe and there is nothing lacking in them in this regard. Further, religious believers tend to worship together in community and to identify themselves with their religious communities; hence 'non-public', although not the ideal term, is nonetheless better than 'private' when describing religious believers' conceptions of the good.

Further, it is not the case that religious believers are required to sequester their conceptions of the good. In political liberalism they are permitted to do intellectual work with them, even in the public square, *as long as* the terms of the translation proviso are met, as we have seen (Rawls 1996: li). As I see things, these terms are not onerous or unfair to defenders of either religious or non-religious comprehensive doctrines. Once one acknowledges that reasonable citizens affirm many different conceptions of the good, one comes to realise that it would be a sign of disrespect to enact laws (especially those that use the coercive apparatus of the state to restrict the freedom of citizens) that are based on the terms of a single comprehensive doctrine that many citizens could not accept.

For example, once again consider the thought of Martin Luther King (or those he influenced), who easily could have met the terms of the translation proviso by providing for his agnostic listeners, in addition to his appeal to religious grounds, a non-religious explanation of why he advocated a discrimination-free society on the basis of race. Or again, Rawls himself, who was a defender of abortion rights for women, nonetheless commended Joseph Bernardin, the Catholic cardinal of Chicago, for trying to defend opposition to abortion in terms that were compatible with public reason. On Rawlsian grounds Bernardin may have been wrong, but by fulfilling the terms of the translation proviso he was at least being respectful of fellow citizens (see Rawls 1996: lvi; also see Dombrowski 2000). If opponents to abortion are not as successful as King was in changing the laws of the land, this in itself is not reason to abandon the translation proviso so as to allow the use of one comprehensive doctrine to trump the concepts of the good found in others.

It is true that *some* religious beliefs (e.g. belief in the trinity or in the dual nature of Christ) might not be amenable to the rational articulation that is the hallmark of public reason, but it is precisely these beliefs that are least political in that we can easily imagine a just *polis* where there is reasonable disagreement on these matters. Whereas some religious beliefs are overdetermined in the sense that they could be justified either in line with public reason or on religious grounds (e.g. that murder is wrong), and hence are easily amenable to the terms of the translation proviso, other religious beliefs seem to be justifiable only on non-public grounds. These latter beliefs are not appropriate bases for public policy in a democracy, as I see things.

The stable beliefs that are the subjects of widespread agreement in contemporary democracies (e.g. that slavery is wrong, that women deserve political equality with men, and so on) are shared by all reasonable parties, whatever their comprehensive doctrine. This is fortunate because abandonment of these beliefs would most egregiously put our moral lives into disequilibrium. In other words, it is rational to think that we pay too great a price for abandoning these beliefs, hence it is more accurate to say that political liberalism *contextualises* religious belief than it is to say that it *privatises* such belief.

The fixed points within political liberalism (e.g. that citizens should be seen as politically free and equal, reasonable and rational), the abandonment of which produces a dangerous disequilibrium with respect to morality, in general, and political philosophy, in particular, are, of course, open for discussion. But this is a far cry from suggesting that the results of such a discussion among reasonable and rational parties would lead to the abandonment of human authenticity, as Gamwell suggests. These beliefs are stable precisely because reasonable citizens who lead authentic lives affirm them (albeit in many different ways).

My response to the fourth criticism, that the most one can hope for in political liberalism is a *modus vivendi* rather than an overlapping consensus, follows from what has been said above. In logic it is clear that one can reach the same conclusion (X) starting from several different sets of premises (a, b, c), either directly:

$$a \qquad b \qquad c$$
$$X$$

or indirectly:

$$a \quad b \quad c$$
$$d \quad e \quad f$$
$$X$$

If something analogous can be said in political philosophy, then overlapping consensus (perhaps even Gamwell's 'comprehensive purpose') is possible in that X can be agreed to by all reasonable parties.

I understand what Gamwell has in mind when he says that political liberalism can only achieve a convenient *modus vivendi* because it is non-teleological. We cannot decide *in politics* among a, b or c's ends. Likewise, it is non-theoretical *in the sense that* we cannot decide in political philosophy about whether a, b or c is true. If these are mutually exclusive options, however, we *can* know that they cannot all be true and that some of them (but which ones?) are false.

What Gamwell wants in politics are both commonly held principles (which is what overlapping consensus is all about) and necessarily true principles. Regarding the latter political liberalism admittedly falls short. Although necessarily true principles are not denied in political liberalism, as Gamwell alleges, they *are* left to metaphysicians like Gamwell and myself to deal with. Decisions regarding necessarily true principles (and I think that Gamwell and I would largely decide in similar ways) should occur at scholarly conferences and in academic journals, in religious councils and in theological discourse, rather than in the halls of congress or in courthouses.

Gamwell is correct to be suspicious regarding a *modus vivendi*, however. The question is whether political liberalism can achieve something greater in terms of overlapping consensus. The problem with a *modus vivendi* is that it lacks stability and can fall apart at any time. The reason for this is that there is no meeting of minds or likemindedness in a *modus vivendi*, only a truce that could easily be violated when the forces arrayed on the other side are diminished. It should be noted, contra Gamwell, that over time a *modus vivendi* can develop into an overlapping consensus as mutual trust develops. It should also be noted as a concession to Gamwell that an overlapping consensus can over time degenerate into a *modus vivendi* as trust wanes and as political opponents in a friendly *agon* gradually come to be viewed as hated enemies (see Dombrowski 2009). The election of Donald Trump as President of the United States leads one to realise that the latter is a real possibility.

The fifth criticism is that Rawls develops a comprehensive doctrine and an established religion in spite of himself. The first point that should be made in this regard is that, if Rawls's view is in fact a comprehensive doctrine, as Gamwell alleges, it is not very comprehensive. There is no statement for or against the existence of God in Rawls, no stance regarding the afterlife, no theodicy. There is not even a theory of human nature other than an articulation of the parameters within which a *political* person as free and equal, reasonable and rational, can manoeuvre. There is no stated view regarding the mind–body problem (the greatest philosophical problem since the seventeenth century) and no resolution to the problem of human identity over time other than how this problem relates to *political* agency. Rawls has no stated metaphysical view regarding the status of universals, the problem of the one and the many, or the relationship between being and becoming. There is not even a general theory of axiology that deals with moral as well as aesthetic value. And, perhaps most significantly, we have seen that there is no developed theory regarding *why* human beings are ends-in-themselves, dignified subjects worthy of respect, as would be the case if he had a truly comprehensive doctrine.

To say that Rawls also implies an established religion (of separation) is to elicit a response to the effect that it would be a very odd established religion in that Jews, Christians, Muslims, atheists, agnostics, and so on, are not only tolerated, but are also afforded political equality with all other citizens. As we have seen, the separation of the just from the good is not absolute or 'religious' in Rawls due to the translation proviso. Between pure exclusivists, like Rorty, who would utterly prohibit religion in politics, and pure inclusivists, like Wolterstorff and Gamwell, lie Rawls and his partial inclusivism. It is true, however, that Rawls is closer to Rorty on this continuum than he is to Wolterstorff or Gamwell in that, if the terms of the translation proviso are not met, Rawls thinks that the exclusion of one's particular concept of the good from politics is itself a good thing. However, some religious convictions *are* very important in politics, that is, those that are reasonable and translatable. An example would be the religious conviction that human beings are made in the image of God, which can be translated (not without remainder, to be sure, but translated well enough to do significant intellectual work, in Wittgensteinian fashion) into the language of rights and respect.

Gamwell is often at his best when he points out performative self-contradictions, but it is hard for me to see how Rawls falls victim. Rawls admits that a thin theory of the good is required in theory of justice, which is a theory of the good that involves basic things that would be required in *any* thicker and wider theory of the good that is reasonable. When Rawls separates justice from the good it is this thicker and wider concept of the good that is separated, not the thin theory. Perhaps it would have been less confusing if Rawls had called the thin theory of the good a theory of (Martha Nussbaum-like) capabilities or (Aristotelian) requirements so as to avoid the appearance of contradiction.

It is futile, Gamwell thinks, to try to avoid metaphysics. In a peculiar way a Rawlsian could agree with this claim in that, because political philosophy is only a part of an overall moral philosophy, *some* conception of the good is required in order to deal with all of the questions that are not spelled out in theory of justice. As the cliché has it, politics is not the whole of life, even if it affects everything else. Another way to put the point is to say that it is misleading to suggest that no concept of the comprehensive good is required in political liberalism; rather, several different metaphysical views and their concomitant comprehensive goods are compatible with justice. Hence there is no incoherence in eschewing any particular metaphysical view *in politics* while permitting one, encouraging one, perhaps even requiring one elsewhere. The fact that political liberalism permits metaphysical views is well known; but the fact that it either encourages or requires them should be more widely known.

Very early in *A Theory of Justice* Rawls makes it clear that justice is the first virtue of social institutions, just as truth is the first virtue of systems of thought (Rawls 1999c: 3). There is no principled opposition in political liberalism to truth. So Gamwell in a way is insightfully correct to say that the Rawlsian distinction between the reasonable and the rationally discoverable true itself must be true. But this very abstract truth is clearly not the whole truth or the less abstract truth found in a comprehensive doctrine or in metaphysics-1. That is, political liberalism is not challenged in any significant way when it is claimed that it cannot remain neutral regarding all of the abstract aspects of truly comprehensive doctrines.

It should now be clear how I would respond to the sixth criticism, that Rawls does not submit to the idea that any moral claim at least implicitly includes its meta-ethical grounding. This is another way of objecting to Rawls's idea that theory of justice should be freestanding. My response relies on a distinction between two different senses of 'freestanding'. The first connotes the idea that a theory of justice should be freestanding in the sense that it does not rely on any *particular* meta-ethical view, whereas the second stands for the idea that a theory of justice should not rely on *any* meta-ethical stance. The second sense is, as Gamwell rightly thinks, problematic for several reasons. But it is the first sense that a political liberal should defend and it is not clear what is wrong with freestandingness in this sense.

The seventh criticism (that political liberalism lacks a true comprehensive doctrine and that only such a comprehensive doctrine can redeem political prescriptions) should be addressed in terms of Rawls's admission that his view of political philosophy is *pro tanto*. Literally, these Latin words mean to pay in part, as when in a legal context someone in debt escapes penalty by paying part of the debt on the pledge to pay the remainder at a later time. *Pro tanto* pledges are quite different from bankruptcies, where one is under no obligation to repay the remaining debt. Given this distinction, one can interpret Rawls to be saying that one pays one's 'debt' in moral philosophy in two stages (or, better, in two different ways, in that I am speaking of logical stages here and not temporal ones). 'First' one needs to get clear on the abstract principles of justice that would guide a democratic society in a condition of reasonable pluralism, 'then' one needs to deal with all of the other questions in moral philosophy that are not primarily questions regarding justice.

Because the second payment involves one of the two moral powers that are individually necessary and jointly sufficient in the moral life – a sense of the right or the just *and* a sense of the good –

no bankruptcy proceedings are appropriate here. Whereas Gamwell speaks as if Rawlsian political philosophy is a type of bankruptcy proceeding (in that the sense of the good is not exercised in the effort to understand the comprehensive order, indeed it is *denied*), it would perhaps be more accurate to say that the sense of the good is *postponed*. Or, better, because one's concept of the good may ante-date one's concept of justice, it might be even more accurate to say that it is not so much postponed as it is *relegated* to a different part of moral theory and the moral life.

Not to engage in this sort of *pro tanto* postponement or relegation is to run the risk that one *would* end up with an explicit or implicit established religion (or anti-religion, depending on the compre-hensive doctrine in question). To say of one's favoured universalist concept of good that it alone can redeem political prescriptions is to flirt with the possibility that overlapping consensus would disin-tegrate into a *modus vivendi* or worse.

Of course there is something messy about *pro tanto* reasoning, in particular, and about reflective equilibrium, in general, as we have seen. But this is because reflective equilibrium is a type of dialectic; and this generic philosophical method (once again, *the* method of philosophy, according to Scanlon – Scanlon 2003: 149) always involves some unfinished business and some questions only partially answered. The hope for a philosophic method that moves beyond dialectic has a long history, dating back to the attempt at the topmost rung in Plato's divided line to achieve a level of reality beyond being (*hyperousia*). But there is an equally long history, also dating back to Plato, of returning to dialectic once the effort to move beyond it has failed.

Gamwell's own effort to develop a universalistic concept of good, such that only in its terms could political prescriptions be redeemed, itself is open to dialectical criticism and to further clari-fication (as Gamwell himself would no doubt admit). The fallibilist, Hartshornian way to make the point is to say that, if we are lucky enough to reach necessary truth, this fact itself will be contingent. We have no viable alternative to the back-and-forth movement involved in the process of reflective equilibrium: intuition, rational argument, counterargument, response to counterargument, new intuition and so forth. The regional resolution of the problem of justice that this processual and fallibilist method has produced is the sediment associated with political liberalism. No doubt improved versions of liberalism may be in the offing, but the disequilibrium that would be brought about by radical shifts to the right or left (as in adopting the Straussian or Marxist views mentioned above) continues to be unpersuasive. There is nothing arbitrary in accepting the provisional results of dialectical argument in political philosophy. The disastrous results of disequilibrium make this readily apparent.

However, in a way I am in agreement with Gamwell's eighth criticism, that religious conviction at the most abstract level (e.g. regarding the existence of God or regarding the features properly connected to the concept of that than which no greater can be conceived) are rationally defensible. My agreement here with Gamwell, however, is as a metaphysician, not as a political philosopher. It should be clear that we are in a minority regarding the defensibility of the ontological argument (see Dombrowski 2006). And our common belief that creation *ex nihilo* is unintelligible is also controversial even in (especially in!) religious circles, as is the belief that opposition to truth inevitably leads one into performative self-contradiction. That is, in political theory, in contrast to metaphysics, we will have to rest content with philosophy rather than Philosophy, with rationality rather than Rationality.

Concluding Reflections

I would like to make it clear that I share Gamwell's concern that religious conviction ought to be exemplified without duplicity (Gamwell 1995: 49). But I do not see duplicity at work in trying to understand philosophically and to implement practically the biblical advice to 'Let both grow together until the harvest' (Matthew 13:24–30). Taken literally, 'both' refers to wheat and weeds, but here I am taking it to refer to true and false comprehensive doctrines. I have previously admitted that some comprehensive doctrines must be false. This is a logical point in that when comprehensive doctrines contradict each other one realises that they cannot both be true.

My point here is not merely logical, however. I agree

wholeheartedly with Gamwell's belief that there are convincing reasons for thinking that neoclassical or process theism *is* true. I do not so much hide this belief in public, and hence behave duplicitously, as I refrain from calling attention to it unless it seems both effective to do so in politics (largely it is not) *and* respectful to do so (sometimes it is, per the translation proviso, sometimes it is not).

I also share Gamwell's fear of postmodern refusal or denial of metaphysics and metanarratives (which often conceal an implicit metaphysics and metanarrative). But I have tried to show how the freestanding character of political liberalism enables one to be non-metaphysical in one sense and as committed to metaphysics as one would like to be in another *as long as* one is reasonable. I have previously argued (Dombrowski 2001a: 159) that the problem here is, in Whiteheadian fashion, misplaced concreteness. The locus for integration of political principles and metaphysical ones is not at the societal level as long as many reasonable citizens either eschew metaphysics or defend different metaphysical views from one's own. Rather, the locus for such integration is at the individual or associational level.

As I see things, until all rational beings agree at the level of comprehensive doctrine (the 'harvest'), we have a duty to be reasonable. As the biblical image makes clear, one danger is that by prematurely pulling the weeds the wheat itself might be ruined. Finally, it seems to me that it would be a mistake to view this stance as religion-lite (I have no reason to believe that Gamwell thinks this); instead it should be viewed as religion come of age, given the long history of religious intolerance that both Gamwell and I deplore.

Rawls and Faith

My engagement with Gamwell's thought can be supplemented by a consideration of Rawls's own nuanced view of faith. One learns about Rawls's own approach to religious faith in published writings at the very beginning and the very end of his career. In his undergraduate thesis at Princeton (1942) he indicated a religious faith under the influence of neo-orthodox Protestant thinkers like Emil Brunner. At this stage he thought that faith in God was not sheer fancy and that one could give reasons for religious belief, even if he did not have a great deal of confidence in rational or natural theology. By 'faith' he meant a spiritual disposition to be fully integrated into community and to be rooted in the divine source who sustains it. That is, faith is inherently personal, in contrast to 'belief', which is a cognitive attitude that holds certain propositions to be true or false. Strictly speaking, he thought, one might believe *that* God exists, but one has faith *in* God as personal. At this very early stage of his career, the opposite of faith was 'sin', which he defined as the destruction of personal community (Rawls 2009: 113, 123–5, 214).

Late in life (1997) Rawls drafted an essay titled 'On My Religion' in which he described the history of his own religious beliefs and attitudes towards religion, including his abandonment of orthodoxy during World War II, largely due to orthodoxy's inability to deal convincingly with the theodicy problem. Apparently, his views changed several times over the years. Although it is clear that he abandoned orthodoxy, it is not clear that he abandoned theism, in general. In fact, he speaks of his 'fideism' (Rawls 2009: 261, 263). In addition to this late essay, it also makes sense to suspect that Rawls's own religion is illuminated by his comments on 'reasonable faith' in Kant in that Rawls's own comprehensive doctrine seems to have been Kantian until the end of his life (see Rawls 2000: 16, 147, 288-9, 306, 309–10, 319–22, 363).

Quite apart from Rawls's own religious faith or lack thereof, what is more important in his thought is his treatment of faith as a *political* problem. Indeed, he is quite explicit that the origin of political liberalism lies in the aftermath of the Reformation, when it became clear that the lack of toleration among both Catholic and Protestant leaders alike created a huge problem: how can people of faith live together in justice when they are divided, sometimes uncompromisingly so, in the comprehensive doctrines that they affirm? Rawls's solution to this problem is to take questions of the highest good off the table as *political* questions (Rawls 1996: xxv–xxxi, 159; 1999a: 412; 2001: 192; 2000: 347–8). In this regard he was heavily influenced by both Locke's famous 'A Letter Concerning Toleration' and the not so well-known 'Colloquium of the Seven' by the sixteenth-century Catholic thinker Jean Bodin (Rawls 1996: 145; 2009: 266–9).

In that many or most of the people that Rawls wanted to bring within the scope of political liberalism were persons of faith of some sort, his hope was that, at the very least, a *modus vivendi* among all reasonable citizens could be established. Or, better, he hoped that stability for the right reasons could eventually be reached among all reasonable citizens, both those who professed religious faith and those who did not (e.g. Rawls 1999a: 616–22). That is, religious faith need not be fanatical or irrational or mad, although admittedly there is the possibility that it could exhibit these qualities if the religious faith in question was not tempered by a healthy fallibilism (Rawls 1999c: 485; 1999b: 126–7, 173).

Now that my positive contributions to the process of political justification have come to a close, it is time to explore some approaches to political philosophy that are far less defensible.

4

Religion, Solitude-in-Solidarity and Snyder's Bloodlands

Introduction

Whitehead insightfully notes that

> the chequered history of religion and morality is the main reason for the widespread desire to put them aside in favour of the more stable generalities of science. Unfortunately for this smug endeavour . . . the impact of aesthetic, religious and moral notions is inescapable. (Whitehead 1968: 19)

Whitehead is like Rawls in seeing political values as a species of moral values, in general. And in order to avoid the smugness that Whitehead mentions, it is difficult to overestimate the importance of healthy democratic institutions. This is because of the dreadful results that are likely to occur if they fail. In the present chapter I will examine the work of someone who is perhaps the most informed and exciting contemporary scholar of the mid-decades of the twentieth century in European history: Timothy Snyder. By examining Snyder's scholarship through a Whiteheadian lens, I hope to show the importance of the concept of solitude in religion, a concept that is integrally connected to the cultivation of an inner peacefulness that is, in turn, conducive to peace-L and peace-W as these ideas were developed in a previous chapter. But the solitude in question is really solitude-in-solidarity with other solitary selves. That is, by learning from the perversions of 'individual' and 'community' as these surfaced in the mid-decades of the twentieth century, we might be in a better position to understand the solitude-in-solidarity with others that characterises justice in a politically liberal context.

One of the most controversial features of Whitehead's enormous influence on how philosophers and theologians think about God and religion is the close connection he sees between religion and solitariness in his classic work *Religion in the Making*. The purposes of the present chapter include the efforts: (1) to understand the connection Whitehead sees between religion and solitariness; (2) to understand why Whitehead's view of this connection is so controversial; yet (3) nonetheless to defend the close connection that Whitehead sees. Regarding this last purpose I will appeal to authors who write from or about the 'Bloodlands', a term coined by the historian Timothy Snyder that refers to a large portion of Eastern Europe where, between 1933 and 1945, over 14 million individuals were murdered by either Nazi Germany or the Soviet Union. In addition to Snyder, I will be engaging with the writings of the Nobel laureate Czesław Miłosz (as well as with Miłosz's communication with Jerzy Andrzejewski), who lived through this disastrous period in the Bloodlands.

Religion as Solitariness

The Whiteheadian view that there is, at the very least, a close connection between religion and solitariness is in part a protest against the view of religion solely as a social fact or as public display. In addition to the pageantry of religion, there is something more important that occurs when someone is seized by the inwardness and peacefulness of a particular religious tradition. 'Religion is the art and the theory of the internal life' of an individual (Whitehead 1996: 16). Whitehead well realises, along with John Donne, that no person is an island and that we cannot understand individuals apart from the social facts within which they have grown. However, collective emotion and societal influences leave untouched 'the awful ultimate fact' that, in a sense, each of us is alone, especially when we die. To be alone, however, is not necessarily to be lonely or to be bereft of meaningful contact with others.

'Religion is what the individual does with . . . solitariness'

(Whitehead 1996: 16), on Whitehead's view. When stress is placed on the word 'does' in this quotation, some misconceptions of his view can be avoided. Perhaps what one can do is to commit oneself to service of one's family or community. Or perhaps what one can do is to imitate God when seen in Whitehead's process terms not as an omnipotent tyrant, but as a companion, a fellow-sufferer who understands (Whitehead 1996: 17; also 1978: 7). In stronger terms, at times Whitehead suggests that there is more than a close relationship between religion and solitariness, there is an identity of the two: 'religion *is* solitariness' (Whitehead 1996: 17 – emphasis added). What this means is that, if one has never been solitary, one cannot be religious. On this account, religion is beyond collective enthusiasm, institutions, churches, revivals, sacred texts, rituals, codes of behaviour, and other trappings or external manifestations. Rather, 'what should emerge from religion is individual worth of character' (Whitehead 1996: 17).

The earliest phases of religion do indeed tend to reduce it to a social fact or a tribal identity, fuelled by herd psychology. But once efforts to rationalise religious belief are initiated, solitariness comes to the fore. Whitehead lists as examples of the solitariness that haunts the imaginations of religious believers scenes where Prometheus is chained to a rock, the Hebrew prophets protest and denounce unjust rulers, Mohammed broods in the desert, the Buddha meditates, and Jesus suffers on the cross. In each case, there is a sense that the solitary individual in question felt forsaken (Whitehead 1996: 19–20, 28, 30). The great rationalised religions are the result of a religious consciousness that is universal rather than tribal. And it is *precisely because* of such universality that solitariness is introduced. The universality of rationalised religion signals both a disconnection or detachment from immediate surroundings and the search for something that is intelligible and everlasting in the midst of the flux. Once again, religion consists in the cleansing of one's inner parts and in what one *does* with one's own solitariness (Whitehead 1996: 47, 58, 60).

It is easy to see why some critics might be skittish about Whitehead's view that religion *is* solitariness (Whitehead 1996: 17), but it is important to notice that this view is not at odds with the more familiar claim that human beings are social animals. The topic of religion, for Whitehead, is individuality *in* community, with the individuality of human beings just as important as their communal existence. In one sense, Whitehead's view seems to be that individuality and community are on a par. But in another sense his view seems to be that the world is a scene of solitariness in community such that religion is primarily individual. Perhaps the safest characterisation of his stance is that, although it is correct to say that one cannot really understand human individuals apart from their societal influences, it is equally true to say that one cannot really understand *human* community without coming to terms with what it means to be a solitary individual. The profundity of this insight will become apparent when we examine what Snyder and especially Miłosz and Andrzejewski say about the Bloodlands.

Snyder on the Bloodlands

Each of the 14 million people murdered in the Bloodlands became a number. (By the 'Bloodlands' Snyder refers to the territories subject to both German and Soviet police power between 1933 and 1945, principally Poland, the Baltic states, Ukraine, Belarus and western Russia.) The killing began with the political famine that Stalin directed at Ukraine, which took 3 million lives. It continued with Stalin's 'Great Terror' of 1937–8, in which about 700,000 people were shot. Then, in 1939, the Germans and the Soviets cooperated in the destruction of Poland. After Germany declared war on the Soviet Union in June of 1941, there were 4 million non-Jews, mostly prisoners of war and the inhabitants of Leningrad, who were murdered. During the war, approximately 5.7 million Jews were killed by the Germans (and the Romanians). It is no wonder that Hannah Arendt, in her classic study of totalitarianism, painted this picture in terms of the contemporary superfluity of the individual (see Arendt 1966). First we slowly lose our humanity in mass society, then it is extinguished altogether in the death camps. As Snyder puts the point in his book on the Bloodlands, 'Auschwitz is the coda to the death fugue' (Snyder 2010: 383).

One of the many virtues of Snyder's magisterial scholarship is that it forces us to slow down the theoretical impulse, including that found in the present book. Europe's mass killing tends to be over-theorised and, as a result, misunderstood. That is, there is a lack of proportionality between theory and historical knowledge. Nazi Germany murdered about 10 million people in the Bloodlands (and about 12 million overall), and the Soviet Union under Stalin murdered about 4 million people in the Bloodlands (and about 9 million total). These numbers, of course, are staggering, even if they lean on the conservative side (Snyder 2010: 384, 412). Nazi Germany, in particular, killed millions of people faster than any state in history to that point. Mao's China exceeded Hitler's Germany in the famine of 1958–62 by killing approximately 30 million people (see Snyder 2010: 504; also see Dikotter 2010). However, if Nazi Germany had won the war Hitler's plan (modelled after Stalin's starvation of Ukraine in the early 1930s) was to kill within a few years another 30 million Slavs such that, by killing all the Jews and culling the Slavic herd, Eastern Europe would be available for German colonisation (Snyder 2010: 416). These enormous numbers do not include those killed in battle, those who died as forced labourers, those who died of hunger due to wartime shortfalls, or civilians who died in bombings. The 14 million in question were *murdered* (Snyder 2010: 410).

It is perhaps not surprising that there is at present an international competition for martyrdom as these numbers, beyond biblical proportions, have become nationalised and politicised. 'Nationalists throughout the bloodlands (and beyond) have indulged in the quantitative exaggeration of victimhood, thereby claiming for themselves the mantle of innocence' (Snyder 2010: 402). But the accurate numbers are nonetheless shocking. The greatest single crime in the Bloodlands was the annihilation of the Jews, but other crimes, including the murder of millions each of Poles, Ukrainians and Belarusians, are quite remarkable (Snyder 2010: 405–6).

The connection between Snyder and Whitehead comes into focus in the following questions asked by Snyder:

> Can the dead really belong to anyone? Of the more than four million Polish citizens murdered by the Germans, about three million were Jews. All of these three million Jews are counted as Polish citizens, which they were. Many of them strongly identified with Poland; certain people who died as Jews did not even

consider themselves as such. More than a million of these Jews also counted as Soviet citizens, because they lived in the half of Poland annexed by the USSR at the beginning of the war. Most of these million lived on lands that now belong to independent Ukraine. Does the Jewish girl who scratched a note to her mother on the wall of the Kovel synagogue belong to Polish, or Soviet, or Israeli, or Ukrainian history? . . . So even when we have the numbers right, we have to take care. The right number is not enough. (Snyder 2010: 406–7)

Although accurate counting is a necessary condition for understanding what happened in the Bloodlands between 1933 and 1945, it is not sufficient. For example, the 5.7 million Jewish dead should be counted as 5.7 million *times one* in that no generic Jews were killed, but specific individuals. We should remain attentive to this point. Snyder offers an instructive way to grasp the individuality and Whiteheadian solitariness of the dead. The official number of those killed at Treblinka is 780,863. The 3 at the end might be seen to refer to Tamara and Itta Willenberg, whose clothes clung together after their bodies were gassed, and Ruth Dorfmann, who was able to cry with the barber who cut her hair before she entered the gas chamber and who consoled her by saying that her death would be quick. Or again, of the 33,761 individuals shot at Babi Yar, the 1 at the end, let us say, was Dina Pronicheva's mother (Snyder 2010: 408).

To put Snyder's point in Whiteheadian terms, if one has never been solitary, one has never been religious. And to put Whitehead's point in Snyder's terms, if one does not grasp the murders in the Bloodlands as 14 million *times one*, then one fails to comprehend the immorality (and hence the irreligiosity) of these events. Once again, we should remain attentive to this consideration. On the religious view, at least in the Abrahamic religions (as evidenced in Genesis) and perhaps in other religions as well, it is individual human beings who are made in the image of God, with this view modified somewhat in Islam where images are prohibited. As this point is made in Christian scripture, God cares even for the fall of a sparrow, but *each* of us is of more value than many sparrows (Matthew 10:28). This omnibenevolent concern for individuals in their solitariness was not lost on Hamlet, who alludes to this piece of scripture shortly before his death (Act 5, Scene 2).

Miłosz, the Individual and the Collective

Much more needs to be said and Miłosz helps us to say it. During World War II Miłosz lived in Warsaw and was part of the Polish resistance to the Nazis. Although he unfortunately lent his services to the communists after the war until 1951 (see Snyder 2006; 2017), eventually he received political asylum from Soviet domination of Poland and lived in Europe and the United States until his death in 2004. In 1996 a collection of essays written from 1942 to 1943 appeared in print that was subsequently translated into English in 2005. These essays, gathered together under the title *Legends of Modernity*, cluster around the themes of religion and the tension between the individual and the collective. In each essay of the book a single author is analysed in terms of the contribution made in the effort to understand both the nature of religion and the related tension between the individual and the collective. My claim is that, by coming to grips with Miłosz's understanding of this tension, and the impact this tension has on religion, we will come to better appreciate the nuances of the Whiteheadian view of religion that is the focus of the present chapter. The high-pressured atmosphere of Warsaw during the war, where brute force reigned supreme, sheds light on human nakedness that can be quite revealing to those who are focused on the value of individuals.

Legend of the Island

Miłosz was formed intellectually as a Catholic. On his view the path to perfection in Catholicism is strictly communal and based on the concept of *the* common good (see Cobb and Daly 1994). This perhaps explains the fascination Miłosz has, by contrast, for Daniel Defoe's *Robinson Crusoe*, which is the subject matter of the first essay in the book and of the first legend of modernity: the legend of the island. When communal life becomes oppressive a longing arises for total isolation, where island life symbolises an absence of human conflict. Miłosz reads *Robinson Crusoe* as a Christian book of removal and repentance. Specifically, it is a Protestant book that, although it does not reveal *in toto* the true nature of a human being, it does nonetheless accurately depict a search for something that is crucial: a place where one can flee in order to rescue. It is well known, however, that Robinson Crusoe is himself not an island in that he brought civilisation with him, including the desire for profit and a willingness to exploit. Thus, neither Catholic communalism nor 'Protestant merchant morality', to use Miłosz's language, is individually sufficient. The legend of the island is supported by Jean-Jacques Rousseau's idea that the source of evil is outside of us and that both goodness and religion are innate. Living on an 'island' enables one to submit human nature to close analysis, the result of which, however, is a certain scepticism regarding Rousseau's buoyancy, as Robinson Crusoe's own guilt makes apparent. There will be no easy, sentimentalised *romantische Strasse* to understanding the solitariness that is the origin of religion, as Whitehead understands it.

Legend of the Monster City

Just as Robinson Crusoe carries civilisation with him to the island, so also people in a capitalist society bring their individualism with them when they enter a city. Miłosz's chapter on the legend of the monster city examines Honoré de Balzac's contribution to the subject matter in question. Indeed, a capitalist city is one where isolated individuals struggle against other isolated individuals. Paris, for example, is the Babylon of our times, according to Miłosz, in that the frenetic tempo of contemporary life found there fosters depersonalisation. Those who live in a small town tend to see the same people over and over, such that any change that occurs there happens only gradually. In big cities, however, we meet and pass by so many people in a short amount of time that we cannot really learn to care for them and we are instead encouraged to foster the desire to preserve our own interests. Balzac himself seems incapable of constructing a noble character in his novels. Quite ironically, living in a throng actually encourages the interiorisation of religion, especially if there is enormous evil that is being perpetrated in the city. Whereas cities seem to be life affirming in that they, like Noah, preserve a pair of every form of life, they actually facilitate various phenomena that are nothing less than monstrous. In effect, the legend of the island and the legend of the monster city hold each other in check in the effort to understand the Whiteheadian view of religion as solitariness. That is, peacefulness-L and peacefulness-W require that we avoid both an exaggerated/distorted individualism *and* an exaggerated/distorted sense of community.

Legend of the Will

The first two legends give rise to a third: the legend of the will. Here Miłosz considers the thought of Marie-Henri Beyle, who is better known by his pseudonym, Stendhal, especially his novel *The Red and the Black*. Because we live in monster cities, like so many Jonahs inside a whale, some individuals arise who think themselves to be superior to others and whose *ressentiment*, which includes a volatile mixture of envy and anger, propels them towards conspiracy theories regarding why they have been kept down. These supposed superior individuals tend to see religion as merely a human fiction. In fact, the tendency on the part of the allegedly superior individual is to think that only *he* sees things as they are and only *he* is not deceived. (In his analysis of Stendhal's character Julien Sorel, Miłosz relies heavily on the thought of Max Scheler.)

Stendhal's novel is consistently individualistic, but, unlike the individualism of Defoe, which is tied to the legend of retreat and repentance, the individualism evidenced in the legend of the will is fuelled by histrionic and hyperbolic ambition. Raskolnikov in Fyodor Dostoyevsky's *Crime and Punishment* has thoughts and urges much like those of Julien Sorel, and these constitute nothing less than the deification of the will, according to Miłosz. It is not surprising that Stendhal exerted a strong influence on Friedrich Nietzsche, who, on Miłosz's interpretation, played a significant role in the formation of the Nazi version of totalitarianism; in fact, such a role 'cannot be denied' (Miłosz 2005: 46). Great individuals rise above both good and evil as well as truth and falsity such that all blame is to be heaped on those who shackle these great individuals or collection of individuals.

These self-proclaimed great men typically construct a mythic version of history according to a romantic template wherein an original golden age is lost due to some big mistake such that only a great individual can recover former glory. In the case of Nazi Germany, this type of history involved the myth of a lost fatherland populated by Siegfried and Barbarossa; only Hitler could bring back and expand lost conquests. The spoils that accrue to great individuals (or to a collection of such, as in the Germans when seen as a master race) are compensation for their having to live among the unwashed masses. Throughout his discussion of the legend of the will, Miłosz emphasises the fact that those along the Stendhal–Nietzsche axis tend to exaggerate both the (real) tension between the individual and the city and the (imagined) superiority of some of the former to the latter. These exaggerations have as their result nothing less than the instrumentalisation of the truth for the ends contrived by the supposed superior individuals. In this regard we should be alarmed at the willingness of those on the postmodern left to readily endorse the Nietzschean commonplace that there are no facts, only interpretations, a view that is not unrelated to the rise of Trump and other notorious liars in politics. As Miłosz sees things, however, when religious ideals (as in Christian *agape*, Buddhist compassion, truth-telling) retreat, the result is like a receding tide that leaves behind a population of sand crabs scrambling in panic, which is an obvious allusion to the chaos he experienced in Warsaw in 1942–3 (Miłosz 2005: 48).

Absolute Freedom

The legend of the will segues easily into Miłosz's treatment of 'absolute freedom', where his focus is on André Gide, who was heavily influenced by Nietzsche. Gide, like Nietzsche, came from a Protestant background, yet he rejected Christianity. He is instructive because, although he advocated an extreme form of individualism, he (like Jean-Paul Sartre) eventually turned to communism. This is analogous to the fact that Nietzsche's hyper-individualism exerted considerable influence over the architects of the fascistic version of totalitarianism. Failure to understand and appreciate the idea, congenial to Whitehead, that we are individuals-in-community can lead to the disastrous consequences that Miłosz witnessed personally under the Nazis *and* the Soviets. That is, the aforementioned histri-onic and hyperbolic version of individualism, termed by Miłosz the legend of the will, is itself susceptible to a diabolical strain of collec-tivisation. This is because the absolute, unrestricted freedom claimed by defenders of the legend of the will includes the freedom to declare not only oneself but also one's *Volk* or one's party to possess a monopoly on, and a licence to use, force. This is why we should pay careful attention to the theme of individual-in-community.

In Gide's book *Travels in the Congo*, the author empathises with the people he saw in that part of the world, but he does so from above, from the perspective of not only a Nietzschean who appar-ently thought of himself as an *Übermensch*, but also from the van-tage point of a wealthy background. From Miłosz's quite different point of view, the people described by Gide were apparently living in what amounted to concentration camps. Gide in effect drapes an aesthetic cloak around certain poisonous international currents. Both Nietzsche's and Gide's inner heroic powers were in real-ity inner demons. As a result, the sword that fell into the hands of madmen like Hitler and Stalin was actually forged by certain romantic thinkers (Miłosz 2005: 57) whose apotheosising of the solitary individual had unintentional yet devastating consequences.

Gide is unfair to Protestantism when he sees Nietzsche as its culmination, although it must be admitted that in the tension between the individual and the communal there is a tendency in Protestantism for the former. Where Gide is very helpful is in his unwittingly alerting us to the close connection that can exist between self-liberation and the rapture of destruction. The noncha-lance with which Nietzsche and Gide talk about destruction, how-ever, pained Miłosz a great deal as a denizen of the Bloodlands. He is intent to defend the claims that the delicate hands of intellectuals are very often stained with blood and that the mottos of totalitarian regimes are simplified versions of philosophy.

It is noteworthy that Miłosz read William James's *The Varieties of Religious Experience* just after he graduated from high school. This book had a profound effect on him in the effort to reach equilibrium among conflicting (not necessarily contradictory) forces (Miłosz 2005: 68). Among these are the tension between the Jamesian will to believe and rationality as well as the tension between the individual and the communal. As Miłosz was writing in 1942–3, World War II was not yet a social, historical fact. It was a personally *experienced* reality. War is by its very nature destructive of equilibrium and produces in its victims a sense of helplessness and biblical destitution. It is also conducive to a loss of faith in both civilisation and religion and encourages a deep yearning for harmony and equilibrium. War brings about a rupture in which it is understandable to ask the question as to which of our ideals and goals are primary.

This is very close to what Whitehead means by claiming a close connection, even identification, between religion and solitariness. War makes us very much aware of the fact that human beings can commit monumental evil, but they are also capable of incredible saintliness. It should not, but often does, hide from us the great and wise harmony or equilibrium of existence in general (Miłosz 2005: 84). Here Miłosz learns a great deal from Leo Tolstoy's *War and Peace*. Does one *need* severity in order to accept civilisation and religion? This is a complicated question, both psychologically and philosophically. Whitehead himself apparently turned towards the religious philosophy he became most famous for as a result of his son Eric's death in World War I (see Russell 1956: 93, 100). Miłosz, too, was well aware of the common Slavic theme of purification through suffering. Solitariness need not be equated with the various types of egoism that are so hard to eradicate.

As Miłosz sees things, there is a question mark that hovers over the future of religion. Solitariness can lead one to some version of theism, to non-theistic religiosity in the case of Buddhism, or to agnosticism or atheism. Miłosz's fear was that ethics would devour theistic metaphysics and religion and that relativistic aesthetics would devour ethics. It was certainly easy in 1942–3 to be persuaded by catastrophism. But the problem he faces is not as particular as it seems initially. Religion started losing its influence once philosophy arrived in ancient Greece. That is, the equilibrium supplied by dominant religion has been challenged ever since Socrates' questioning. Miłosz and Whitehead are alike in thinking that, if we are to achieve some sort of really wide reflective equilibrium on cosmological issues (which involves an overcoming of the bifurcation of nature, in Whitehead's terms), then a theistic metaphysics is required, although Miłosz is less advantaged than Whitehead in this regard in that he would have been familiar only with the Thomistic, classical theistic view (and with certain forms of German idealism) and not with Whitehead's and Hartshorne's neo-classical or process theistic alternative. (On Whitehead and Miłosz, see Latour 2014: 92.) Miłosz well knew, however, that neo-Thomism did not bring us close to the equilibrium that is needed wherein the great achievements in the humanities along with those in the sciences would be brought under the umbrella of one conceptual system, albeit a fallible and revisable one as the ongoing process of critical inquiry advances.

Despite the fact that Miłosz felt that he was saturated with collective categories imposed by both the political right and left, he thought, along with Whitehead, that it was anxiety regarding one's individual existence that led people not only to religion, but also to art, which is a poor substitute for religion, he thinks. In an essay on a thinker well known in Poland but not elsewhere (Stanisław Witkiewicz), Miłosz suggests that religion arises in an individual who is astonished that one is oneself. Coming to terms with one's personal identity involves a process whereby religious questions are inevitable. Miłosz is also like Whitehead in thinking that each moment brings with it a partially new reality, such that hope, however faint, is awakened with each drop of experience. When everything seemed to be hatred and despair, Miłosz's method was to look within and write measured, perfectly calm and peaceful sentences expressing his deepest thoughts and feelings (Miłosz 2005: 260).

Miłosz and Andrzejewski on Equilibrium

At the end of *Legends of Modernity*, an extended exchange of letters between Miłosz and his less famous friend Andrzejewski has as its focus the individual and his or her solitariness. It is not surprising that, under the circumstances in the Bloodlands when these letters were written, society is seen as a terrifying desert because of the loss of a sense of the tragic. Individuals are precious precisely because they are fragile; they can fall and break. To be religious is to recognise this preciousness of the individual and to strive to preserve an ethical sense of the tragedy involved when one of them falls unnecessarily. This sort of individualism, it should be emphasised, is not to be confused with the legend of the island or capitalist self-interest or anarchism. The times in which Miłosz and Andrzejewski lived enabled them to awaken to the sound of individual voices that in normal circumstances might have been taken for granted. In a sense, we live *and die* in isolation, as Joseph Conrad also noticed. And it is precisely this sort of isolation that counterintuitively makes it possible to achieve a solidarity that is deeper than any hoped for in the slogans of the French Revolution. Isolation is a burden that crushes individuals, thereby fuelling the desire to be together voluntarily with other individuals who have preserved a sense of the tragic (Miłosz 2005: 149, 154–5, 158, 160–1).

The solitariness of life in the Bloodlands led to a desire to get past one's time, to imagine a period in which the tyranny of the collective would end. But the end of such tyranny does not necessarily point towards individual*ism* in the pejorative sense of the term. Rather, as indicated in the previous paragraph, it could lead to genuine communion with others, to the sort of *solidarnosc* later developed by Lech Wałęsa and others. We are all familiar with the desiccated husk of religion. However, life in the Bloodlands can remind us of the solitary origins of the concepts of God and communal solidarity, of what Catholics call the Mystical Body of Christ, although there are rough equivalents to this in other religions. Instead of individual*ism*, Miłosz and Andrzejewski seem to be pointing us towards the individual*isation* of human beings in solidarity with the same. Becoming a true individual is an arduous process rather than any accomplished fact or ready-made product. There is no need to overstep the mark by claiming that individuals are so different from each other that no commonality can be found. By contrast, on the Miłosz–Andrzejewski account, *we are united in our solitariness*, which can be seen to be Whitehead's very point (Miłosz 2005: 163–4, 168).

The fact that individuals can communicate with each other helps to ease the tension between solitariness and communal values. It is such ability to communicate that leads to a deeper fraternity/sorority, indeed to a deeper solidarity, than might be suspected initially. The fact that we can talk with disgust about the Gestapo killing Jews or the communists liquidating the bourgeois intelligentsia is itself important in that such talk helps us to realise that a value is not necessarily defensible merely because it is communal. Likewise, it would be a mistake to think that a value is necessarily indefensible merely because it arises individually. In this regard it is worth remembering that Socrates' daemon and Kant's categorical imperative so arose. When people are killed like bedbugs or flies, some respond to such insectivity by becoming indifferent to the death of others. But this is not the only response that is possible in that some are fettered by pangs of conscience even if they are not the ones responsible for the exterminations. Human nature is quite elastic. As we have seen Whitehead suggest, religion is what one *does* with one's solitariness. There is no guarantee that what will be done is good (Miłosz 2005: 169–70, 174–7, 182, 189).

There is a vague sense in Miłosz–Andrzejewski that the concept of God is improved through time and experience and that eventually there will be a new and really wide equilibrium where various conceptual tensions (e.g. religion and science, individuality and community) will be relaxed. In the Bloodlands, however, it is difficult to escape from the sense that solitariness brings one face to face with inner darkness. The hoped for new equilibrium would also bring about a relaxation of the tension between faith and reason. Tertullian's *credo quia absurdum est* ('I believe that which is absurd') has a certain beauty and usefulness when it is uttered to fill in certain gaps in human understanding, but it is extremely dangerous when it is placed on a banner as the chief slogan. Although Marxism, in particular, has been beneficial in exposing what often goes on behind the scenes in religion, the truly sacred things that are sometimes felt or thought in solitude are nonetheless left untouched by Ludwig Feuerbach and Karl Marx (Miłosz 2005: 197, 199–200, 203, 206–10).

Those who have very strong social instincts will likely consider cloistered monasteries, or the solitary equivalent of these in everyday life ('a room of one's own' or 'quiet time'), as shallow, empty, useless, perhaps even parasitical. But this knife can cut both ways in that those who have developed contemplative lives will likely find odious the blithe energy with which active people move through their lives like ants. Both sides in this tension are subject to caricature. Miłosz–Andrzejewski are aware of how difficult it is to achieve measure or Aristotelian moderation or reflective equilibrium between the individual and the communal, but the task is not impossible, say when communal values mirror, indeed amplify, the value of the individual and when one is able to rise above the quotidian. The Whiteheadian insight in this regard would seem to be that one cannot be a contemplative-in-action without first being a contemplative, someone who is renewed by solitariness. The sort of solitariness that is being extoled here is very much at odds with hubris or arrogance. The fact that collective currents affect who we are as individuals is not to be confused with the claim that they are sufficient in explaining the activity of solitary contemplation. And solitude *is* an activity, specifically an activity in which we can be astonished by both the transitoriness of momentary experience and the degree to which solitude and peacefulness are actually shared by reflective human beings (Miłosz 2005: 215–57).

Preliminary Conclusion

The purpose of the present chapter has been to explore the nuances of Whitehead's thesis that there is a crucial connection between religion and solitariness and to argue in favour of the claim that this thesis is not only not as implausible as many think, but actually provides insight into the origins and nature of any religious belief that moves beyond mere conformity to social convention or obeisance to communal pressure. The effort to understand Whitehead's view is facilitated by Whitehead himself when he makes it clear that what he means by solipsism in *Process and Reality* (Whitehead 1978: 81, 152, 158) is markedly different from what he means by solitariness in *Religion in the Making*. But the effort to understand Whitehead's view also depends on a firm grasp of those communal values that are in dialectical tension with the solitary. Here it is crucial to note that we may just now be in an enviable position to come to grips with communal values in the contemporary world when they run amok.

Of course it has been my intent to say that even during the darkest days in the Bloodlands there were solitary individuals like Miłosz and Andrzejewski who are instructive even today regarding the connection between solitariness and religion and regarding the dangers involved when communal values become simultaneously distorted and hegemonic. But their views were never made public until 1996 and did not appear in English until 2005. It should also be noted that, because most of the killings in the Bloodlands took place in regions under Soviet control after the war (including those committed by Nazi Germany, especially the Holocaust of the Jews), we have only recently been in a position to adequately assess these atrocities. Only since 1989 has the archival evidence in Eastern Europe really been opened up to historians like Snyder. This evidence makes clearer than had been the case previously that the similarities between Nazi Germany and the Soviet Union are as intelligible as the differences between the two, especially given the hatred each of these exhibited towards peaceful solitude and hence (pace Whitehead) towards religion. That is, we are in a better position at present to assess Whitehead's view of the connection between solitariness and religion than at any point since he made the connection in 1926. Further, scholars have hardly started the process of morally assessing China's version of the Bloodlands in the late 1950s and early 1960s, despite the fact that the Communist Party is still in power (see Dikotter 2010). We should not ignore the non-violent individuals in Hong Kong who, from 2014 until the present, have heroically protested against the continued tyranny of the collective.

Snyder points out in an instructive way that not only Miłosz, but also Vasily Grossman (a Jewish journalist who travelled with the Red Army), saw the few remaining Poles and Jews living in Warsaw at the end of the war as latter-day Robinson Crusoes. Each was aware of the other, but very often they were not in solidarity with each other as common victims of both the Soviets and especially the Nazis (for various complicated reasons, including anti-Semitism, that are not the foci of the present chapter). But Snyder also notes that Miłosz tried to bridge the gap between Pole and Jew by highlighting what I have referred to above as shared solitude. As a Pole in solitude he could not help but notice that the Jews who died in the Warsaw Ghetto (which did not exist before the war in that most Warsaw Jews were 'assimilated') did so alone. As Snyder puts the point, 'no earthly agent could sort the Jewish ashes from the Polish ones' (Snyder 2010: 297, also 280, 290).

The Miłosz–Andrzejewski solitude-in-solidarity in the Bloodlands, as well as Whitehead's solitude after the death of his son in World War I, obviously encourages serious engagement with the theodicy problem. Such an engagement is not my focus here. Suffice it to say that the keystone of process theodicy is provided by a critique of the concept of divine omnipotence (see Hartshorne 1984c). This critique is analogous to Andrzejewski's prediction that 'the time will come to bid farewell, and not without regret, to the vanishing throne of God the Father' (Miłosz 2005: 197). If God *is* omnipotent, then moral responsibility for the enormous suffering and death in the Bloodlands would seem to lie at the divine doorstep. We have seen that Whitehead even goes so far as to compare the omnipotent God of classical theism with Hitler (see Whitehead 1954: 172–3, in an entry from 30 August 1941). However, theists can receive solace in knowing that there is a neoclassical, process alternative to classical theism (see Dombrowski 2004a; 2005; 2006).

The Importance of Pinker

World War II was not the end of history. Steven Pinker is a social scientist who collates the results of many other natural and social scientists who study the human tendency towards violence. The overall conclusion of such research is that, despite the enormity of violence in the world wars, human beings worldwide are becoming *less* violent, a result that should give us at least some solace. Although it is true that historical decline in violence is no guarantee that such a decline will continue into the future (pessimists will no doubt think that our present situation is like that of early 1914 when the naively optimistic world was unwittingly on the brink of disaster), it is important to resist the mistaken impression many people have that violence has increased. Granted, the *absolute* number of people who die violent deaths is sufficiently large to continue to fuel the beliefs of pessimists, but declining *percentages* of people who die violent deaths give a more accurate sense of our historical situation, a fact that should not escape our notice.

Although the 55 million people killed in World War II is the worst thing people have done to each other in absolute terms, the number of people killed in World War II as a percentage of the total population of the world at the time barely gets World War II into the 'Top Ten' of such events in world history. On this basis, the worst atrocity of all time was the An Lushan Revolt and Civil War, an eight-year rebellion during China's Tang Dynasty in the eighth century that resulted in the death of 36 million people, about a sixth of the world's population at the time (see Pinker 2011: 194–5).

The 'better angels of our nature', to invoke Pinker's use of a phrase from Abraham Lincoln, incline us towards cooperation and peace. Pinker focuses on six processes that help us to orient ourselves towards peace, despite the horrors of the Bloodlands: (1) The *pacification process* is Pinker's label for the ancient transition from hunter/gatherer societies, with their proclivity towards violence, to sedentary agricultural societies, a transition that resulted in an enormous decrease in the rate of violent deaths. It is hard to overestimate how violent our evolutionary ancestors were. (2) The *civilising process* further reduced the percentage of people who died violent deaths as states were established that had a formal monopoly on the use of force. Of course, ever since the rise of the state there has been the serious problem of the state itself behaving immorally, but Pinker thinks that we should not be fooled into thinking that the solution to this problem lies in abolishing the state in anarchistic fashion. To paraphrase Henry David Thoreau's famous essay on civil disobedience, what we want is not no state at all, but a better one.

(3) From the *Enlightenment* in the seventeenth to eighteenth centuries until the present there have been many organised efforts to abolish various types of violence that were previously seen as either desirable or at least acceptable: despotism, slavery, duelling, judicial torture, domestic violence to women, cruelty to non-human animals, and so on. (4) The next major transition, which Pinker calls the *long peace*, is directly related to the horrors in the Bloodlands described by Snyder. Since the end of World War II until the present something has occurred that is unprecedented in human history: the great powers have stopped warring against each other. That is, the period from 1945 until the present is the longest and most productive period of peace in the entire history of Europe, a period of peace that is rivalled only by the Pax Romana in antiquity and the relatively warless period between the end of the Napoleonic Wars

in the early nineteenth century and the start of World War I.

(5) This long peace is amplified by the *new peace* that has occurred after the end of the Cold War in 1989. Organised conflicts of all kinds (civil wars, ethnic and religious wars, etc.) have declined throughout the world, once again despite popular misconceptions to the contrary. And (6), further amplifying the long peace that has occurred after World War II is what Pinker calls the *rights revolution*, found especially in the Universal Declaration of Human Rights in 1948. There is growing revulsion to violence against ethnic minorities, women, children, gay people, disabled people, non-human animals and others.

A hermeneutics of suspicion abounds, however. Perhaps it will be objected that the Universal Declaration is a piece of intellectual imperialism wherein smaller countries around the world were pressured into accepting the Western concept of rights. An instructive book by Mary Ann Glendon, however, paints a quite different picture. The hero of the story concerning this document is Eleanor Roosevelt, who led the effort to get the great powers to approve the Universal Declaration. The United States and the United Kingdom were initially reluctant to work in this direction because they thought that the effort would be futile in that the Soviet Union would never even try to live up to the terms of the document if it were approved at the United Nations. However, due to the insistence of several smaller countries (e.g. Lebanon, Venezuela, Taiwan) the effort went forward and Roosevelt was able to get the project off the ground. That is, the historical details do not support the (widely held, yet inaccurate) view that it was the big countries that forced the Universal Declaration on everyone else. Further, one of the principal authors of the Universal Declaration, Jacques Maritain, provides an instructive example of the translation proviso that was discussed in a previous chapter. He used rights language from the Thomistic natural law tradition that was easily translatable into other languages from around the world that were compatible with the theses that human beings should be seen as dignified and as worthy of moral respect (see Glendon 2001).

The better angels of our nature mentioned above include the natural capacities of human beings (which are admittedly mediated by various layers of social construction) to exhibit empathy/sympathy to other sentient beings, self-control and rationality regarding moral issues. These capacities, when enhanced by the feminisation (and hence partial pacification) of politics and a cosmopolitanism that partially mitigates tribal impulses, are the grounds for cautious optimism. The overall impact of Pinker's scholarship is that careful study makes the past look less innocent than it may have seemed to romantics and the present less sinister than it appears to supposed realists. The small gifts of coexistence (as in Abrahamic theists and atheists befriending each other, or as in an interracial family playing in a park) should also not escape our notice. The gradual shift towards liberal peace is not a shift towards complacency so much as it is a commitment to the ongoing process of enlightenment and to the moral defensibility of non-violent methods of conflict resolution.

Although to some extent it may be true to say that the aforementioned long peace is a nuclear peace based on fear, to a far greater extent it is a democratic, liberal, in-the-process-of-enlightenment peace. In any event, we should not be surprised to learn that the percentage of people who die violent deaths is at present, both in the United States and worldwide, at its lowest point in human history! However, this 'decline of violence may be the most significant and least appreciated development in the history of our species' (Pinker 2011: 692). It is a commonplace among those who take Martin Luther King seriously that the long arc of history bends towards justice. It is to be hoped that it will become a commonplace due to Pinker that the long arc of history also bends towards peace.

Rawls on Sin and Religion

Given the grim realities discussed in this chapter, albeit contextualised by Pinker's cautious optimism, it will be worthwhile to consider Rawls's own sober yet equally cautious optimism regarding the topics of sin and religion.

Rawls's undergraduate thesis at Princeton dealt primarily with the concepts of sin and faith. The former was defined as the repudiation and destruction of community, whereas the latter was defined as the affirmation and enhancing of community. The sort of relations that were *communal* were those between persons (including God as personal), relations that were *natural* were those between a person and an object, and relations that were *causal* were those between objects (Rawls 2009: 113–14, 122, 193).

Egoism was seen as a type of sin wherein communal relations were turned into natural relations (e.g. when people were treated as objects). Egotism (with a 't') was a more basic type of sin that consisted in self-love. In fact, egoism was claimed to be an external manifestation of egotism such that the latter was really the master sin (Rawls 2009: 122–3, 193, 203, 209, 211). Whereas egoism fails to embrace personal relations and settles for natural relations, egotism embraces personal relations only to destroy them from within.

At this early stage in his career Rawls anticipated a third sort of sin to appear in the future: despair. This was because the prime result of sin was loneliness, which was seen as the most terrible condition for a human being. Even Rawls's early view of sin was primarily social rather than metaphysical (Rawls 2009: 206, 213). Despair is a type of hopelessness, suggesting that living without hope is a type of sin. One is reminded here of Rawls's later attempt to sustain reasonable hope for liberal democracies.

Although the root of sin was passion (specifically, in the passionate tendency towards self-love), and although the ancient Greeks gave a great deal of attention to passion, they did not arrive at an adequate conception of sin. The early Rawls's view of sin was heavily influenced by the Augustinianism of neo-orthodox theologians popular in the mid-decades of the twentieth century. This included the influence of original sin (Rawls 2009: 145, 152, 171–3).

It is ironic, given his later defence of social contract theory, that the early Rawls saw the view of society as based on mutual advantage as sinful. At this point in his career he also saw both bad institutions and anxiety as signs of sinfulness. That is, he rejected the Manichean view that sin was due to a cause external to us. Rather, we deprave ourselves, which is the heart of the doctrine of original sin (Rawls 2009: 189–92) when interpreted not literally as the inheritance of Adam's sin, but as a metaphor for humanity's tendency to foul its own nest, as it were. The killing in the Bloodlands keeps this doctrine alive in the minds of many sober thinkers. Later in his career Rawls identified Kant's moral psychology as Augustinian in that our moral failures were seen by Kant as due to the exercise of our free power of choice (Rawls 2000: 294, 303). By contrast, Rousseau criticised the Augustinian doctrine of original sin in that he saw our moral failures as due to external causes (Rawls 2000: 205, 208–9).

In this regard the mature Rawls was more like Rousseau than Kant. He even came to see Augustine (along with Dostoyevsky) as one of the two 'darkest minds' of Western thought (Rawls 2007: 302). Indeed, in his very late essay 'On My Religion' he came to see the doctrine of original sin as 'repugnant' (Rawls 2009: 263). This strong language is surprising given that one of the reasons for deliberation behind a veil of ignorance is the pervasiveness of bias in theorising about justice, a pervasiveness that makes sense on the Augustinian belief in original sin.

Rawls's repudiation of the doctrine of original sin is required to understand his view at the very end of *Law of Peoples* to the effect that, if a reasonably just society, or a global society of peoples, is not possible, then the explanation would probably be due to the inability of the members to subordinate their power to reasonable aims. If human beings are incurably self-centred (which Rawls denies), then Rawls wonders 'whether it is worthwhile for human beings to live on the earth' (Rawls 1999b: 128).

Despite appearances, there is much in the very early Rawls (when he was an orthodox Episcopalian and entertained the thought of entering the seminary) that prefigures the political philosophy for which he was later to become famous. For example, sin is a thoroughly social phenomenon in that it is defined as that which repudiates or destroys community. Likewise, faith is defined as that which constitutes and integrates community. And the thesis that human beings are made in the image of God is interpreted not so much in terms of the presence of rationality in human beings, but rather in terms of human beings being uniquely capable of entering into community. As a result of these concepts of sin, faith and *imago Dei*, the very early Rawls thought that religion and ethics could not be separated (Rawls 2009: 113, 116, 193, 205, 207, 214, 219).

The less than adequate features of traditional Christianity that Rawls noticed in World War II led him to study in detail the history of religious intolerance, as well as the rise of political liberalism, which was meant to respond to the disastrous effects of the wars of religion in the early modern period. We have seen that in addition to Locke's famous 'A Letter Concerning Toleration', Rawls was heavily influenced by a little-known work by the sixteenth-century Catholic thinker Jean Bodin, 'Colloquium of the Seven'. Bodin saw toleration not only in political terms, but as the expression of true Christianity. The seven speakers at an imaginary banquet represented different religious traditions, but they were happy to abandon attempts to refute each other's religious beliefs (Rawls 2009: 264–5; also 2007: 311).

The deeply religious temperament in Rawls surfaces in his philosophy in many ways. Political philosophy itself involves a reasonable faith that a just society is possible, despite what happened in the Bloodlands; otherwise one might wonder whether it is worthwhile for human beings to live on this earth. Further, Rawls also aims to establish that human nature is good in the sense that it is capable of justice, which entails a rejection (à la Rousseau) of original sin (Rawls 1999b: 128; also 1999a: 448; 2007: 205–9). And Rawls concludes *A Theory of Justice* by appeal to a view of our social world *sub specie aeternitatis*, which is also an indication of what Thomas Nagel would call his religious temperament, although it should be noted that this view is one within history, not beyond it (Rawls 1999c: 514; also 2009: 5–6).

The most extended treatment of the role of religion in politics is in *Political Liberalism*, where Rawls contrasts the Homeric religion of the ancient Greeks with Christianity. Specifically, the Reformation fragmented the religious unity of the Middle Ages by creating a situation of religious pluralism. This led to problems as rival versions of authoritative and salvationist religion vied for control of the populations of Europe. Luther and Calvin turned out to be as dogmatic and intolerant as the Catholic Church had been. This led to the question: how is a just society possible among those of different faiths? Political liberalism arose in the sixteenth and seventeenth centuries as a response to this very question (Rawls 1996: xxiii–xxvi, 303; also 2001: 192; 2000: 3, 6–14).

Rawls seems to identify a view as religious if it involves a conception of the world as a whole that presents it as in certain respects holy or worthy of devotion (Rawls 2000: 160). But in

Political Liberalism Rawls tends to refer to comprehensive doctrines rather than to religions. A comprehensive doctrine involves a general conception of what is of value in human life. Contemporary society is characterised by a plurality of comprehensive doctrines, both religious and non-religious, but this situation need not be seen as disastrous due to the conceptual and practical progress brought about by political liberalism. A just society does not depend on agreement on a common comprehensive doctrine, despite claims to the contrary by either fascists or communists (or other dogmatists). This is because the problem of political justice does not depend on a resolution of the problem of *the* highest good. Political liberalism starts with the realisation of the depth and breadth of irreconcilable differences regarding which comprehensive doctrine, if any, is the true one (Rawls 1996: xvii–xxviii).

Rawls makes explicit in *Political Liberalism* what was only implicit in *A Theory of Justice*: political liberalism is not the same thing as comprehensive liberalism. The latter is a comprehensive doctrine that arose in the Enlightenment period in figures like Kant as a secular replacement for traditional Christian comprehensive doctrines, whereas the former has no such aspirations. Political liberalism is not a comprehensive doctrine, but a framework within which those who affirm uncompromisingly different comprehensive doctrines can live together in a just society (Rawls 1996: xxix–xxx, xl, li–lii; also 2000: 14–16).

One comprehensive doctrine can retain power in a condition of pluralism only by way of an oppressive use of state violence. This was true in the Catholic Church's use of the Inquisition and it would be equally true if a non-religious comprehensive doctrine were seen as normative in the political sphere, once again as in fascism or communism (or other sorts of dogmatism). I have noted that Plato, Aristotle, Augustine, Thomas Aquinas, Luther and Calvin all thought that there was only one comprehensive doctrine that was true and that a just society consisted in getting those who knew *the* good into power and to punish those who worked against the good. On this basis, toleration of reasonable differences among comprehensive doctrines was actually a vice. In political liberalism, by contrast, citizens are expected to have two views: a political conception of justice and a view of the good life. The latter should at least be consistent with the former; indeed, it is wider than the former. Rawls's justice as fairness intentionally stays on the surface so as to sidestep deep and divisive problems surrounding the nature and content of the good (Rawls 1996: 37, 134, 138; also 1999a: 329, 360, 391–5, 453, 475, 490; 1999c: 189–91; 2001: 34, 187).

A stable society is one in which there is not a mere *modus vivendi*, where adherents to different comprehensive doctrines would impose their will on each other if they could, but an overlapping consensus among adherents to different comprehensive doctrines. That is, reasonable religious believers can wholeheartedly affirm politically liberal principles in their own ways. Except for certain forms of fundamentalism or religious authoritarianism, all of the major historical religions, including Islam, are capable of being reasonable comprehensive doctrines. Granted, some religious comprehensive doctrines provide limit cases regarding what can be tolerated in a just society, but if children in such religious traditions are educated in the democratic virtues and values then there is a good chance that such religious comprehensive doctrines can be brought within the sweep of politically liberal institutions. Religious comprehensive doctrines should not try to do too much in the political arena in a condition of pluralism; and democratic political institutions should not try to do too much at the associational level of religious institutions. The doctrine *extra ecclesia nulla salus* (outside the church there is no salvation) may or may not be true, but it should not have any political force (Rawls 1996: 148, 170, 195–9; also 1999a: 411–12, 426, 433–4, 483, 590, 597; 2001: 164, 183).

The only comprehensive doctrines that run afoul of public reason are those that cannot support a reasonable balance of political values. Some, but not all, opponents to abortion on religious grounds do this. This does not mean that religious believers cannot bring their comprehensive doctrines to bear on public policies, but it does mean that they must meet the demand of 'the proviso' that they translate their comprehensive doctrine into terms that any reasonable person could understand and could possibly accept. That is, difficult problems are not settled in advance against religious believers, as Rawls argues in his treatment of the debate between Patrick Henry and James Madison over religious freedom. Further, the demands of this proviso are placed on the shoulders of defenders of non-religious comprehensive doctrines as well. This proviso is historically indexed, however, in that Lincoln's introduction of religious language into his speeches may have met the demands of public reason in his day, when religious pluralism was not recognised to include those with no faith at all (Rawls 1996: li–liii, 243–5, 254; also 1999a: 280, 462, 586–7, 595, 601–13).

As before, much of Rawls's later thoughts on religion are implicit in *A Theory of Justice*. Religious intolerance would never be chosen behind a veil of ignorance. However, an 'omnicompetent laicist state' would also be rejected, whether it came from the political left or the political right. Neither having religious beliefs nor conversion (a theme that goes back to Rawls's undergraduate thesis) nor apostasy should be seen as crimes. In *A Theory of Justice* Rawls is neither sceptical towards nor indifferent regarding religion in that, although the right is prior to the good, the good is nonetheless a necessary feature of the moral life, in general, and a just society, in particular. Parties behind the veil of ignorance know that they will have *some* interests that concern religion, but which ones? That is, the priority of the right to the good does not mean that political values necessarily outweigh transcendent ones. Indeed, the importance of religious beliefs, including their role in constituting personal identity, plays a key role in the argument for the priority of liberty. However, strength of religious conviction does not trump justice (Rawls 1999c: 17, 181, 186, 188, 288; also 1996: 31–2, 109; 1999a: 17, 87, 91–2, 372, 405; 2001: 23, 37).

Further, it should be noted that Rawls's difference principle shows a noticeable similarity to the preferential option for the poor found in various religious traditions. Rather than a 'trickle down' approach, he defends a 'suffuse upwards' approach wherein a key feature of a just society is to make sure that everyone's basic needs are met and that any inegalitarian distribution of wealth be to everyone's advantage, especially to those who are least advantaged. This helps us to understand how Rawls could respond to certain religious ethicists who might be bothered by what appears to be the secondary place of love in Rawls's philosophy. The mutually disinterested agents of construction found in the original position *when constrained by* the veil of ignorance produce a conception of justice that is very close to what would result if a just society were planned by purely loving agents (Rawls 1999c: 57–73, 128–9, 167–8, 205). This confluence of opinion should strike theists as quite remarkable.

Rawls does defend the right of conscientious refusal, which is typically based on religious reasons, as in Christian pacifist opposition to conscription. But this defence is based on political rather than religious reasons. Likewise, the principles of justice, in general, should be freestanding, not in the sense that they could exist alone apart from any additional philosophical or metaphysical support, but in the sense that the principles of justice can be inserted into or embedded in several different comprehensive doctrines so long as they are reasonable. We have seen that religious belief need not be irrational or unreasonable, even if some versions of religious dominant ends are indeed mad (Rawls 1999c: 323–4, 331, 338, 398, 485–6, 492; also 1996: 374–5, 393; 1999a: 388; 2001: 151).

These considerations regarding religion *in* society obtain as well in international justice *among* societies. Here Rawls makes some concessions to societies that are 'decent' (in the sense that they do not commit grave human rights violations and they are non-aggressive), but who have a 'consultation hierarchy' that is dominated by one religion, as in the mythical Kazanistan described in *Law of Peoples*. The fact that such societies are decent requires us to try, as far as possible, to bring them into the law of peoples. One wants to ensure that they, and thus their religious traditions, may develop in their own way and in their own terms, provided basic human rights and relations of international right are secure. There is no a priori reason to think that our history from the late Middle Ages to the present will necessarily be their history. Further, when international law breaks down Rawls defends a theory of just war that has several similarities to the traditional Catholic view, but without any appeal to the dominance of one comprehensive doctrine (Rawls 1999b: 16, 21–2, 65, 69, 74–8, 103–5, 126; also 1999a: 537, 547).

Although 'religion' does not even appear in the Index to *A Theory of Justice*, it is a theme that runs throughout his writings from beginning to end. Rawls was concerned about the survival and flourishing of constitutional democracy in countries where the majority of people claim in some fashion to be religious. He vigorously denied that his political philosophy was a veiled argument for either religion or for secularism. In fact, he defends Tocqueville's idea that religion flourishes in the United States *precisely because* of the separation of church and state. Both religion and democracy were *processually on the way*, in his estimation, in the effort to bring about a common good of common goods in that religions that once rejected toleration of reasonable differences as a virtue can come to accept it as such (Rawls 1999a: 616–22; also see 235, 256, 446, 582, 593–4; 2001: 198). Likewise, the peoples who committed the crimes in the Bloodlands could come to see, and in the case of most Germans did come to see, the defensibility of political liberalism and of the virtue of toleration of reasonable differences.

5
Heidegger, Political Philosophy and Disequilibrium

Introduction

The problems with seeing Heidegger as instructive in politics are put into sharp relief when the following 1949 quotation from him is considered, a quotation to which I will return throughout the chapter:

> Agriculture is today a motorized food industry, in essence the same as the manufacture of corpses in gas chambers and extermination camps, the same as the blockade and starvation of countries, the same as the manufacture of atomic bombs. (*Ackerbau is jetzt motorisierte Ernahrungs-industrie, im Wesen das Selbe wie die Fabrikation von Leichen in Gaskammern und Vernichtungslagern, das Selbe wie die Blockade und Aushungerung von Ländern, das Selbe wie die Fabrikation von Wasserstoffbomben.*) (quoted in Schirmacher 1983: 25)

We will see that the problems with Heidegger's political philosophy are integrally connected to issues surrounding both his early anthropocentrism *and* his later anti-anthropocentrism. The levelling effect of his later anti-anthropocentrism is in evidence in this troubling quotation, which is disruptive of the process of reflective equilibrium. But in neither period was Heidegger a supporter of democratic political philosophy or the concept of human rights.

It is common to hear those who are sympathetic to Heidegger's ideas say that he teaches us how to 'think' properly and how to dwell authentically on the earth and, presumably, with other human beings. It will be my purpose in the present chapter to dispute these claims. To be frank, I think that there is something odious about his critique of technology and the democratic state, a critique that is summed up in the above quotation.

The critic of Heidegger with whom I will be primarily engaged here is Michael E. Zimmerman, and this for two reasons. First, Zimmerman has made what is perhaps the most detailed yet balanced case for Heidegger as an important theoretician. Indeed, Heidegger's thought is largely kept alive through talented scholars like Zimmerman. Second, although to some extent a defender of Heidegger, Zimmerman is nonetheless willing to listen attentively to criticisms of Heidegger's Nazism. Heidegger's Nazism, I will suggest, highlights why he is not at all instructive regarding how we should view political philosophy. I will avoid *ad hominem* arguments in that I will be claiming that Heidegger's metaphysical views (which have influenced many of the most important thinkers, both religious and non-religious, over the past century) interpenetrate with his intellectualised version of Nazism, as we will see. My own criticisms of Heidegger's thought, and to a lesser extent of Zimmerman, have to do with the failure to acknowledge (Heidegger) or to defend consistently (Zimmerman) the rights of sentient individuals. Heidegger's own hatred of individualism and of rights was a contributing factor in his becoming a fascist.

Further, Ronald Beiner has argued convincingly that (Nietzsche and) Heidegger are 'dangerous minds' who provide the roots for the contemporary growth of right-wing ideologues who revile both the Enlightenment and the liberal-democratic way of life. For this reason alone we should take Heidegger's politics seriously from the perspective of process liberalism. The fact that Richard Spencer, Julius Evola, Aleksandr Dugin and other thinkers behind the current fascist resurgence largely take their cues from (Nietzsche and) Heidegger is noteworthy. And, as Berel Lang has argued, it will not suffice to say that the matter can be settled with the simple declaration that (Nietzsche and) Heidegger have been misinterpreted if what they have in fact said is inimical to any democratic government that at least approximates justice (see Beiner 2018; Lang 2002).

Heidegger's Metaphysics

The fundamental insight of Heidegger's *Being and Time* is that there is a difference between Being and entities (or beings). We are familiar with entities, like shoes or cows or numbers. But we have a hard time specifying what Being or is-ness means. On Heidegger's well-known view, Being is not an entity, but refers to the self-manifesting, presencing, or revealing of entities. For an entity to be (i.e. for it to present or manifest itself), a corresponding absencing is needed, a clearing constituted by human existence. In effect, humans are both a kind of entity *and* the clearing in which entities can be manifest. In this regard there is a sort of anthropocentrism in his thought, but not one that is conducive to liberal democracy or to human rights.

For the Heidegger of *Being and Time*, entities in some sense would persist if no humans existed, but they would not 'be' in Heidegger's sense of being manifest within the clearing of human existence. The anthropocentric tendencies of *Being and Time*, however, yield in Heidegger's later thought, according to Zimmerman, to a sort of biocentric egalitarianism (see Zimmerman 1983: 123; 1986: 21–4), an egalitarianism that, I will argue, is the most dreadful imaginable, as is evidenced in the quotation at the top of the present chapter. In *Being and Time*, at least, there is a certain degree of Kantianism in Heidegger's view, as Zimmerman notes:

> In *Being and Time* Heidegger fails to clarify the following puzzle: do natural entities show themselves either as instruments or as objects because these are the two major ontological dimensions of natural entities in and of themselves, *or* instead do natural entities show themselves as instruments or objects because these are the only two ways in which human existence is open for entities? (Zimmerman 1986: 28, also 23)

Zimmerman thinks that we should commend the somewhat anthropocentric Heidegger of *Being and Time* for avoiding the really ethically bothersome anthropocentrism of Descartes. Because human beings are finite, in Heidegger's view we cannot be open to entities in ways that exhaust what they are. But ever since the time of Plato, and especially since Descartes, we have tended to be open to them in extremely constricted, one-dimensional ways. For Heidegger, who originally defined human existence as care (*Sorge*), we fulfil our humanity when we exist in a way that lets entities be what they are instead of forcing them to serve our needs only. By allowing our understanding to be used solely for the purpose of dominating entities, we have left the world as inert and without purpose. Because *Dasein* (literally 'being there': the experience of Being that is peculiar to human beings) is the measurer in Heidegger's philosophy, it is important to notice that human temporality is such that, as epochs change, entities show themselves in different ways. In modern philosophy they tend to appear as strictly material mechanisms. These mechanisms are seen primarily as instruments for socio-economic purposes or for scientific investigation. It is Heidegger's belief that only by re-appropriating our philosophical tradition, by rethinking Plato and Descartes and almost everyone else between the Pre-Socratics and Heidegger himself, that this manipulative sort of anthropocentrism can be ameliorated (Zimmerman 1986: 19, 22–5).

Heidegger's replacement for the bothersome sort of anthropocentrism seems in his later philosophy to be what he calls 'the fourfold' (*das Geviert*), a configuration of earth and sky, mortal beings and the gods, wherein the order of nature emerges not out of a divine or human plan, but out of the capacity of individuals to behave in their own ways such that they nonetheless produce an overall harmony: individuals adjust themselves to other individuals. Zimmerman mentions the similarities between Heidegger and Whitehead with respect to their criticisms of the view that the cosmos is a rigidly defined machine and their desire to recur to pre-seventeenth-century modes of thought. But there is a decisive difference in this recurrence: Whitehead was a political liberal (see Morris 1991; also see Heidegger 1971; finally, see Weinberger 1984). Nonetheless the clearing of an open space in our culture so as to see entities largely reveals them as use values or as commodities, in Heidegger's view. In a very real sense, preliterate people did not see the same sorts of entities that we see. Entities, including human beings, are put in a frame (*Gestell*) for us by science/technology. It should also be emphasised that there is no crucial distinction in Heidegger between science and technology, since science has in recent centuries been integrally connected to the will to power.

In this chapter I am largely criticising the political implications of Heidegger's metaphysics, but there are problems with his theory even on a purely metaphysical level. For example, the clearing opened by *Dasein* should not, indeed cannot, as Heidegger alleges, lead us to wonder why there is something rather than absolutely nothing *if* absolute nothingness is, as Plato and Bergson and Hartshorne and many others have argued, unintelligible. Zimmerman, however, sometimes speaks as though it is only recently that *das Nichts* has become a mere vapour. His view is that *das Nichts* for Heidegger is not a mere nothing, but the withdrawing of Being, which necessarily leads to political destruction (see Zimmerman 1975: 404–5). Although not a theist, Heidegger nonetheless operates in the tradition of the classical theistic view that sees a crucial role for absolute nothingness. The classical theistic view is that an omnipotent God creates the world out of absolute nothingness by exerting coercive power.

In his later philosophy, Heidegger did not attribute inauthenticity to a lack of personal resoluteness (as he did earlier), but to a cultural phenomenon: anthropocentrism. Authentic human existence in his later philosophy consists in the realisation that humans are but one element in the fourfold and not necessarily the most important one. This realisation was never lost on peasants, on Zimmerman's interpretation of Heidegger, even if it has been lost (or, better, killed) by deracinated urbanites.

Several questions need to be asked here, however: (1) There is the question of whether the anti-anthropocentrism entailed in the fourfold is also a variety of anti-humanism, as I allege, or, as Zimmerman alleges, is a type of 'higher humanism' or 'beyond humanism' – Zimmerman cannot decide which to defend (see Zimmerman 1986: 43; 1993). (2) What are we to make of Heidegger's claim that in technological culture moral distinctions, including those in political philosophy, lose their meaning? Is this claim actually a ruse for Heidegger's own inability in his philosophy to make moral distinctions? (3) Is it not the case that there is something a bit too convenient in the suggestion that, from a

Heideggerian point of view, World War II was due not to Hitler and the Nazis, but to forgetfulness of Being? And (4), is it not also a bit too convenient to hold, if one was a dues-paying member of the Nazi Party from the early 1930s until the end of the war, as was Heidegger, that technological framing of nature is a defect found especially in democratic cultures, but not fascist ones? That is, what are we to make of Heidegger's belief that the Germans (under Hitler) were the only people capable of bringing about a new beginning for the West, in a way at least somewhat analogous to the Greek beginning two millennia before (see Zimmerman 1977: 76–80; 1979: 100, 103)?

It must be admitted that at times Heidegger suggests that the history of Being is a kind of play in which one mode of self-manifesting follows from the previous one without any mode being more adequate than any other. At other times Heidegger suggests that the current technological disclosure of the Being of entities is particularly restrictive. It is this latter tendency that has the upper hand (see Zimmerman 1983: 103).

Zimmerman's Criticisms

It should be noted that before 1987 Zimmerman's view of Heidegger corresponded to the 'official version' of Heidegger's political views. His more recent criticisms of Heidegger, brought on by the work of Hugo Ott and Victor Farias (see Ott 1993; Farias 1989), constitutes an admirable example of intellectual honesty and the use of critical reason on Zimmerman's part. In 1990 he called Heidegger to task on at least three points: (1) Zimmerman thinks that there is a residual anthropocentrism in Heidegger's later thought. Even though the later Heidegger abandoned the idea that *Dasein* is essentially different from all other entities, he did not integrate humanity into the seamless web of life described by ecologists; this is largely because Heidegger was always a severe critic of naturalism.

Closely related is (2), Zimmerman's critique of Heidegger's antipathy to science. It is true that many scientists are implicated in scientism or the view that all entities are mere objects and that science is the only reliable source of information. Hence regarding these issues Heidegger was correct, according to Zimmerman, to be distrustful. However, 'insofar as Heideigger refused to take seriously the organic dimension of human existence, he may well be accused of having remained in a curious way tied to the human-centered, dualistic metaphysical tradition of which he was so critical' (Zimmerman 1990: 244). The problem from a political point of view is that Heidegger's residual anthropocentrism did not include a defence of basic human rights or more specific democratic rights for human individuals. Further, there is the obvious point that, behind a Rawlsian veil of ignorance, no rational person would agree to the sort of authoritarian rule, indeed fascism, favoured by Heidegger. This is because behind a veil of ignorance there would be no assurance that when incarnated we would be 'Aryans', but perhaps Jews or Slavs or gays.

(3) Heidegger's philosophy is, as Zimmerman notes, integrally connected to a politically reactionary critique not only of industrialisation, but also of the whole modern world, including its notions of rights and political autonomy. By way of contrast, the process thinker David Ray Griffin defends a sort of *constructive* postmodernism (which is to be distinguished from the more famous *deconstructive* sort) that is critical of modern industrial civilisation, but *not* at the expense of the great gains made in the modern period in terms of human rights and political autonomy. Zimmerman's criticism of Heidegger goes as follows:

> [We] must examine seriously the implications of Heidegger's involvement with National Socialism. His willingness to support an authoritarian regime to 'solve' the problems posed by modernity and industrialism, the ease with which he abandoned the principles of the respect of the rights of others, his talk about a mystical 'union' between the *Volk* and earth, and his hierarchical views about those 'gifted' with insight about the meaning of history – all of this must give pause to those [who] . . . recognise that authoritarianism, hierarchism, and communitarianism without respect for individual freedom are by no means 'solutions' . . . [We] want to be able to speak about the organic relatedness of all life on earth *without* being accused of reverting to fascist mythologising. (Zimmerman 1990: 243)

Murray Bookchin is another thinker who reminds us that Heidegger's thought is tainted with fascism and hence is a dubious source of wisdom regarding a closer tie to nature, if only because the Nazis themselves quite clearly exploited the earth as a symbol for their movement (see Bookchin 1988; Bromwell 1989). I am trying to advance the thesis that there is a world of difference between, first, an anti-anthropo*centrism* that nonetheless acknowledges that *anthropoi* (human beings) are worthy of respect and are possessors of rights and, second, an anti-anthropocentrism that is perversely anti-human, to the point where, as the quotation at the top of the present chapter indicates, there are no moral differences among machines that harvest wheat and those that milk cows and the gas chambers. Here Heidegger puts us in a condition of severe disequilibrium with *both* considered intuitions and theory.

Heidegger provides an example of a politically dangerous sort of anti-anthropocentrism, whereas Isaac Bashevis Singer provides an example of a morally responsible sort (regarding Singer, see Wynne-Tyson 1985: 335–7). When Singer suggests that animals are constantly in danger of being sent to a humanly imposed 'Treblinka' or that we often act like Nazis towards animals, he nonetheless makes it clear that: (1) the real Treblinka was a morally evil place; and (2) the 14 million people murdered in the Bloodlands constitute a still greater evil than the very real evil of, say, 14 million non-human animals killed in slaughterhouses or in laboratories (and this due to the highly rational capacities of almost all of the human beings killed in the Bloodlands). Heidegger, by contrast, never condemned Treblinka, leaving people to wonder whether he, as a good Nazi to the end, perhaps approved of it. But even if he had condemned Treblinka, it is by no means clear that he would have, or even could have, done so in any terms stronger than he could have offered against the killing of 14 million (non-rational yet sentient) animals or 14 million (non-rational and non-sentient) blades of grass. Even mowing the lawn violates the vague Heideggerian imperative to let things be (*Gelassenheit*). Admittedly, to let things be is not to be purely passive. It is: (1) to open up a clearing in which things disclose themselves without undue interference; and (2) to interact with entities in respectful ways. But Heidegger is not at all helpful regarding what such respect means and how we can, on the basis of his philosophy, approximate reflective equilibrium.

It is dangerous in the extreme to abandon rights in favour of the obscure notion that we should let things be. Although Zimmerman finds the quotation at the top of the present chapter 'astonishing', and although he has left behind his earlier (Heideggerian) criticism of rights, he continues to show traces of Heidegger's apparent stance that the Holocaust is more due to advanced technology than it is to a denigration of individual moral patients. When the later Zimmerman says that 'mass extermination in the Nazi camps was possible only because of developments within industrial technology', it should be noted that the crucial piece of technology needed for the death camps to occur was the railroad and precise rail scheduling, which had been in existence since the nineteenth century. The 'final solution' was far more of a low-tech operation than Heideggerians like to admit. A great number of victims of the Nazis died, it should be noted, by a gunshot to the back of the head so that the victims would fall forward into a trench that they themselves had dug. It will not do to blame technology *simpliciter* for disrespect shown to persons (see Zimmerman 1990: 43; 1983: 102, 107).

Several of the features of Heidegger's thought that some find appealing, such as his idealisation of peasant life in his notion of the fourfold, are nonetheless bothersome both because they appear to suggest simply a rejection of modern science and technology altogether, rather than a critical engagement with it, and because they seem to be connected with a notion of tradition that entails a rather vicious version of nationalism. Indeed, Heidegger refers to a new appropriation of Western tradition that is made possible by *German* language and philosophy. This newness suggests that proper limits for human behaviour cannot be established through current legal or moral norms, but only by Being itself, whatever that means. As Zimmerman notes, the new *ethos* suggested by Heidegger only seems to make sense if Being is hypostasised and personalised into a divine agent, as in his well-known claim published posthumously that only a God can save us now (Heidegger 1976; Zimmerman 1983: 116–19). Even if Heidegger is correct in claiming that human beings go astray when they forget that they are not self-created, it is not clear that reminding us of this fact helps very much without an explicit statement of theistic belief on Heidegger's part. If Being is not to be divinised, why should we believe, along with Zimmerman, that we are 'brought forth *so that* entities can manifest themselves' (Zimmerman 1986: 29 – emphasis added)? Zimmerman's earlier thought was very much in the spirit of Heidegger in the claim that the philosophical doctrine of human rights justifies exploitation. Zimmerman seems to favour Heidegger's idea that ontology precedes ethics. Although he thinks that rights cannot be abandoned *at present*, he claims, if I understand him correctly, that it is rights, rather than fascist or communist ideology, that spawn totalitarianism. He identifies 'service' as the true aim of life (but whom are we to serve?) and he views rights as fictions. Because of these dangerous, disequilibrium inducing claims, I think that we should take with a grain of salt what Zimmerman and other Heideggerians say about learning how to dwell appropriately on the earth as the most pressing moral issue of the day (Zimmerman 1983: 99, 102, 106–7; 1985: 44, 47, 49–51).

Rights, it seems, get in the way of our 'primary obligation': to be open to the Being of entities. But not even the early Zimmerman favours Heidegger when he attacks not only rights, but the whole project of morality, as is evidenced in the following puzzling quotation from Heidegger: 'Every valuing, even where it values positively, is a subjectivising. It does not let things be. Rather, valuing lets beings: be valid – solely as the object of its doing' (Heidegger 1977: 228). Richard Wolin aptly calls this approach, which lies behind the quotation at the top of the present chapter, a 'leveling gaze' (Wolin 1990).

Our supposed obligation to Being does in fact threaten the loss of hard-won rights. On early Zimmerman's Heideggerian view, political activism is itself part of the problem in that it indicates a confidence that frenetic human activity can really improve things. As Heidegger himself continued to work his way out of subjectivism and anthropocentrism, he made it harder and harder to deal with ethical and political questions, although it would be a mistake to think that he really dealt with them well even in his more anthropocentric phase when he wrote *Being and Time*.

The later Zimmerman shows at least some willingness to 'make use of ethical and political theories, including theories that defend rights, to prevent exploitation from occurring, but this is not his usual view, which remains a sort of holism. Zimmerman thinks that somehow or other we will find adequate ways of dealing with inevitable conflicts among individuals without either utilitarianism or rights theory. He hopes that, somehow or other, by letting things be these conflicts will sort themselves out (Zimmerman 1987: 43; 1986: 21, 23). But surely Zimmerman errs here by following Heidegger's vagaries. Ethical and political problems do not sort themselves out, nor do the resolutions to these problems shine forth with middle-voiced clarity, as the laborious processual character of reflective equilibrium makes clear. What is frustrating about Heidegger's thought is the inconsistent way in which he *does* implicitly make moral and political distinctions. Despite the fact that he does not see any ethical distinction between mechanised agriculture and the Holocaust, he does see one between a dam on the Rhine and a Hölderlin poem about the Rhine: to equate *these* two is an example of 'monstrousness' (quoted in Zimmerman 1990: 129).

Both Max Scheler and Emmanuel Levinas have rightly criticised Heidegger for elevating Being over ethics. The later Zimmerman at least partially follows Scheler and Levinas in this regard:

To some extent, Heidegger was following his predecessors Hegel and Nietzsche in claiming that the world-historical individual is 'beyond good and evil'. By portraying ethical matters as secondary considerations which arise within and which are limited to a particular historical world, however, Heidegger ran the risk of justifying whatever ethical form of life happened to emerge in a world 'founded' by a new work of art. The demented 'world' of National Socialism reveals what may be 'justified' when artistic considerations are allowed to triumph over supposedly outmoded ethical ones. Heidegger's refusal to describe his behaviour between 1933 and 1945 in terms of moral guilt stemmed from his belief that his 'ontological calling' to found a new world removed him from the moral censure that pertained only to ordinary people. Of course, since the German people themselves were 'extraordinary' in being called to the dangerous

There is something worse than useless in a misology that culminates in an incapacity to distinguish among the killings of a rational human being, a non-rational yet sentient animal, and a non-sentient shaft of wheat.

The upshot of what has been argued thus far is that: (1) Zimmerman has done an excellent job of indicating the implications of Heidegger's thought for ethics, in general, and for political philosophy, in particular; (2) the later Zimmerman makes at least some progress with respect to criticism of Heidegger's thought in this regard; but (3) even the later Zimmerman fails to sufficiently emphasise the dangers involved in a denigration of rights and political autonomy and in a lack of concern for sentient *individuals*.

Steve Sapontzis is correct in claiming that there is a false dilemma between individualism and holism. Rights theory (as connected to a Kantian kingdom of ends), utilitarianism, virtue-based ethics, Whitehead's value of the whole, and Hartshorne's theistic contributionism are alike in being *partially* holistic. The more robust holism of the early and later Zimmerman, as well as the total holism of the early and later Heidegger, makes it not only possible, but likely, that we would develop an indifference to the suffering of sentient individuals:

> The common moral goal of reducing the suffering in life and otherwise making life more enjoyable and fulfilling would not obviously be more effectively pursued by valuing individuals only as contributors to a community. Indeed, since it is individuals, not communities, that experience enjoyment, fulfillment, distress, and frustration, and since total holism proposes regarding individuals as disposable items in the pursuit of the integrity, stability, and beauty of the community, it seems reasonable to conclude that total holism would not provide as likely a path to this moral goal as our current, mixed morality, which directly values individuals and their quality of life. (Sapontzis 1987: 263)

Jews and Poles suffer, not Jewishness or Pole-hood.

Total holists are, as Sapontzis notes:

. . . fundamentally out of touch with contemporary morality, which emphasises compassion for the injured, the sick, and the handicapped, tolerance for diverse ways of life, concern to expand the diversity of opportunities and experiences available to people, protecting the weak against the strong, and hope for progress. (Sapontzis 1987: 264)

Further, once we abandon Heidegger's levelling gaze we are not necessarily committed to the belief that nature is valuable only as resource, as some Heideggerians might assume. For example, sentient non-human individuals have rights, too (see Dombrowski 1997a), as we will see in the final chapter to the present book.

I am not claiming that a denigration of democracy and rights *necessarily* leads to fascism, only that such denigration makes fascism or some other sort of authoritarianism much more likely. This easy transition to authoritarian rule is facilitated by what Whitehead calls the fallacy of misplaced concreteness wherein abstractions are treated as though they were concrete particulars. Consider Heidegger when he says:

Since the beginning of my installation, the initial principle and the authentic aim [of my Rectorat] . . . reside in the radical trans-formation of intellectual education into a function of the forces and demands of the National Socialist state . . . One cannot presume [to know] what will remain of our transitory works . . . The only certainty is that our fierce will, inclined toward the future, gives a meaning and brings support to our most simple effort. The individual by himself counts for nothing. It is the destiny of our nation incarnated by its state that matters. (see Ott 1993; also quoted in Zimmerman 1989: 332)

Heidegger also claims that 'In truth . . . my works belong not to my person, but instead they serve the German future and belong to it' (Ott 1993; also quoted in Zimmerman 1989: 334). This makes it too easy, in my estimation, to also sacrifice *other* individuals for the sake of the state. Zimmerman's view, which is admittedly a noticeable improvement over Heidegger's, nonetheless involves scare quotes around the word 'rights' (Zimmerman 1993). When a utilitarian does this we should be concerned, I think, but at least I think I understand why a utilitarian uses the scare quotes. When Heideggerians like Zimmerman use the scare quotes, I develop a nervous twitch. I would like to emphasise, however, that Zimmerman at his best is a more enjoyable dialectical partner than those defenders of Heidegger who do not so much explain Heidegger's Nazism as explain it away (see Gadamer 1989; Harries 1990; and, at times, Zimmerman himself, e.g. 1989).

Wolfgang Schirmacher is to be especially thanked for having unearthed the quotation from Heidegger at the top of the present chapter. Heidegger was a Nazi and one operational definition of a Nazi is someone who has lost the capacity for horror (see Davidson 1989, who relies on Stanley Cavell). Even in a work as abstract and arcane as his book on Parmenides, Heidegger asserted the need to defeat the Soviets at Stalingrad. In this book he also took a swipe at the 'so-called philosophy' practised in the United States with its at least approximately democratic institutions (see Heidegger 1992).

The disequilibrium created by Heideggerian politics is, as Levinas insightfully sees things, 'beyond commentary' and diabolical (see Levinas 1989: 487–8). Mark Lilla even goes so far as to suggest that the Heidegger quote that is the focus of the present chapter is obscene, as is Heidegger's 1953 discourse regarding the 'inner truth and greatness' of the National Socialist movement (Lilla 1990). There is a rhetoric, a cadence and a point of view in the Heidegger quote at the top of the present chapter that are damning beyond commentary (also see Sheehan 1988: 41–2).

The *Ad Hominem* Fallacy

Some critics might object at this point that Heidegger's philosophy is being treated unfairly due to the fact that it has been tainted by scare words like 'Nazi' and 'fascist'. Heideggerians are wont to say that the *ad hominem* fallacy is being used against Heidegger and that criticisms of his personal character are being used to discredit his metaphysics, or at least that criticisms of his political views are being used to discredit his metaphysics. The latter procedure, if not an example of the *ad hominem* fallacy, is nonetheless an example of a category mistake similar to the *ad hominem* fallacy.

In the present section I will attempt to accomplish two things. First, I will suggest that critics of Heidegger need not commit the *ad hominem* fallacy in that Heidegger's personal character, his political views and his metaphysics are each, singly, deserving of criticism such that one can criticise each one of these without entering into the other two areas. I will offer some examples of Heidegger's personal character, of his political views and of his metaphysical views that deserve to be criticised, especially because of the disequilibrium-producing potential of these views.

As I see things, there is nothing wrong in criticising Heidegger's personal character if one is clear that this is what one is doing, and as long as one does not use this critique in the effort to discredit his political views or his metaphysics. And there is nothing wrong with criticising Heidegger's political views as long as one does not use this critique in a clandestine way so as to discredit his metaphysics. And finally there is nothing wrong with criticising his metaphysics. None of these procedures involves the *ad hominem* fallacy, which is committed only when one assumes that one has adequately criticised a position by discrediting the person (or discrediting the political views of a person) who holds the position, as when Johannes Stark thought that he had delivered a telling blow to relativity theory by pointing out (in reference to Albert Einstein) that it was 'Jewish physics' (see Heilbron 1986).

But, second, the waters are muddied quite a bit when we consider Heidegger's own view of the connection between his metaphysics, on the one hand, and his political views and the ability of certain individuals (most notably himself and Hitler) to disclose Being, on the other. That is, I will treat some troubling examples from Heidegger's own writings that indicate that it is Heidegger himself who invites the *ad hominem* fallacy by indicating that his metaphysics and his political views and his personal ability to act as an amanuensis for Being all stand or fall *together*.

It is now clear that Heidegger was a member of the National Socialist Party from 1933 until the end of the war. In fact, at various times he wore the Nazi uniform or wore a Nazi insignia, he began his classes and ended his letters with a robust 'Heil Hitler!' and so on. The French investigators who conducted the denazification proceedings in Freiburg at the end of the war saw him as a *nazi typique*, a typical Nazi.

Consider Heidegger's remarks as Rector, remarks made shortly after thirteen faculty members were expelled from the university at Freiburg on racial grounds:

> We lecturers seek to rise up and come to ourselves again. We seek to cleanse our ranks of inferior elements and thwart the forces of degeneracy in the future. By nurturing our sense of honour we seek to teach and instruct each other, thereby ensuring that there is no possibility of falling back into the old ways. (quoted in Ott 1993: 155)

Heidegger was not scandalised by these expulsions, nor did he quietly permit them. He welcomed them. In fact, Heidegger was an enthusiastic supporter of *Gleichschaltung*, the 'homogenisation' of the university. We now also know that Heidegger made disparaging remarks about Jews in his letters and notebooks (see Farin and Malpas 2016).

Examples of Heidegger's duplicity now seem to surface at every turn. Heidegger sugar-coated his remarks to Edmund Husserl and ridiculed him behind his back. Heidegger claimed that he never used his power as Rector to harm others, but in point of fact he denounced to the authorities the chemist (and future Nobel Prize winner) Hermann Staudinger because of the latter's formerly held pacifist beliefs. Heidegger denigrated Catholicism and Catholic priests, yet he pleaded for assistance from Archbishop Gröber when it appeared that only he could help Heidegger with the French authorities at the time of the denazification proceedings. And Heidegger claimed to have left his manuscript titled *An Introduction to Metaphysics* unaltered when it was published in 1953, in the same state it was in when written in 1935, including his aforementioned infamous reference to 'the inner truth and greatness' of the Nazi movement, yet he did, in fact, add a phrase (as Otto Pöggeler details) to get people to believe that what he meant by the Nazi movement was merely the attempt to control rampant technology and so on.

Most problematically, Heidegger never apologised for his own

Nazism, nor for his rather important role in solidifying the Nazis in power at a time when it was not clear that they could keep their hold of Germany, nor for the Nazis causing a world war and the Holocaust. Heideggerians used to say that Heidegger's 'silence' after the war was an appropriate response to an event as incomprehensible as the Holocaust, but we have seen that Heidegger was not silent about this event.

The above should indicate that there are sufficient grounds for calling Heidegger's moral character into question. There is equally sufficient evidence that his political views should be criticised. Regarding a basic question in political philosophy regarding the relationship between the individual and the state, we have seen that Heidegger adopts the especially problematic view that the former is completely subservient to the latter: 'The individual, whatever his place, counts for nothing. The destiny of our nation within the state counts for everything' (see Ott 1993: 240). This defence of totalitarianism, I think, deserves to be criticised no matter who holds it in that it seems to have despaired altogether of the effort to seek a balance between the legitimate interests of the individual and the legitimate interests of the state.

Along with a defence of totalitarianism, Heidegger defended the *Führerprinzip*, the view that, as he put it, 'The Führer himself and he alone *is* the German reality, present and future, and its law' (see Ott 1993: 243; also see Wolin 1990). Heidegger's careful use of the copula here intimates the presence of Being itself. And Heidegger succeeded in getting himself appointed not only as Rector, but also as Führer of the university at Freiburg, the first to do so in the German university system. At one point he had to deal with Erik Wolf, the dean of the faculty of law, who was intent on following principles of procedural fairness and democratic egalitarianism with his faculty, principles that Heidegger hated: 'The whole point of the new constitution and the struggle we are presently engaged in is that you enjoy *my* confidence first and foremost, and not so much that of the Faculty' (cited in Ott 1993: 239).

But it is not only Heidegger's totalitarianism and his defence of the *Führerprinzip* that deserve to be criticised among his political views, but also his extreme nationalism. And, once again, these positions deserve to be criticised no matter who holds them, even

HEIDEGGER AND DISEQUILIBRIUM

those whose personal characters might be more admirable than Heidegger's. An example of Heidegger's own extreme nationalism is his communication to Herbert Marcuse that he thought that the Allied treatment of the Germans after the war was worse than the German treatment of the Jews during the war (see Farias 1989: 283–7)!

Finally, Heidegger's metaphysics deserves to be criticised quite apart from his own personal failings and quite apart from his odious political views. Such a critique will obviously not be offered here in any detail, but only hinted at. Perhaps a good place to start is with a little-known passage that nonetheless contains many of the elements of Heidegger's philosophy that make him appealing to his many followers: a certain literary flourish used to counteract epistemological aggressiveness (as found, say, in the dialectical method of reflective equilibrium) and to encourage 'responsiveness to Being', in Heidegger's sense of this phrase. In this quotation Heidegger is speaking to Elisabeth Blochmann; 'Beuron' refers to a Benedictine monastery near Heidegger's hometown of Messkirch; and 'compline' refers to the last of the seven canonical hours in the monastic day:

The past of human existence as a whole is not a nothing, but that to which we always return when we have put down deep roots. But this return is not a passive acceptance (Übernehmen) of what has been, but its transmutation. So we can only abhor contemporary Catholicism and all that goes with it, and Protestantism no less so: and yet 'Beuron' – to use the name as a kind of shorthand – will unfold as the seed corn of something essential. This is already clear from your feelings about compline, which *had* to give you more than you could ever get from the High Mass. To say that we walk daily into the night is a truism at best for modern man, who for the most part sees the night simply as an extension of the day as he understands it, as a continuation of the busy, intoxicating round. But compline embodies still the elemental power of the night as a mythical and metaphysical presence, which we must constantly break through in order truly to exist. For the good is only the good side of evil. Modern man is more than accomplished in the organisation of every conceivable thing, but he is no longer capable of composing himself for the night. We *appear* to *be* something and to achieve something in a state of 'motion'; but when rest and leisure come our way, we simply do not know what to do with ourselves. So compline has come to symbolise for you the projection (*Hineingehaltensein*) of existence into the night, and the inner necessity of being prepared for it each and every day. (see Ott 1993: 377–8; letter of 12 September 1929)

Even for a critic of Heidegger like myself this is a powerful passage in that it strikes some of the same chords struck by the Romantic poets (who greatly influenced both Whitehead and Hartshorne – see Dombrowski 2017: ch. 6) when they were at their best, say in William Wordsworth's 'Expostulation and Reply' and 'The Tables Turned'.

The key point here is that one can criticise Heidegger's views without committing the *ad hominem* fallacy. One problem with Heidegger's opposition to epistemological aggressiveness (my phrase) and with his fondness for 'responsiveness to Being' is that it is not through public discourse or dialectical exchange or the process of reflective equilibrium that one uncovers the truth in metaphysics, nor even do these procedures help one on a Heideggerian basis to purify one's position of error. Although, as the above quotation indicates, Heidegger does not want to be interpreted as encouraging a mere passive acceptance of tradition or of Being, it is clear that *some* sort of wise passiveness is his object of admiration such that those who are truly responsive to Being are above and beyond the confines imposed by rational criticism from others.

Further, as the above quotation indicates in the line that claims that the good is only the good side of evil (?), Heidegger notoriously held that responsiveness to Being has hegemonic control over the human impulse to use practical reason and the method of reflective equilibrium to make ethical judgements, including those in politics. In a word, metaphysics replaces ethics in Heidegger's view. This leads to what Wolin once again refers to as a leveling gaze in Heidegger where it is not this or that being that deserves respect, but Being.

Thus far I have tried to keep each of three sorts of critique sequestered from each other, but Heidegger himself tempts us to mingle them. The perpetual Advent and the effort to regain the greatness 'of the beginning' that Heidegger emphasises can only be appreciated through the German language and through German philosophy; indeed, only through *his* development of German philosophy in the German language. Obviously, this will strike outsiders as hyberbolic, but what should be noticed is that for Heidegger responsiveness to Being hinges on German philosophy at the present stage of its history as articulated by Heidegger himself.

Outsiders also have a hard time appreciating Heidegger's claim that the Führer is the crucial event not only for political history, but also for the history of Being. It seems that he was dispatched by Being to fulfil the historical mission of the West, a mission understood most clearly by Heidegger himself. We have seen that even in his book on Parmenides, which one would suspect would remain distant from contemporary political issues, Heidegger himself welds his political views with his metaphysics: the German attempt to save Being hinges on the defeat of the Russians at Stalingrad in that the Russians (and the Americans) were alleged to be wholly in the grip of *techne* and hence were incapable of the historical mission to respond adequately to Being (see Lacy 1989).

In that Heideggerian Being withdraws itself from the assertive grasp of descriptive statements, as Wolin emphasises, it can only be encircled in indirect discourse and 'rendered silent'; thus the conceptual content of Being remains undiscoverable. Speech about Being, Heidegger thinks, must remain propositionally content-less; hence this stance also has the illocutionary sense of demanding resignation to fate and the perlocutionary effect in politics of a diffuse readiness to obey in relation to an indeterminate authority, as we have seen Habermas claim. In simpler language, despite what Heidegger and Heideggerians say, Heidegger's metaphysics is supportive of an obsequiousness in politics that can easily be put to use by fascists (see Habermas 1987: 151, 167).

It should be noted that the process whereby instrumental reason, as tied to the forces of modern technology and modern political economy, has crowded out both *sophia* and *phronesis* does, in fact, deserve to be criticised such that we can tease out both the strengths and weaknesses of contemporary technology, contemporary political economy and contemporary fascination for instrumental reason. By way of contrast, Heidegger's theoretical orientation in his metaphysics promotes a rejection of rationality itself, or at least a rejection of practical reason and the processual method of reflective equilibrium where meaningful ethical and political distinctions can and must be made (cf. Young 1997, who incredibly thinks that Heidegger's thought is compatible with liberal democracy).

It should now be clear that critics of Heidegger have a great deal of conceptual mobility to move within three separate areas: Heidegger's personal character or lack thereof, his political views and his metaphysics. There is no need to confuse these categories given the enormous amount of material worthy of criticism within each area, but if critics do, in fact, mingle the categories it is, given Heidegger's own mingling of them, understandable if not justifiable that they do so.

The Noble Lie

Thankfully, no process thinkers of which I am aware have been tempted by the sort of extreme right-wing politics exemplified by Heidegger. This is no doubt due, in part, to the aforementioned idea that the *strict* conservative is working against the nature of the universe in that with each moment something *new* emerges. It is also no doubt due, in part, to the fact that process thinkers are not susceptible to etiolatry (worship of causes) in that there is more in effects than in causes in that, on the process view, effects prehend (or grasp) causal influence from the past *and* creatively advance beyond such influence. However, the fact that the past does causally influence the present (by providing necessary, if not sufficient, conditions for what is decided in the present) means that conservativism cannot ever be *completely* denied. Disputes that arise in this area very often are due to the use of different terminology. For example, Roger Scruton thinks of 'reactionary' thinkers as those who want to return to the past *simpliciter*, whereas he thinks that 'conservatives' are those who try to preserve the best in the past so as to advance fruitfully into the future (see Kearns 2018). On this usage, one could, in fact, imagine a conservative process thinker.

Problems arise when conservative principles are overemphasised or fetishised, as in Heidegger. Problems also arise when the disequilibrium produced by extreme versions of right-wing politics starts to resemble that produced by extreme versions of left-wing politics. And many process thinkers *have* been enticed by these left-wing views. It is to this topic that I will turn in the next chapter of this book.

Before doing so, however, I would like to note one more disequilibrium-producing political problem found in many versions of political thought along the Nietzsche–Heidegger axis: endorsement of the noble lie. Contemporary disinformation campaigns around the world are common. It is crucial to notice that any defensible response to the question 'Is it ever morally permissible for a government official to lie to the citizens?' would have to take seriously Plato's nuanced and apparently positive response to this question (see, e.g., *Republic* 414–15). It is one thing for government officials to lie to citizens, it is quite another to philosophically justify such lies.

Leo Strauss, who, like Heidegger, was heavily influenced by Nietzsche, is one political philosopher who defends the noble lie (see Page 1991). This is a defence that got some traction in George W. Bush's administration, which contained several officials who either studied under Strauss himself or under Straussians (see Dombrowski 1997b; 2004b). From Strauss one learns that Plato's dialogues contain concealed, esoteric meanings, the truth of which can be understood only by a few. The masses cannot understand them. In this regard Straussian Platonists are like many Heideggerians in being in debt to the Pythagorean distinction between the numerous *akousmatikoi*, who hear the message of the master in diluted form, and the relatively rare *mathematikoi*, who are able to really appreciate the truth found in a leader who facilitates lack of concealedness.

Strauss's epigones see the world as a place where isolated liberal democracies are in constant danger from hostile elements, which must be confronted with vigorous leadership and, at times, with lies and violence. The Straussians often criticise those who fail to comprehend the duplicitous character of the regimes with which democracies have to deal. And they adopt Strauss's idea that political life itself is integrally linked to deception. As Seymour Hersh describes Strauss's view: 'Indeed . . . deception is the norm in political life' (Hersh 2003). One major difference between Heidegger

and Strauss is that the latter reluctantly and begrudgingly toler-
ates democracy despite its defects because it can act as a bulwark
against the worst form of government, tyranny, a tepid toleration
of democracy not exhibited by Heidegger.

Any contemporary attempt to defend the noble lie (*gennaion
pseudos*) is only as strong as the effort to demonstrate that the rulers
really are superior, both intellectually and morally, to those who are
deceived. By way of contrast, contemporary political liberals like
Rawls, who opposed the noble lie (see Rawls 1999c: 398), are to
be commended for following Kant in thinking that our rulers can
only come from the ranks of human beings with the same sort of
intellectual ability and moral dispositions as the rest of us. We now
claim to know – accurately, I think – that our rulers can only be
marginally brighter or better than the rest of us; and we are lucky if
even these sorts of leaders can be found.

The agent-centred dimension of Platonic and Straussian justifications of the 'noble' lie (the ancient Greek word *gennaion* actually
indicates 'well born' in that the word for 'noble' is *kalos*) is likely to
cause such attempted justifications to fail. Plato is nonetheless to be
thanked for shedding light on the casuistry that would be needed
in order for a virtuous ruler to justify the noble 'lie' (defenders of
which will translate *pseudos* not as 'lie', but as 'convenient fiction'
or some other euphemism). The ruler needs to ask not only 'Will
the lie foster the common good?', but also 'Am I intellectually and
morally superior to those to whom I am about to lie?' It is hard to
imagine that Heidegger and Strauss could persuasively answer these
questions in the affirmative about themselves (although Heidegger
no doubt was willing to try to do so); and it is even harder to
imagine persuasive answers in the affirmative made in favour of
Hitler, Bush or Trump.

It is to process thinkers' credit, as it is to Rawls's credit, that
the perspective of the deceived (see Bok 1999) is not ignored, a
perspective from which those lied to almost invariably respond
by claiming that as dignified subjects they should not be treated as
lied-to objects. To ignore this perspective, as Heidegger and Strauss
do, is to put our commitment to veracity in a dangerous disequilibrium with everything else we believe to be important in political
philosophy.

One might have expected so much more from Heidegger's political philosophy in that his major philosophical concern was *Being and time*, hence one might have hoped for a processual view that would have been friendlier to Whiteheadian or Hartshornian concerns. However, Heidegger's process approach, if we can call it that, is distorted by a reactionary (as opposed to liberatory) romantic template that is imposed on the attempt to figure out how we are to live together politically. This template includes at least the following six features, on my interpretation:

(1) Heidegger's political philosophy operates against an assumed backdrop of a *primordial golden age* in the past. His idealisation of Pre-Socratic philosophy is a prime example here, but there is a family resemblance among related designations like the following: home, hearth, earth, the fatherland, shelter, wholeness, and integration. (2) There was a *fall* away from this primeval bliss, as is indicated by terms in Heidegger like the following: separation, concealedness, dissonance, fracture, strife, estrangement, alienation, inauthenticity, anxiety, distress, despair, nihilism. This fall in large measure is due to very specific philosophical commitments to logic, science, analysis, argument and dialectic (including the processual method of reflective equilibrium). (3) Because of the fall, a *return* of some sort is needed, as is indicated by terms like these: road, way, will, back-to-the-beginning, and destiny. This is made possible by (4) a *leader* who points the way. Plato's philosopher-king (or queen) is one such leader and Pythagorean *mathematikoi* are a group of such, but Heidegger often alludes prophetically to a poet (Hölderlin) or a hero (Hitler) who fearlessly wanders above the mist and who alone is able to facilitate the proper journey to be taken. We have seen that Heidegger also saw himself in these heroic, Siegfried-like terms. (5) The leader's task is precipitated by a *crisis*, which, as we have seen, should be welcomed because it leads to recovery. Here several cognate terms come to mind: angst, encounter, epiphany, authenticity, transcendence, apocalypse, consummation, conflagration. The key idea here is that the leader's redemptive sufferings are necessary for us to vicariously participate in ecstatic recovery. And (6), all of the above steps are indicative of the unfolding of an historical script, otherwise indicated by terms like tidings and message, and a theory of interpretation that enables us to understand this unfolding.

Although it is hard to know where to begin to criticise this ambitious theoretical construct, it is important to notice that its practical result was politically disastrous, as in the aforementioned (disequilibrium-producing) claim by Heidegger unearthed by Farias that the Allied treatment of the Germans after the war was worse than the German treatment of the Jews during the war. At the theoretical level, it has been the aim of the present book to support the claim that the type of dialectic that I have designated as the processual method of reflective equilibrium is not, as Heidegger thinks (see step 2 above), the cause of our problems. By contrast, it provides our best hope to approximate a just society.

6

Organic Marxism and Process Liberalism

Introduction

A key aim of the present book is to emphasise the close connection between political liberalism and the processual method of reflective equilibrium. As a result of this emphasis we have seen that, whereas some strands of conservative political thought can be parts of an overlapping consensus in an approximately just society, there is no room for rapprochement with an extreme right-wing view such as that found in Heidegger's Nazism. Hence it is understandable that process thinkers have avoided Heidegger's (and Strauss's) political views like the plague (see Dombrowski 2004b). By way of contrast, several process thinkers have advanced the case for rapprochement between process thought and Marxism, despite Whitehead's and Hartshorne's own political liberalism (see Morris 1991: especially ch. 8; Marsh 1999; Pomeroy 2004; and Sturm 1979). The purpose of the present chapter is to engage one set of authors who defend a view called 'organic Marxism' and who use the ideas of Whitehead and Marx to reinforce each other: Philip Clayton and Justin Heinzekehr. These thinkers have recently co-authored one book and co-edited another that are eminently worthy of attention both because of the ways in which common ground between political liberalism and postmodern Marxism can be articulated and because of the ways in which these two views remain at odds. My procedure will be to briefly summarise the salient parts of Rawls's view that are relevant to a fruitful comparison to organic Marxism, then to see the strengths and weaknesses of Clayton–Heinzekehr and related views.

Justice as Fairness

Because of pervasive pluralism in society, Rawlsians think that objective decision-making procedures are needed so as to avoid the settling of political disputes strictly in terms of force. Rawls famously has us imagine ourselves deliberating about justice behind a veil of ignorance where, although we would have as much knowledge as possible of general truths, we would remain ignorant of what our own particular characteristics would be in the society we are designing. Although for the sake of method we are to advance our interests behind a veil of ignorance, as well as the very long-term interests of family members we represent, because we do not know in any detail what our interests would be, we are forced to be fair.

The first principle of justice that would be agreed to by reasonable-rational agents in such a decision-making procedure would be the *equality principle*, which has priority over any other principles that would be decided upon: all basic goods, both material and formal, should be distributed equally in a just society. That is, Rawls is well aware of the fact that formal liberties like freedom of speech do not amount to much if there is not also material freedom from hunger. As a result, one of the standard (and understandable) Marxist criticisms of classical liberalism has been addressed in Rawlsian political liberalism, although the equality principle is arrived at not as a concession to Marxism, but as a result of the painstaking and nuanced terms of the fair decision-making procedure found in the original position.

The second principle of justice concerns the unequal distribution of goods beyond those that it takes to fund the basic goods, which are distributed equally to everyone. If someone gets a larger slice of the pie than others, the possibility of such unequal distribution has to be: (1) open to all (the *opportunity principle*) so that women and blacks, for example, cannot be shut off from such opportunities; and (2) to everyone's advantage, especially the least advantaged (the *difference principle*). It would be an egregious mistake to think that the difference principle was a concession to human egoism, which Rawls does not defend. Rather, parties behind the veil of ignorance would agree to the difference principle for the sake of the least advantaged members of society themselves.

In sum, all three principles of justice work together because they are lexically ordered and tightly knit. The first order of business in a just society is to make sure that basic goods are distributed equally to everyone in society, *then* if there is sufficient wealth for some to get a larger slice of the pie than others, the opportunity for such unequal distribution has to be open to all and it has to be to everyone's advantage (say through a fair system of taxation), especially the least advantaged.

This scheme is diametrically opposed to any 'trickle down' system of justice. Its egalitarian character is such that if a Rawlsian scheme were implemented in practice it would lead, as we have seen, to the most egalitarian society on the face of the earth. It is a 'suffuse up' system rather than one that trickles down. Further, it is clear that this politically liberal view of justice is at odds with any laissez faire version of capitalism, otherwise known as neoliberalism or libertarianism. Although many people in reality defend a laissez faire view, no rational person behind a veil of ignorance would do so! However, it is also clear that *some* version of a market economy could be just. Likewise, it is clear that this politically liberal view of justice is at odds with any version of a command economy, which would not be chosen in the original position, but *some* version of socialism could be just. It follows *a fortiori* that a mixed economy that included both market elements and socialist elements could be just. To ask the question 'Which is more just, capitalism or socialism?' is to ask the wrong question in that types of each are incredibly unjust and types of each could be just. The task, political liberals think, is to keep one's eyes on the prize of justice under *any* economic system (see Rawls 1999c: chs 1–3; 2001: parts 1–3).

Strengths of the Clayton–Heinzekehr View

John Cobb, in a 'Foreword' to the co-authored book by Clayton and Heinzekehr, is insightful in noting that the serious errors of Marxism more or less stem from Marx himself and not merely from the ways in which his views were instantiated in nominally Marxist governments. But this does not mean that we have reached a Francis Fukuyama-like 'end of history' (see Fukuyama 2006) in that, in process fashion, we should instead be impressed by the facts that history goes on and that all governments around the world are, in varying degrees, in continual need of philosophical justification and improvement. Both liberalism and Marxism should be allowed to improve on earlier missteps. Continuing problems call out for fresh responses, indeed for solutions. Clayton–Heinzekehr are to be commended, for example, for moving beyond Marx's belief, inspired by Ludwig Feuerbach, that religion is the opium of the people and that social criticism has to start with atheist or agnostic criticism of religion. Likewise, they are to be commended for leaving open the possibility, not left open by most previous versions of Marxist theory, for some market forces in addition to state-run enterprises. In this regard both political liberalism and Clayton–Heinzekehr's organic Marxism are characterised by hybridity in that suitably constrained market forces as well as suitably constrained state-run organisations can benefit the public good (Clayton and Heinzekehr 2014: i, 1–6, 47–8, 233–6). Such hybridity is very much in line with Whitehead's and Hartshorne's own views, as we have seen.

I assume that the adjective 'organic' in the label *organic Marxism* is meant by Clayton–Heinzekehr to highlight the facts that this position is not, like previous versions of Marxism, inimical to religion and it is not, like earlier types of Marxism, resistant to all sorts of rapprochement with market forces and with liberalism. Clayton–Heinzekehr's version of Marxism is organic because it is still growing and can be grafted onto a process worldview. They are also presumably relying on Whitehead's own label for his view, which was not 'process philosophy', but 'philosophy of organism'.

It is also encouraging that Clayton–Heinzekehr sometimes (unfortunately, not always) distinguish between libertarianism and liberalism; it is only the former that should be their intellectual opponent, on my view. Libertarians, for example, tend to have no problems with inherited wealth, whereas political liberals and organic Marxists do. This is a significant omission on the part of libertarians when it is considered that at least half of the large fortunes in the United States are inherited and not earned (see Haslett 2013). This *should* be an issue for libertarians themselves, given the fact that inherited wealth is not earned and unearned wealth has been, from the beginning of capitalism, one of the most hated vices of the aristocratic class that the capitalist middle class supplanted. Further, political liberals and organic Marxists can join forces in defence of the claim that there are numerous factors outside the control of individuals that can significantly affect their fate in a nominally free market (Clayton and Heinzekehr 2014: 21, 45, 47, 58, 123).

Or again, both political liberals and organic Marxists can agree that markets that operate without government constraints are like athletic events that operate without referees: sometimes things will run smoothly and sometimes all hell will break loose. I personally have seen a gun appear as a resolution to a dispute in a pickup basketball game. But the need for government regulation of market forces does not mean that we should run to the other extreme where the government itself is given total or Promethean control over citizens and over nature. Neither political nor environmental fascism (to be discussed in the next chapter) are likely to produce equilibrium. In addition to ignorance of race and class and sex/gender in the original position, participants behind the veil of ignorance are also ignorant of their generation, thus forcing them to consider the effects of their actions to 'the seventh generation', to use a phrase from Clayton–Heinzekehr that is in turn borrowed from Native American environmentalism. In the effort to construct a government of the right size and of the right sort, what is most crucial is that what Rawls calls 'the curse of money' has to be removed. That is, elections should be like the system of national defence or the interstate highway system in being strictly public goods. On these points as well, political liberals and organic Marxists can agree (see Clayton and Heinzekehr 2014: 54, 62, 106, 178, 211).

At times (unfortunately, not always) Clayton–Heinzekehr emphasise the importance of human rights documents like the Universal Declaration of Human Rights, which includes political rights, material rights and environmental rights (blue, red and green rights, respectively). Clatyon–Heinzekehr even go so far as to adopt the Rawlsian language (without acknowledging Rawls explicitly) of seeing *justice as fairness*. One fruitful way to achieve fairness is to start with obvious cases of injustice and then calibrate one's way toward a resolution of these cases in light of considered principles in equilibrium with each other. In fact, Clayton–Heinzekehr use the language of imbalance and disharmony, which have a family resemblance to what I have called disequilibrium. Both political liberals and organic Marxists should welcome the withering away of modern determinism and mechanism in the effort to realise a defensible political philosophy on a processual, organic and relational basis, much as Rawls and Habermas have achieved a certain degree of compatibility between their own versions of political liberalism and critical theory, respectively (see Clayton and Heinzekehr 2014: 109–117, 121–3, 133–5, 152; also see Rawls 1996: lecture ix).

The above positive features of the Clayton–Heinzekehr view, however, are not the whole story. A transition to what I see as the problematic features of this view is facilitated by a consideration of what Clayton–Heinzekehr see as a continuum of positions in political thought (Clayton and Heinzekehr 2014: 130–1). Furthest to the right, they think, is the 'desert theory of justice', wherein one deserves only what one works for, a libertarian or neoliberal view that we have seen has implications not only for supposed welfare cheats, but especially for recipients of inherited wealth, although defenders of this libertarian theory of justice seldom notice the latter implication of their stance. In the middle are to be found both defenders of 'egalitarian justice', who advocate for equal distribution of basic resources across a population, and defenders of maximisation of certain key values across a society. Clayton–Heinzekehr rightly locate Rawls's thought somewhere in the middle region, although their description of the middle region does not exactly fit with the Rawlsian critique of utilitarian reasoning, including the utilitarian thought of Adam Smith. It should also be noted that the social thought of Whitehead and Hartshorne fits into this middle region, as detailed earlier in the book. In any event, Clayton–Heinzekehr's own stance is at the furthest left, Marxist end of the political spectrum in which the goal is to maximise the contribution of those most able to give and to prioritise distributions to those who need the most. What Clayton–Heinzekehr neglect is the possibility that, by not following through carefully enough on the distinctness of individuals and their legitimate claims, the far right and the far left tend to curve around at the ends of the political spectrum and meet at the back, as was intimated in the above chapter on the Bloodlands. Further, the Rawlsian 'maximin' view, as enshrined in the two (actually three) politically liberal principles of justice, is much closer to what they conceive as just than they realise. The difference principle, in particular, encourages hard-working and talented people to maximise their potential *precisely because* such maximisation can benefit everyone else in society, especially those with the most minimal resources.

Weaknesses of the Clayton–Heinzekehr View

The chief defect of the Clayton–Heinzekehr view, as I see things, is that, although they are rightly attentive to developments in Marxist thought, they are apparently oblivious to the same in liberal thought, which has come a long way from the comprehensive liberalisms of modern philosophers. Clayton–Heinzekehr are correct that many critics of Marxism have never actually read Marx, but the same could be said of many critics of liberalism who have never really read Rawls (who is admittedly not easy to read). Because Whitehead and Hartshorne themselves were political liberals, I think there is an obligation on the part of process thinkers to read carefully the most sophisticated contemporary versions of the politically liberal position. Clayton–Heinzekehr are surely correct that what one learns in American popular culture about socialism is a mere caricature, but the same could be said about what is claimed about supposed defects in liberalism that do not take Rawls into account and that have turned him into a straw man. Of course one cannot start *completely* afresh, given the fact that each actual occasion prehends (includes) its past into itself. Although Clayton–Heinzekehr think that they have written the very first book on Marxism from a process perspective (Clayton and Heinzekehr 2014: v–vii, 12), even this limited project has had predecessors, as was noted above (once again, see Morris 1991: especially ch. 8; Marsh 1999; Pomeroy 2004; and Sturm 1979).

Both political liberals and organic Marxists want to criticise both unrestricted and restricted economic systems of utility, but it is important that even Adam Smith not be mischaracterised. Clayon–Heinzekehr claim that Smith's system is based on a principle of selfishness, yet Smith almost always makes it clear that he is defending self-interest, not selfishness. When one acts in one's self-interest, one pursues one's own interest without necessarily harming others or violating their rights (as in tying one's shoes before going down the stairs), whereas when acting selfishly one pursues one's own interest at others' expense. Further, Smith's overall utilitarian view is fuelled by an egoism of self-interest (not selfishness) that is both descriptive and prescriptive. Smith's key idea is that capitalist markets can imperceptibly transform self-interest (not selfishness) into the greatest good for the greatest number. Although I am sceptical as to whether Smith's invisible hand is as efficacious as his defenders claim, Clayton–Heinzekehr are overly optimistic in thinking that references to this alleged invisible hand of capitalism have virtually disappeared. Unfortunately, they have not. In fact, invisible hand reasoning is still at the core of much of what goes on in economic theory, *hence the need for* critique of this idea from the perspectives of political liberalism and organic Marxism (Clayton and Heinzekehr 2014: 18, 29, 39, 125).

As before, although in reality it is obvious that some people defend laissez faire economics based on the concept of the invisible hand (i.e. a system of unrestricted utility), no rational person would do so when deliberating in a fair decision-making procedure, such as that found in a Rawlsian original position behind a veil of ignorance. Likewise, no rational person would defend behind a veil of ignorance welfare capitalism (i.e. a system of restricted utility) because welfare redistribution of wealth puts too much emphasis on, and hence partially legitimates, the initial distribution, which relies on unjust factors such as inherited wealth.

What is needed is a sober assessment of the strengths and weaknesses of markets stripped of the idea that capitalism has a magical invisible hand that automatically transforms egoism into mutual benefit. This assessment is not likely if Clayton–Heinzekehr's organic Marxism has a family resemblance to the influential thought of Slavoj Žižek, as appears to be the case. Žižek is a former member of the Communist Party who is famous or infamous for hyperbolic statements, as in the claim that he is at heart a Stalinist (!), or that he hoped in 2016 that Donald Trump would defeat Hillary Clinton in the United States presidential election, or that it is legitimate for radical political change to be brought about through violence or terror. I would have thought that Žižek's thought, although nominally a new version of Marxism by self-proclamation, shows signs of old-style Marxism that would frighten Clayton–Heinzekehr. Apparently not (Clayton and Heinzekehr 2014: 86–9, 95; also see Žižek 2003; 2008; and various YouTube videos where Žižek appears). The explicit aim of Clayton–Heinzekehr is to rethink freedom and human rights 'after liberalism'. Indeed, they refer to the 'myth of liberalism' as it relates to freedom and human rights (Clayton and Heinzekehr 2014: 99). This myth has a conservative or libertarian version and a progressive version. The former is especially hostile to organic Marxism, they correctly note, but they also see quite a distance between their own view and progressive liberalism. In this regard, two points are worthy of special attention.

First, Clayton–Heinzekehr think that what they call progressive liberalism consigns moral and religious values to the private realm. My hope is that my treatment of Gamwell's thought in an earlier chapter shows convincingly that the issue is much more complicated than Clayton–Heinzekehr indicate, both because of: (1) nuanced differences among public, non-public and private discourses, with religious and other comprehensive doctrines flourishing in non-public as well as private realms; and (2) the translation proviso, wherein the terms of various comprehensive doctrines, both religious and non-religious, *can* legitimately enter into the public square, so long as they are *reasonable*, once again as this technical term is used in political liberalism to refer to a willingness to abide by fair terms of agreement and a willingness to offer reasons that adherents to differing comprehensive doctrines can understand and possibly accept (Clayton and Heinzekehr 2014: 100, 103).

Second, Clayton–Heinzekehr urge that even contemporary versions of liberalism still contain the DNA of capitalism and are inextricably tied to welfare capitalism, at best. Once again, the issue is much more complicated than Clayton–Heinzekehr indicate. We have seen that Rawls is quite open about the possibility that principles of justice are compatible with some versions of socialism or a mixed economy. On a Rawlsian basis, welfare capitalism is a version of restricted utility that, although superior to the laissez faire economy of unrestricted utility, is not itself just. The social basis of self-respect, which looms large in Rawls, is not given to those who receive welfare in a capitalist society. Welfare is a stopgap measure rather than an aspect of a truly just society. Rawls's remarks regarding a property-owning democracy and regarding the government as an employer of last resort are closer to what he has in mind than anything resembling the welfare state, contra Clayton–Heinzekehr (Clayton and Heinzekehr 2014: 100–1).

One of the standard worries about Marxist thought is that there is little evidence in either Marx himself or in Marxist governments that is conducive to human rights, in general, or to democratic rights (like free speech, due process and so on), in particular. Clayton–Heinzekehr think that there is such evidence and in this regard they cite chapter 2 of Marx's *Critique of Hegel's Philosophy of Right*. (However, in the two editions of this work that they cite there is no chapter 2.) They seem to think that socialism is actually a necessary condition for democratic rights (Clayton and Heinzekehr 2014: 117, 121, 158). I am not as sanguine as organic and other Marxists are regarding this and other parts of Marx that discuss democracy, especially in light of the fact that in many other texts Marx denigrates democratic rights as bourgeois fetishes. And I am even less impressed with the human and democratic rights records of Marxist governments, whether historical or contemporary. I would like to reiterate the point, legitimately made as well by Clayton–Heinzekehr and many other Marxists, that democratic rights are not *sufficient* for a just society (in that free speech does not amount to much if one is starving or homeless), but from this admission it is not legitimate to infer that democratic rights are not *necessary* for a just society.

Clayton–Heinzekehr think that libertarians have more consistently thought through the consequences of the individualistic (indeed selfish) *starting point* of the classical liberals than contemporary liberals. Hence, Clayton–Heinzekehr seem to view the best parts of political liberalism as a watered-down version of Marx, instead of as the results of a fair decision-making procedure behind a veil of ignorance. It should not escape our notice that the Clayton–Heinzekehr language of starting points in political philosophy seems to imply a rejection of reflective equilibrium and an endorsement of the proof paradigm that was criticised in Chapter 1 above (Clayton and Heinzekehr 2014: 124).

Only Marxism, it seems, can pull us away from individualism

and selfishness and towards communitarian values. This point of view undervalues not only Rawls's stance, which is actually hyper-communitarian in the sense that the politically liberal societies he defends provide space for many different communities to flourish, but also the liberal stances of Whitehead and Hartshorne and the progressive or 'new' liberals (not libertarians or neoliberals) who influenced them (like T. H. Green, L. T. Hobhouse and so on. – see Morris 1991: ch. 4). That is, Clayton–Heinzekehr create a false dichotomy between the most egoistic sorts of libertarianism (e.g. Ayn Rand's), on the one hand, and their own organic Marxism, on the other. Given a forced choice between these two, they are certain of victory (Clayton and Heinzekehr 2014: 128).

One very interesting (and, I think, dangerous) metaphor used by Clayton–Heinzekehr is that of a scalpel, which can be used for good or for ill, depending on who is using the instrument. The point to the metaphor, if I understand correctly, is that Marxist tools are not problematic in themselves, but only when put to improper use, as in the Bloodlands by Stalin (Clayton and Heinzekehr 2014: 141). The metaphor is something of a cipher, however, when it is considered that Clayton–Heinzekehr, despite their defence of both human rights (as in a right to bodily integrity) and democratic rights (as in a right to vote for political leaders), do not say anything about the egregious violations of such in China (including the persecution of Muslims in north-west China for no other apparent reason than the fact that they are Muslim) in their chapter on Chinese process thought (Clayton and Heinzekehr 2014: ch. 10). In fact, once again if I understand correctly, they think that China is the country we are to look to for the most efficacious leadership regarding the current environmental and climate change crisis. I will return to this theme in the following chapter. One also wonders about Clayton–Heinzekehr's optimism regarding the fate of religion in organic Marxism. At times it seems that their interpretation is that it is only very conservative, supernaturalistic versions of theism that should be criticised by Marxists in that such versions of religiosity distract us away from historical injustices (Clayton and Heinzekehr 2014: 185), but their neglect of the abrogation of religious rights in communist China leads one to suspect that they are turning a blind eye towards a more energetic opposition to religion in Marxist circles.

Once again, Feuerbach was not ancillary to Marx's own thought, but a necessary condition for it.

From the above it should be clear that I think there is much room for collaboration between process liberals and organic Marxists in the effort to approximate a just society. But such rapprochement would be facilitated if Clayton–Heinzekehr backed down from their apparent claim (inspired by Tom Rockmore) that there is no obvious competitor to Marx as a political theorist (Clayton and Heinzekehr 2014: 235). As I see things, the matter is, well, much more complicated than this hyperbolic claim would indicate.

Marx's *Critique of Hegel's Philosophy of Right*

Because Clayton–Heinzekehr single out this work of Marx's as support for their view that a democratic Marxism is most desirable, it will be worthwhile to examine this work with this claim in mind. There are some obvious features that make this work an ideal choice. One is the condemnation of state censorship in this work. Another is the condemnation of private economic interests posing as political, public reason. These rightly criticised defects are not recognised as such by Hegel, whose purported effort to merely understand society just as often involves a conservative defence of the status quo. However, the Hegelian state is an abstraction, Marx rightly notes, such that a commendably concrete democracy is a truer form of government than the monarchy and system of primogeniture that existed in Hegel's day (Marx 1970: 28–31).

But it is by no means clear in this work (or elsewhere) what Marx means by democracy, hence Clayton–Heinzekehr's appeal to him in this regard is problematic. As I see things, there are two major criticisms that need to be made regarding their use of *Critique of Hegel's Philosophy of Right*.

First, Marx's approach to Hegel's distinction between civil society and politics is troubling from the perspective of political liberalism, which involves an analogous distinction between a comprehensive doctrine that stipulates a concept of the good and the principles that should govern a just society. We have seen that the pluralism of comprehensive doctrines that citizens affirm could create (and historically has created) severe problems if these doctrines are not largely taken off the table in politics (as mitigated by the translation proviso). Marx, however, has a theory regarding humanity's 'essential nature' that should not be alienated from the political. This essential nature involves a view of a human being as a *zoon politikon*. It is an aberration of this essential nature to impose an opposition between the particular features of human beings and the general political system within which they live. Partially echoing the language of Jean-Jacques Rousseau, Marx recoils at any division between what it means to be *l'homme* and what it means to be *le citoyen*: one's humanity and one's political being as citizen are identical. We have seen, however, that there are good reasons for the politically liberal distinction between the various conceptions of the good that can flourish and the concept of justice that allows them to do so. That is, in a condition of pervasive pluralism we should be skittish about Marx's desire to have an abolition of the civil society/ state distinction, at least if religion is an integral part of civil society (Marx 1970: xli–xlv, li, 49, 67).

Marx notices that the good and the right (or the just) were fused (or at least appeared to be fused) in the Middle Ages, but they were explicitly separated (Marx would say alienated) in the modern period. One might wonder about what would give Marx confidence that he could fuse them once again. The answer seems to lie in his belief that he had discovered the criteria for the genuine universal class who could speak and legislate for everyone. This will turn out to be the proletarian class whose role of universality is derived from its historical deprivation. Marx faults Hegel for leaving the distinction between civil society and political state intact, even though Marx thinks that Hegel vaguely sensed the 'contradiction' between the two. By contrast, Marx predicts that civil society itself, including religion – indeed the state itself! – will be dissolved when universal suffrage empowers those who have previously been denied political life. My criticism here is that Marx has utterly failed to stare in the face the fact of pervasive pluralism and he has assumed that everyone should, and that eventually everyone will, view species humanity the way he views it. The purpose of the legislature, in this view of 'democracy', is to represent 'the species will' (*das Gattungswillen*) as an organic unity. Quite ironically, Marx here sounds like traditionalist religious believers who are pure inclusivists in resenting the fact that at present they have to 'leave behind' part of who they are when they enter the public square. Analogously, Marx resented any sort of renunciation of class membership in the (then current) transition from civil society to the political (Marx 1970: liii–liv, lviii, lxii–lxiii, 32, 58–9, 72–5, 78 110, 121, 141).

The second criticism is actually a subset of the first and deals with religious pluralism, in particular. Marx's 'Introduction' to his 1843 *Critique of Hegel's Philosophy of Right* was actually written a year later in 1844 (and the work as a whole was never made available to the public until 1922). It contains his (in)famous judgement that religion is 'the opium of the people'. In fact, Marx thinks, relying on Feuerbach, until religion is thoroughly critiqued no other critique is possible. Feuerbach reversed the poles in religion by claiming that, in contrast to the standard theistic view that God created humans, it is humans who created God. Until this point is firmly established, Marx thinks, we are not in a position to say analogously that it is not the natural prerogative of those who control the state to dictate the terms of social existence to us, rather it is we who create the state. It is the task of philosophy to unmask the mystification fostered by theists (contra Hegel) and then to continue the process of demystification into politics (contra Feuerbach). The mystical aura that surrounds both religion and politics is due to a confusion regarding determining and determined, producing and product. It is not the constitution that creates citizens, but rather citizens who create the constitution. Theism is an indication of, indeed the cause of, both a defective philosophical anthropology and a ruinous social analysis. Marx thinks that the sort of mystification found in the ontological argument for the existence of God, for example, spreads everywhere in a dangerous way (Marx 1970: xxx–xxxiii, lviii, 30, 35, 131–2; cf. Dombrowski 2006).

The problem here, once again, is that Marx speaks as if he has *the* truth regarding religion and hence he implies a comprehensive doctrine. This alleged truth is either that he is leading us to the abolition of religion or that 'history' is doing so. If religious pluralism continues to exist, it is a sign of people's stubborn recalcitrance. Here one is reminded of the French phrase *les extrêmes se touchent* in that Marx, like Heidegger, trivialises (or, better, condemns) all views different from his own, to the extent that he even notices any views different from his own. Further, he, like Heidegger, claims to have identified *the* historical forces that will determine future social reality for everyone else and that will 'redeem' humanity. For both Marx and Heidegger there are two sorts of people in the world: those who agree with them and those who misunderstand them. Granted, there is much sober and insightful and nuanced social analysis in the book in question, but Clayton–Heinzekehr should also notice much that is dogmatic and that uses metaphors regarding political philosophy as a battlefield, as hand-to-hand combat, and as striking one's opponent, of philosophical criticism as a weapon, and of praising arguments *ad hominem*. As with Nietzsche and Heidegger, one wonders (along with Berel Lang) regarding Marx about the degree to which all three authors are partially responsible for their readers' responses when they take these violent metaphors quite literally and act on them. Further, Marx's commendable concern for the proletarian class, which today we might refer to as 'the working poor', need not culminate in Marx's claim that this class should have 'universal dominance'. For example, Rawls's equality, opportunity and difference principles, if applied consistently, would accomplish the practical goal of eliminating grinding poverty without threatening (indeed they would improve) democratic rule and the approximation of justice (Marx 1970: xvi, 41, 89, 133, 137, 140, 142). Even if some religious beliefs *do* have a soporific effect on people, as Marx urges, this is not always or essentially the case, as I see things.

There is one additional issue concerning which neither organic Marxists nor political liberals have paid sufficient attention: the continued (Hegelian) importance of civil society, including changing attitudes toward drug use as well as the massive changes that have occurred to the family in democratic countries in the past several decades. As I write in 2018, the streets of Seattle where I live are strewn with homeless people, the majority of whom face addiction problems of various sorts. These people are not exactly proletarians or the working poor, but are members of what Marx would have called the *Lumpenproletariat*. How to deal with these people still (incredibly) remains under-theorised, although there are some promising proposals coming from political liberals that should not be ignored, especially the Rawlsian equality principle (also see, e.g., Moynihan 1996), even if these proposals are not my primary concern in the present work.

Socialism in Process

In a second book, which is a collection of essays by various authors edited by Clayton–Heinzekehr, the same theme of organic Marxism is explored. As might be expected in an anthology of this sort, socialism is seen as in process and pluralistic. Heinzekehr strikes a common note in disavowing any connection with Marxist orthodoxy, yet also in finding inspiration in Marx's texts. He insightfully notices that it is the Western tradition of discrete substances that provides the metaphysical basis for competitive, invisible hand economics, a metaphysics that Whitehead and Hartshorne criticised (Clayton and Heinzekehr 2017: 6, 11).

Against this background, Carol Frances Johnston makes some points which indicate that rapprochement can be reached between political liberals and organic Marxists not only on substantive matters, but also regarding the even more important method of reflective equilibrium. She highlights a theme in Whitehead's *Science and the Modern World* that we should beware of the transfer of the success of the deductive method from geometry to other areas. This is very much like Rawls's rejection of the proof paradigm in political philosophy. Modern adherence to mechanism can easily convince social theorists of all stripes that a simple method like deduction can easily apply to the machine-like parts of society. Likewise, in *Adventures of Ideas* Whitehead, on Johnston's helpful interpretation, did not take the simple route of defending either laissez faire capitalism with its industrial slavery or the orthodox Marxist alternative, but favours a more complex mixed economy that balances or harmonises what might otherwise be seen as discordant elements: free markets and social controls so as to ensure the common good. It is true that, other things being equal, deduction is conducive to clarity and explanatory power, but it also has the defect of concealing unexamined assumptions and disastrous externalities, negative features that are addressed in the dialectical exchange that is the hallmark of reflective equilibrium. The use of deductive arguments *within* an overall process of reflective equilibrium should be our goal (Clayton and Heinzekehr 2017: 22, 28, 32).

However, it is not necessary to demonise Adam Smith while criticising his thought. Christina Neesham and Mark Dibben notice that all three – Smith, Marx and Whitehead – share a fundamental unease with the nature and role of business. This attempt at a balanced reading of Smith requires that we use Smith's *The Theory of Moral Sentiments* as a searchlight to see *The Wealth of Nations* in perspective. The former book has a prominent role for sympathy in partial contrast with self-interest. That is, *The Theory of Moral Sentiments* makes it easier to see Smith's person-in-community context. Further, they are attentive to the fact that in the *Economic and Philosophic Manuscripts of 1844* Marx makes it clear that he leaned a great deal from Smith, despite the defects in Smith's thought. In particular, Marx's concept of class is heavily indebted to Smith's concept of social order.

Balance, a theme that resonates well with the theme of reflective equilibrium, is at the heart of Leslie Muray's excellent essay. His background in Hungary makes him well aware of the reasons why scholars such as myself get nervous when certain forms of Marxism are defended in academe. This is because 'Marxism excommunicated, tortured, and executed its "heretics"' (Clayton and Heinzekehr 2017: 71), as was intimated in a previous chapter on the Bloodlands. The most historically dominant form of Marxism as found in Soviet ideology was decidedly *not* favourable to reflective equilibrium due to its essentialising of capitalism *and* of deterministic socialism (based on the later Marx, in contrast to the freedom and creativity of the 1844 manuscripts). Political liberals and organic Marxists can agree that we prehend our pasts, but what exactly is it that we should include from Marx in our present political philosophising? Muray notices the obvious anthropocentrism of much of what Marx says, which leads one to be sceptical about the degree to which he can be instructive regarding our current environmental and climate change crisis, to be discussed in the following chapter. That is, the non-mechanistic and non-deterministic view that is central to process thought fits poorly with many versions of Marxism, he thinks. Or at least this is his worry, such that by ignoring the problematic parts of Marx we do not thereby make the tendencies in Marxism that led to Stalin and Mao go away.

Both political liberals and organic Marxists seek fulfilment for human beings. Jung Mo Sung rightly notices that the Marxist concept of commodity fetishism helps us to understand why many people today seek fulfilment or Aristotelian *eudaimonia* through shopping, in contrast, say, to people in the medieval period seeking solace by going to a church so as to feel purer and stronger. Although Sung seems to think that the latter approach to happiness only characterises pre-capitalist societies, I confess that it still resonates with my own personal experience. It will be remembered that one of the key features of political liberalism is that it creates a space for theists and non-theists alike to flourish so long as they are reasonable (Clayton and Heinzekehr 2017: 90–1).

The remaining essays in the second Clayton–Heinzekehr volume tend to deal in various ways with the tension between the abstract and the concrete. For example, Anne Fairchild Pomeroy is attentive to Whitehead's fallacy of misplaced concreteness and the danger involved in having our abstractions be confused with concrete reality. But she realises that such confusion need not occur if abstractions are seen for what they really are: conceptual tools that are useful in the effort to understand multifarious concrete reality. In this regard she refers to 'fortunate abstraction'. Problems arise, from my perspective, only when Pomeroy favourably quotes Marx from the 1844 manuscripts as saying that communism is the riddle of history solved. This sort of language calls to a premature halt the process of reflective equilibrium (Clayton and Heinzekehr 2017: 110, 126). Further, Timothy Murphy is helpful in alerting us to one more version of process Marxism, as mediated by Gilles Deleuze, in the book by Michael Hardt and Antonio Negri titled *Empire*.

The need for the method of reflective equilibrium to be ongoing is highlighted by Barbara Muraca, who notes the coagulation and sedimentation of repeated patterns of belief and action that are desperately in need of present questioning and criticism. After a while we forget how these patterns originated and we take them for granted as something unchangeable, as in the tradition of denying basic health care in the United States to citizens who cannot pay for it. By continuing to critically examine this coagulation and sedimentation we might asymptotically approach what Muraca calls a 'concrete utopia' and Rawls calls a 'realistic utopia' (Clayton and Heinzekehr 2017: 157–60).

Political liberals are not opposed to emphasis placed on the concrete experiences of particular peoples with idiosyncratic living conditions in the effort to approximate a just society, at least as long as a consideration of their particular experiences is but one moment in the overall effort to reach reflective equilibrium. Indeed, consideration of concrete experience should be encouraged so as to keep the abstract deliberations in the original position honest, to 'keep them real', as it were. Heinzekehr himself is instructive in this regard concerning the very particular version of Marxism developed in the early twentieth century in Peru by José Carlos Mariátegui. However, abstract reasoning can help to bring clarity and consistency when concrete experiences of different peoples conflict. I have noticed several times in my own life how the experience of Marxism in Latin America is often quite different from the experiences of those in Poland who were oppressed or killed by the Soviets.

Christine D. Miller Hesed's project is like Heinzekehr's in emphasising the need for consideration of concrete, lived experience, in this case the experience of blacks living in flood-prone parts of Maryland's Eastern Shore. Here the abstract reasoning that must be held in check is that of environmental scientists and policy experts who never even think to consult the people who have lived in these flood-prone areas for generations. This is especially bothersome because these potential victims of climate change would be those who are least responsible for it. Hesed is (unwittingly) helpful in restoring the complementarity between the abstract and the concrete that is conducive to reflective equilibrium. Joerg Rieger's way to make a similar point is to say that neither a crude idealism nor a crude materialism alone is sufficient to support a defensible social critique.

The anthology ends with an essay by Clayton where the author argues that the 2010 Supreme Court decision regarding Citizens United provides one of the strangest and most disturbing manifestations of the American DNA by continuing to allow a huge influx of money into political campaigns. Clayton's view shows a close similarity to Rawls's politically liberal desire to rid 'the curse of money' from politics in that, in Habermas-like fashion, our goal should be political discourse that is not distorted by money. That is, it is a big mistake to think that money *is* speech such that to shut down the flow of the former in politics is to restrict the latter. Political liberals and organic Marxists can agree on this crucial point even if they tend to disagree about whether 'the core insights of Marx remain accurate' (Clayton and Heinzekehr 2017: 241, also 233).

Malone-France as Political Liberal

There is a growing tendency among process thinkers to interpret the political implications of process thought in Marxist terms or at least in terms congenial to the non-liberal left. However, Derek Malone-France reminds us that Whitehead and Hartshorne themselves were political liberals and that there are persuasive reasons to continue to work within the tradition of political liberalism in the effort to approximate justice in a way informed by process thought. It will be the purpose of the present and the following sections to explore further this important work.

The underlying assumption in Malone-France's 2012 work titled *Faith, Fallibility, and the Virtue of Anxiety* is that human beings are *fallible*. As Hartshorne famously put the point, as we have seen, a liberal is someone who knows that he or she is not God. Malone-France is skittish regarding those who exhibit an aggressive sort of certainty in their beliefs, whether they be religious fundamentalists or 'new atheists' or comprehensive liberals or organic Marxists. That is, we should not equate religious belief in general with such certainty. In fact, the psychology of political liberalism involves a sort of *epistemic* anxiety in the face of the pluralism of reasonable comprehensive doctrines that human beings affirm. Anxiety is integrally connected to a profound awareness of human finitude, but Malone-France does not intend that his use of the term be confused with anxiety as a negative psychological state or as neurotic. As the title of his book indicates, the epistemic anxiety he has in mind should be seen as a *political* virtue. Epistemic anxiety actually functions as an antidote to irrational nervousness.

By emphasising fallibilism and epistemic anxiety, Malone-France is *not* legitimating anarchy or libertarianism or neoliberalism, as some of liberalism's critics might assume. Rather, he is to be located within the fallibilist tradition of pragmatic, progressive liberals like Charles Sanders Peirce and Karl Popper. Democratic forms of deliberation are the most morally appropriate forms of political decision making. Even when we are *logically* certain (e.g. regarding the principle of non-contradiction) we ought to avoid *epistemic* or *political* certainty, as Gamwell also carefully argues. Both epistemic conditions (fallibility) and ontic conditions (mortality) should chasten us. Here sin is understood as an illegitimate adoption of an absolutist stance or as the self-delusion of epistemic privilege. As Malone-France puts the point, orthodoxism, whether religious or political, is idolatry.

The task is to retain both epistemic and ontic anxiety in the face of committed belief in that Malone-France is defending neither scepticism nor relativism. In fact, he thinks of such anxiety as *the* liberal virtue because it is wider than toleration, which is usually seen as the preeminent liberal virtue. That is, anxiety is an epistemic as well as a political virtue and this counts in its favour.

Once the inadequacies of John Milton, Locke and Mill are explained, Malone-France is intent on preserving and amplifying the best in these three thinkers, as in Locke's groundbreaking 'A Letter Concerning Toleration'. As the title to Malone-France's book also indicates, faith makes special sense in the contexts of uncertainty and the pragmatic-evolutionary character of scientific inquiry. Faith also drives the political quest to approximate justice. Faith is not beyond knowledge so much as it motivates the quest for knowledge in a condition of epistemological and ontic anxiety.

Epistemic anxiety is conducive not only to the politically liberal virtue of toleration of reasonable differences, but also to the virtue of humility. By way of contrast, the delusional certitude of some religious believers and social critics is most often detected in defence of the claim that certain texts can only be known in secret, in some sequestered region of faith or an inner circle that is immune from criticism. It is precisely this belief that Malone-France tries to flush out into the open so as to criticise it. No type of religious exceptionalism is compatible with politically liberal principles. If there are such things as revealed truths or even secular 'sacred cows' that are not publically accessible, these surely can be cherished by citizens so long as they are not used to restrict the autonomy of others.

In this regard Malone-France is wise to steer a moderate course between pure inclusivists, who think that it is always legitimate to have the terms of one's particular comprehensive doctrine intrude into the public square, even to justify the restriction of others' freedom, on the one hand, and a pure exclusivist position, where one can never bring one's particular comprehensive doctrine into the public square, on the other. This moderate position permits the introduction of one's particular comprehensive doctrine into the public square, but only when such introduction enhances public reason itself, as we have seen in Martin Luther King's religious efforts to enhance public reason.

Malone-France's fallibilist faith and democratic political norms go hand in hand. In turn, politically liberal faith in a future that is at least partially open pushes him toward a defence of a Whiteheadian version of open theism. In contrast to classical theistic omniscience, with its implicit determinism, Malone-France's God faces an open future and, as a result, can even be said to exhibit divine anxiety in analogy with our own anxiety regarding the future. That is, Malone-France defends a revised process version of divine omniscience and also a Whiteheadian–Hartshornian critique of divine omnipotence.

There is a sort of anxiety that the process God shares with us (e.g. regarding future determinables that are not yet determinate) and a sort that is peculiarly our own (e.g. regarding our mortality). God's anxiety is explicated in Whiteheadian terms as the divine Eros. Thus, we do not make ourselves more like God by utterly rejecting anxiety, but rather by avoiding its negative, neurotic expression and by embracing its politically virtuous potential. By contrast, the classical theistic God as a strictly permanent Unmoved Mover is in no way anxious or internally affected by the creatures.

Although it is accurate to claim that neither Whitehead nor Hartshorne engaged in a detailed way with political theory, they nonetheless made it clear that their own political commitments were in favour of some form of liberal democracy or to what today is called deliberative democracy, which exhibits a hybridisation of liberal political theory, on the one hand, and virtue ethics, on the other. Once again, this is not libertarianism, given the atomic, rather than relational, notion of the self in this neoliberal view that is also understandably criticised by Clayton–Heinzekehr. In fact, there is a strong analogy between the libertarian self and the strictly self-centred and self-motivated God of classical theism.

On Malone-France's view, it even makes sense to say that process opposition to determinism and emphasis on the literal decision made by each actual occasion (where some possibilities are cut off so that others are allowed to become actual) amounts to the exaltation of deliberative theory beyond its application in liberal political theory to its productive use in ontology. On this view, persuasion becomes normative not only in politics, but also in reality generally. Snyder's book on the Bloodlands and Dikotter's equally instructive book on Mao illustrate how disastrous politics can be when persuasion gives way to force. These two books detail what are arguably the worst crimes in political history. It is to be hoped that Malone-France's book will be read not only by religious thinkers (who tend to be aware of developments in political theory), but also by political theorists (who tend not to be aware of developments in religious thought, as Malone-France himself insightfully notices).

Hartshorne would seem to agree with Malone-France in his defence of the dialectical method of reflective equilibrium. Hartshorne's method involves certain features that are commonplace in some circles and largely neglected in others (that are unfortunately hegemonic in certain parts of contemporary academe). The Hartshornian features in question involve the following: working as hard to find common ground with one's intellectual opponent as the effort to criticise this opponent, defending one's view against the strongest and most intelligible version of the view of one's interlocutor – in contrast to the 'straw man' approach, and seeking a moderate position when confronted with polar opposites that are extreme (Hartshorne 1984b: 68). It is to be hoped that the present book at least approximates these virtues.

Walzer as Political Liberal

The hope is that the family resemblance among my view, that of Malone-France and that of Rawls should now be apparent and that this family of politically liberal views provides counterweight to the organic Marxists. Another figure in the politically liberal family is Michael Walzer, who helps in the effort to reach rapprochement with organic Marxists in that his view is a bit more communitarian and a bit more energetically socialist than Rawls's view.

At several points in his writings Rawls indicates a debt to Walzer. Most noteworthy in this regard is the fact that Rawls's defence of just war theory in *The Law of Peoples* (Rawls 1999b: 95) does not depart in any significant respect from that of Walzer in his now-classic work *Just and Unjust Wars*. Rawls largely agrees with Walzer regarding issues in *jus ad bellum* (i.e. the justice *of* war), wherein a just cause to fight requires either that one be fighting in self-defence or in defence of the rights of aggrieved others, as well as issues in *jus in bello* (i.e. justice *in* war), wherein the rights of non-combatants should be respected.

Throughout his career, even when opposing the war in Vietnam, Rawls was like Walzer in seeing the refusal to participate in all war under all conditions as an 'otherworldly' view that was integrally connected to sectarian doctrine. Such a view no more challenges the right to self-defence than a defence of celibacy challenges the right to get married (Rawls 1999c: 335).

Rawls also relies on Walzer in defence of the claim that a state has a right to defend its borders and to limit immigration (although the details of such limitation are not specified by Rawls) on the assumption that, unless a definite agent is given responsibility of maintaining an asset, the asset tends to deteriorate (Rawls 1999b: 39). Rawls even follows Walzer rather closely in the latter's controversial defence of a 'supreme emergency exemption'. Here Rawls claims (Rawls 1999b: 98–9) that when civilisation itself is threatened (as when the Allies were on the verge of defeat early in World War II before the Battle of Stalingrad) then *jus in bello* constraints could be violated for the sake of justice.

Rawls relies on Walzer in another area of non-ideal theory. He holds that there is more than one path that leads to toleration. In addition to the toleration of reasonable differences found in politically liberal states, there is something like this in consultation hierarchies as well, as evidenced historically in the Ottoman Empire and imaginatively in Kazanistan, the mythical consultation hierarchy discussed in *The Law of Peoples* (Rawls 1999b: 76).

In ideal theory Rawls also acknowledges a debt to Walzer in claiming that expertise in political philosophy does not entail a claim to rule or a claim to have authority, as would be suggested by philosopher-kings/queens. Nor is political philosophy required in the day-to-day activities of politicians, but this does not diminish the significance of questions in political philosophy. Rather, political philosophy finds its place in the education of citizens regarding the character of democratic thought and attitudes (Rawls 2007: 2, 7; 1996: lxi). Or again, we turn to political philosophy when our shared political understandings break down or when we are divided within ourselves on some political question. The deeper the conflict (as in the contemporary pervasiveness of pluralism), the higher the level of philosophical abstraction that is required in order to get an uncluttered view of its roots. That is, the Rawlsian work of abstraction is set in motion by deep political conflicts (Rawls 1996: 44, 46), as in the divisions created by various nationalist politicians around the world who flourish as I write in 2018.

It should be noted that Rawls does not go as far as Walzer in seeing all political ties deriving from consensual acts, in that Rawls also acknowledges the force of natural duties (Rawls 1999c: 99). Even subjected minorities, for example, have a natural duty not to be cruel (Rawls 1999c: 330). It also seems fair to say that, despite Rawls's defence of associational freedoms, he is not as much of a 'communitarian' as Walzer, whose view seems to require something like a shared (partially) comprehensive doctrine, in contrast to Rawls's stronger recognition of the fact of reasonable pluralism. That is, Walzer's view incorporates culture, and not only institutions, in a way that Rawls would resist.

Rawls makes it clear that justice could be reached either through a kind of liberal socialism or through a kind of liberal property-owning democracy (e.g. Rawls 1999c: 239; 2001: 135–40). Walzer seems to lean more forcefully in the direction of liberal socialism, yet both he and Rawls share many important critiques of contemporary society. One example is Walzer's emphasis on the unjust boundary crossing found in the abuse of money in politics and Rawls's aforementioned emphasis on the 'curse of money' in politics (Rawls 1999a: 580). On this point the family resemblance commendably extends to Clayton–Heinzekehr and other organic Marxists.

Now that my own view is on the table for rational criticism (Chapters 1–3), as well as my criticisms of prominent views that I find deeply problematic (Chapters 4–6), I would like to turn to the issue of how processual political liberals should respond to one of the greatest challenges facing political theorists in the twenty-first century, that is, how to respond to the enormous environmental crisis that faces us. My response will have the status of non-human animal rights play a more significant role than is usually played in the work of other political theorists and will, once again, rely heavily on the method of reflective equilibrium.

7

From Non-human Animals to the Environment

Introduction

Historians of philosophy have sometimes noted how crucial it is to one's interpretive stance in the present to be as clear as possible regarding the 'from . . . to . . .' perspective that one is adopting in one's scholarly work. For example, the Descartes that one would study in a book with the title *From Aquinas to Descartes* would presumably be quite different from the Descartes one would study in a book titled *From Descartes to Kant*. In the first case one would probably be considering the medieval sources of Descartes's thought and in the second case one would probably be viewing Descartes as preparing the way for Kantian dualism (see Collins 1972: 165–77).

In the present chapter I will be exploring the possible benefits for environmental ethics, in general, and for environmental ethics in the process tradition, in particular, of approaching questions in environmental ethics by way of non-human animals. We will see that there are significant differences between my 'from non-human animals to the environment' approach and the more popular 'from the environment to non-human animals' approach. It is often assumed that in order to deal adequately with the current environmental crisis one must first develop a reticulative vision of the whole and, as a consequence, develop a version of deep ecology wherein our primary ethical obligations are to ecosystems rather than to individual human beings or to individual non-human animals.

There are obvious benefits to the deep ecology or ecoholist

positions. I am not so sure, however, that the ecoholism that is thought to be necessary solves as many problems as its defenders assume; and I also think that ecoholism, if unchecked, creates serious moral problems from the perspective of political liberalism. Tom Regan has famously (or infamously) argued that the idea that our primary ethical obligations are not directed to individual human beings or to individual non-human animals but to ecosystems amounts to a sort of environmental fascism wherein individuals are for the sake of the whole *simpliciter* (see Regan 1983: 245, 361–2, 396). Although Regan's language here might seem hyperbolic, the legitimate concern he has for sentient individuals (whether human or non-human) should not be ignored. By contrast, one persuasive way to read Aldo Leopold's classic *A Sand County Almanac* is that it basically contains a hunter's ethic that attempts to justify with equanimity culling members of overpopulated herds (see Leopold 1987: viii, xviii, 34, 37, 40, 54–8, 62–6, 71–7, 110, 117, 120–2, 129–30, 132–4, 139, 144–6, 149–54, 166–77, 187). The odious Malthusian implications of this view for the overpopulated human species are not usually noted. For example, Leopold's famous characterisation of the land ethic states that 'a thing is right when it tends to preserve the integrity, stability, and beauty of the biotic community. It is wrong when it tends otherwise' (Leopold 1987: 224–5); this would seem to counterintuitively imply, even if Leopold did not realise this, that war, disease and malnutrition in human beings are actually *good* things.

The 'from the environment to non-human animals' approach starts with a legitimate concern for ecosystems and almost as an afterthought then considers the implications of this view for individual human beings and individual non-human animals. My alternative 'from non-human animals to environment' approach (1) starts with the politically liberal assumption that individual human beings are moral patients worthy of moral respect, then (2) moves to a consideration of those beings who are closest to us in moral patiency status (non-human animals with central nervous systems) so as to see if we have moral duties to them as well, then (3) considers a crucial distinction between domestic and wild non-human animals, with the latter pointing us towards (4) a consideration of ecosystems and the natural world in general. Further, I will explore

these steps with a Whiteheadian framework in mind so as to further enrich the process tradition's already significant contributions
in environmental ethics (see, e.g., Cobb and Birch 1981; Henning
2005). The ultimate hope is that the 'from non-human animals to
the environment' and the 'from the environment to non-human
animals' approaches can mutually benefit each other by keeping
each other honest, as it were, in a friendly dialectical tension that is
conducive to reflective equilibrium.

Revolt against Dualism

Throughout his career Whitehead was, for various reasons, an
opponent of dualism. Not least among these reasons was the fear
that dualism could easily lead to reductionistic materialism once
it was realised that mind (or life or self-motion) is, as a result of
dualism, an irrelevant ghost in the machine. The materialist merely
exorcises the ghost (Whitehead 1967b: ch. 5).

Whitehead's response was to advocate a fusion of mind (or life
or self-motion) and physical nature in the composition of the 'really
real things'. This revolt against dualism has the following implication for non-human animals: in abstraction from its animal body,
a living nexus is not understandable at all (and vice versa). Indeed,
each actual occasion is a bipolar fusion of the physical and the appe-
titive or mental (e.g. Whitehead 1978: 104, 108; 1968: 150; 1967a:
210, 212–13, 253, 259).

Scale of Becoming

This fusion (or better, *inter*fusion) is spread throughout nature in
something like a scale of becoming, which is the process version of
the traditional scale of being. At one point, Whitehead distinguishes
among six types of occurrences in nature. In descending order,
these are human existence, the kind of life found in vertebrate
animals generally, vegetable life, living cells, large-scale inorganic
aggregates, and finally the happenings on an infinitesimally small
scale as disclosed by physicists (Whitehead 1968: 156–7; 1978: 98).
At another point, he distinguishes in an analogous way among four
grades of reality, with the highest level exhibiting a reorganization

of experience characteristic of reason (Whitehead 1978: 177–8).

Whitehead makes it clear that these are not airtight boundaries, but are rather heuristic and explanatory devices. That is, different types of existence 'shade off into each other'. By implication, there is no absolute difference between human beings and non-human animals; indeed human beings *are* animals. Likewise, the most primitive plants fade into the lives of a cluster of living cells. There is not even an absolute gap between living and non-living societies. Ours is a 'buzzing world, amid a democracy of fellow creatures' (Whitehead 1978: 50, 102; 1968: 157).

The problem for Nature (Whitehead himself capitalises here) is the production of complex societies that are unspecialised; in this way 'intensity is mated with survival' (Whitehead 1978: 101). This problem is solved by the enhancement of the mental pole. It should be noted that Whitehead does not restrict such enhancement to human beings (as in Kant), rather he extends it to 'higher organisms'. These are organisms that 'think', at the very least in the sense that they do not thoughtlessly adjust to causal factors affecting them (Whitehead 1978: 101–3). I will return to non-human animal mentality momentarily.

Non-human animal bodies are living societies that contain both living cells as well as 'inorganic' subservient apparati at the level studied by physicists. In a famous turn of phrase, we have seen that Whitehead describes life as 'the clutch at vivid immediacy' (Whitehead 1978: 103–5). We will see that this immediacy is noteworthy from an ethical point of view if what is vividly experienced is pain, especially if it is unnecessary pain.

Non-human animals clearly exhibit modes of behaviour that are directed not only towards the avoidance of pain, but also towards 'self-preservation', Whitehead thinks. In fact, they give every indication of having some sort of feeling of causal relationship with the natural world. Even a jellyfish advances and withdraws in response to causal influence; and plants reach down to find water and nutrients with their roots (Whitehead 1978: 176). Although feeling of some minimal sort is spread throughout nature, in that there are 'throbs of pulsation' in molecules, plant cells, and the lives of non-human animals and human beings, it is only with non-human animals that we find sense perception per se. It is probably true that non-human animal perception does not rise to the level of presentational immediacy found in human beings. In human beings there can be immediate absorption in the projected present, as opposed to being (largely but not exclusively) a vehicle for receiving the past. But whereas the laws of nature are constituted by large average effects that are impersonal, those beings capable of both sense perception and 'expression' exhibit a significant degree of personal individuality (Whitehead 1978: 176–8; 1968: 21, 86).

Continuity with Non-human Animals

We have seen in the previous section both that Whitehead defends a hierarchy of becoming in nature *and* that there are no wide gaps, but rather continuity and shades of difference, between each hierarchical stage. There is no sharp division between mentality and nature. Likewise, there is no sharp division among the levels of mentality found in nature: we live *within* nature (Whitehead 1968: 156; 1967a: 186).

Like us, non-human animals have minds that are temporally ordered. Further, their minds are incorporated in bodies that are constituted by a vast number of occasions of experience that are spatially and temporally coordinated. Such coordination is a major factor in the activities of the parts (Whitehead 1978: 106). In addition, vertebrate animals with central nervous systems, at the very least, have their social systems dominated by mentality to such a significant extent that it is fair to say that their lives are *personally ordered*. Although a dog does not rise to the height of human mentality (and hence, in a sense, is not a person in the commonsensical version of personhood), a dog nonetheless has a mental life that is temporally coordinated, with continuity among its occasions of experience (and hence, in a different and technical sense, *is* a person). To take a simple example, if a dog is kicked by a particular human being on Tuesday, then when the same human being approaches the dog on Wednesday the dog either cowers or growls because she *remembers* what happened the previous day and *has good reason* to be afraid. Lower animals and vegetation, by way of partial contrast, lack the dominance provided by a (quasi-monarchical) personal society of occasions. As Whitehead puts the point, 'a tree is a democracy' (Whitehead 1967a: 205–6, 215, 291).

In technical language, personal order characterises a society when 'the genetic relatedness of its members orders these members "serially"' or when a society 'sustains a character' (Whitehead 1978: 34–5). Immediately we think of human persons, and rightfully so. In some sense we think of human persons as the same realities from birth to death, but the issue of personal identity is complex in process philosophy, as is well known, due to the belief that the primary, concrete realities are momentary experiences. There is something more abstract involved in attributing identity to these experiences when they are strung together over long stretches of time. As a result, the abstract identity of a human being or of a non-human animal should not be overemphasised. This is because if, as Whitehead thinks, 'life is a bid for freedom', then human identity cannot be seen as a strictly enduring substance. Both we and non-human animals *change* from moment to moment. That is, human beings and non-human animals are living organisms that exhibit self-motion in their reactions to any tradition (Whitehead 1978: 90, 104).

Hartshorne's Whiteheadian way of putting the issue is to speak of personal identity in terms of temporal asymmetry: we are internally related to our pasts, which are already settled (e.g. I cannot change the fact that I was born in Philadelphia), but externally related to our futures, which are partially open to our plastic control (who knows what city I will be in when I die?). 'Life is a passage from physical order to pure mental originality' (Whitehead 1978: 107). Whitehead's use of 'pure' here is misleading, however, in that it suggests *complete* central control or strictly mental activity without the body. Rather, Whitehead seems to think that we are somewhat more decentralised than this in that our hearts beat and our hormones secrete largely in ways outside of our control (Whitehead 1978: 106–8).

The key point here is that, whereas primitive feeling is to be found at lower levels of reality, 'we have passed the Rubicon' when sense perception is acquired; here 'we' refers to *both* human beings and other sentient animals. Sentient non-human animals (albeit to a lesser degree than most human beings) use sense perception to learn from their mistakes; they 'profit by error without being slaughtered by it'. And in our own 'upward evolution' we proceed not only by way of error-elimination, but also by a positive, confident 'animal faith' (à la Santayana) that the world is intelligible (Whitehead 1978: 113, 142, 168; 1967a: 4, 20, 177–8, 214, 247). Donald Griffin has us notice here that the aforementioned Whiteheadian 'Rubicon' is not crossed when human rationality comes on the scene, but when sense perception is acquired by non-human animals.

It is because human beings have animal bodies capable of sense perception that we can use these bodies as 'the great central ground underlying' more intellectual pursuits. This central ground makes possible the 'inflow into ourselves of feelings from enveloping nature', an inflow that sometimes overwhelms us such that it is only gradually, after much thought and experimentation, that we can understand it. In Whiteheadian terms, the supposedly more exalted perception in the mode of presentational immediacy is dependent on perception in the mode of causal efficacy. Hume and other modern epistemologists erroneously invert this relationship (and thereby obliterate causal efficacy); hence they misunderstand the nature of the continuity between non-human animals and human ones. We, as with non-human animals, feel *with* our bodies in terms of a 'vector transmission of emotional feeling', with such feeling being not only transmitted but also modified along the way (Whitehead 1978: 170, 178, 181, 312, 315).

Even in *Modes of Thought*, where a human being's partial transcendence of animality is a major theme, Whitehead notes that the rise of human genius and of human civilisation has a long history that stretches back to non-human animals. That is, the highest reaches of the human psyche cannot be dissociated from our animal physiology. Indeed, sense perception already involves abstraction in the sense that it encourages (in fact, requires) selective emphasis. Thus, when a human being tries to be as clear as possible regarding sense perception, he or she 'sinks to an animal level'. Non-human animals, too, in a certain sense specialise their perceptions, as when a pig picks up a scent for food when hungry and then will not let it go. Our 'triumph of specialisation', although distinctive, is continuous with non-human animals' transmission and modification of massive and vague experiences in the mode of causal efficacy (Whitehead 1968: 65, 73, 113, 121).

To put the aforementioned point in a phenomenological way, the sharp distinction between mentality and nature is not what we experience. In a courtroom trial we are skittish about merely circumstantial evidence; we also want to know what the accused's *motive* was. Likewise, a lost dog that exerts great effort to get home is believed to have *aimed* to do so. Despite the fact, rightly noticed by George Lucas, that Whitehead does not explicate the thoughts of Darwin or other major evolutionary biologists with the same attention that he gives to major figures in the history of physics, nevertheless everything that he says about non-human animals pre-supposes a worldview thoroughly consistent with the theory of evolution. Consider vision. We are obviously not the only animals who can see, even though vision is considered by some scholars to be the most intellectual sense because of its abstract, impartial spectator quality (in contrast, say, to the concreteness of touch). In fact, some non-human animals (e.g. eagles) see better than we do. Hence, Whitehead sees evidence of 'flashes of mentality' in non-human animals (Whitehead 1968: 156–9, 167–8).

Partial Transcendence of Animality

Despite the considerable continuity between human beings and non-human animals detailed in the previous section, Whitehead nonetheless is committed to the contrast between the high-grade functioning of human beings and 'mere animal savagery' (Whitehead 1967a: 48). The contrast is a subtle one, however, despite the startling language regarding savagery. For example, the high-grade functioning of human beings in Whitehead is quite different from the traditional anthropocentric, essentialist claim that human beings are rational. 'This is palpably false: they are only intermittently rational' (Whitehead 1978: 79); and only some of them are intermittently rational, as we will see. The higher non-human animals (i.e. vertebrates with central nervous systems) are persons, in the sense specified above, but they are not necessar-ily aware of themselves as such, as we *at times* are. Our intermittent self-consciousness allows us a partial transcendence of animality (Whitehead 1978: 107, 109).

Much of our lives is spent aesthetically appreciating the world in ways continuous with those of the non-human animals. Thus, Whitehead thinks that Kant's 'Transcendental Aesthetic' is a distorted fragment of what should have been his main topic. When Whitehead says that 'intensity is the reward of narrowness', he seems to be referring to those relatively rare moments of self-consciousness when we reflect on our lives as conscious animals (Whitehead 1978: 112–13). We pay a price for this narrowness, however. That is, we pay a price for our partial transcendence of animality. This is because it is precisely narrowness in the selection of evidence that is the chief danger to philosophy, especially when such narrowness is confused with synoptic vision of all aspects of a problem (Whitehead 1978: 319, 337). It seems that narrowness of focus (and the intensity of experience it brings) is both necessary to, and destructive of, systematic philosophy.

A human being's partial transcendence of animality is found in most of Whitehead's major philosophical works (e.g. 1967a; 1967b; 1978), but it is especially prominent in *Modes of Thought*. Here he makes it clear that he thinks that although songbirds (the hermit thrush, the nightingale) can produce real beauty, they are not civilised beings. Note in the quotation below, however, evidence of both the partial transcendence of animality *as well as* the seeds of a Whiteheadian ethic of non-human animal rights:

> The hermit thrush and the nightingale can produce sound of the utmost beauty. But they are not civilised beings. They lack ideas of adequate generality respecting their own actions and the world around them. Without doubt the higher animals entertain notions, hopes, and fears. And yet they lack civilisation by reason of the deficient generality of their mental functionings. Their love, their devotion, their beauty of performance, *rightly claim our love and tenderness in return* . . . Civilised beings are those who survey the world with some large generality of understanding. (Whitehead 1968: 3–4; emphasis added)

Along with many other twentieth-century philosophers, Whitehead sees language as the key to our advanced mental functioning, but even the most articulate among us often find it difficult to speak with learned precision about what we feel *as animals* (Whitehead 1968: 5).

In Whitehead's terms, non-human animals as well as human ones have intense 'interest' in various particular things as well as some inchoate sense of the 'importance' of the whole environment. Further, Whitehead thinks that it is importance that generates interest and that such generation gives rise to discrimination among interests and hence gives rise to language and advanced consciousness. Once again, there is continuity with non-human animals here. They can clearly engage in both signalling and emotional expression, but Whitehead thinks that non-human animals are limited in the degree to which they can engage in abstraction from the immediate situation. The biblical metaphor used by Whitehead to make the point is that on the sixth day God gave human beings speech and they thereby became souls (Whitehead 1968: 11–12, 20–41, 44, 52–3, 57).

At one end of the continuum of nature there are human beings with a profound experience of 'disclosure' of nature's secrets; at the other end there is supposedly inorganic nature. Towards the upper end of this continuum there are non-human animal satisfactions as well as a certain degree of clarity found in human understanding. Or again, non-human animals *enjoy* the structure of the world, but human beings can *study* it. We can see form within fact. By way of contrast, Whitehead cites an example from personal experience of seeing a mother squirrel remove her young from a dangerous place one by one until all three were safe, but she returned a fourth time to the old place because she could not count (Whitehead 1968: 62, 76–8).

We can try to understand nature in terms of concepts like 'space', 'time' and 'deity'. Non-human animals only anticipate this understanding when they sometimes pass beyond the enjoyment of immediate fact. The aforementioned mother squirrel, for example, presumably stored up acorns for the winter. In Whitehead's strongest statement in favour of partial human transcendence of non-human nature, however, he suggests that 'when all analogies between animal life and human nature have been stressed, there remains a vast gap in respect to the influence of reflective experience' (Whitehead 1968: 102–3). Or again, 'take the subtle beauty of a flower in some isolated glade of a primeval forest. No animal has ever had the subtlety of experience to enjoy its full beauty. And yet this beauty is a grand fact in the universe' (Whitehead 1968: 120). Even less capable of experiencing such beauty are the living cells in the flower.

Yet Whitehead nonetheless thinks it is an example of 'holiness' that one notices the 'sacredness' of natural beauty in both flowers and non-human animals. Partial transcendence of animality depends on the level of abstraction at which we (some of us, some of the time) can think. Granted, non-human animals live at a much more abstract level than cells, but we emphasise and are explicit about such abstraction (Whitehead 1968: 120, 123).

Two Arguments in Favour of Non-human Animal Rights

There has recently been an explosion of interest in philosophy regarding our current environmental crisis, in general, and regarding the moral status of non-human animals, in particular. This interest often intersects with philosophical arguments in favour of non-human animal rights. The purpose of the present section is to present two such arguments and to eventually argue for their philosophical soundness on a Whiteheadian basis.

The first of these two arguments is called the argument from sentiency and it is the simpler of the two:

A. Any being that can experience pain or suffer has, at the very least, the right not to be forced to experience pain or suffer (or be killed) unnecessarily or gratuitously.

B. It is not necessary that we inflict pain or suffering (or death) on sentient non-human animals in order for us to have a healthy diet.

C. Therefore, eating sentient non-human animals is an example of unnecessary infliction of pain or suffering (or death) and ought to be avoided.

The intuitive appeal of the argument from sentiency is enough to convince many philosophical vegetarians. Whiteheadians who are convinced by it might speak in terms of tragic loss. However, the realisation that it is not necessarily rationality that is the criterion that must be met in order to deserve moral respect leads to further considerations that are treated in the second argument, which is often called the argument from marginal cases (hereafter: AMC).

Defenders of this argument agree with almost everyone else regarding the criterion that must be met in order to be a moral *agent* (i.e. someone who can perform moral or immoral actions and who can be held morally responsible for his/her actions): rationality. At times it might be difficult to apply this criterion if the alleged moral agent is not obviously rational, but almost everyone agrees that rationality is the property that would be required in order to hold someone morally accountable for his/her actions.

The key question, however, is the following: what property needs to be possessed in order to be a moral *patient* or a moral beneficiary (i.e. someone who can receive immoral treatment from others, or who can have his/her rights violated, or who can be treated cruelly)? Here the issue is quite complicated and contentious. One of the complicating factors is that to speak without qualification of 'properties' of 'subjects' is both to run the risk of remaining within the subject-predicate mode of thought and to continue the fiction of a substantial self, which Whitehead legitimately wants to criticise. The proper task is to temporalise moral patiency status so as to avoid both of these defects, as we will see, while nonetheless paying sufficient attention to the infliction of unnecessary suffering or death that understandably results in a Whiteheadian sense of tragic loss (see Dombrowski 1997a: 189–93).

The most parsimonious response to the question regarding moral patiency status leads to a type of symmetry that some find attractive: make *rationality* do double-duty by serving as the criterion for moral patiency status as well as for moral agency. But this response leads to disastrous consequences in that on its basis many human beings (the marginal cases of humanity) would not be moral patients and hence would not deserve moral respect.

An understandable reaction to the difficulties involved in demanding a very high criterion for moral patiency status like rationality is to lower it significantly. For example, some religious believers (e.g. Albert Schweitzer and other 'pro-life' proponents in Christianity, or the Jain sect in Hinduism) wish to make *life* the criterion for moral patiency status. All life, we are told, deserves moral respect. But this response also leads to disastrous consequences in that on its basis we would not be morally permitted to mow, or even walk on, grass because living insects would be killed; cut out cancerous tumours because cancer cells are (unfortunately) quite alive and well; or even breathe if perchance we would suck in living organisms that would be killed; and so forth. What would we be able to eat on a consistent pro-life basis? Schweitzer's own writings indicate what some of the absurd consequences would be. And Jain purity was historically often purchased at the expense of the Dalit caste as these 'untouchables' cooked for, and swept the paths of, those Jains who refused to take the life of a living thing. That is, AMC forces us to be a bit more specific than we have been thus far regarding moral patiency status.

Defenders of AMC work their way, both theoretically and practically, to a place in between these two extremes so as to find a defensible criterion for moral patiency status in *sentiency*. On this basis all human beings deserve respect (even the most marginal of marginal cases still have a functioning central nervous system and hence are sentient), but non-human animals with central nervous systems, and hence sentiency, are also protected.

Before moving to the connection between AMC, on the one hand, and Whitehead, on the other, an ordinary language statement of the argument might be helpful:

A. It is undeniable that members of many species other than our own have 'interests', at least in the minimal sense that they feel and try to avoid pain, and feel and seek various sorts of pleasure and satisfaction.

B. It is equally undeniable that human infants and some of the profoundly mentally impaired have interests in only the sense that members of these other species have them and not in the sense that normal adult humans have them. That is, human infants and some of the profoundly mentally impaired (i.e. the marginal cases of humanity) lack the normal adult qualities of purposiveness, self-consciousness, memory, imagination and anticipation to the same extent that members of some other species of animals lack those qualities.

C. Thus, in terms of the morally relevant characteristic of having interests, some humans must be equated with members of other species rather than with normal adult human beings.

D. Yet predominant moral judgements about conduct towards these humans are dramatically different from judgements about conduct towards the comparable non-human animals. It is customary to raise the non-human animals for food, to subject them to lethal scientific experiments, to treat them as chattels, and so forth. It is not customary – indeed it is abhorrent to most people even to consider – using the same practices for human infants and the mentally impaired.

E. But lacking a finding of some morally relevant characteristic (other than having interests) that distinguishes these humans and non-human animals, we must conclude that the predominant moral judgements about them are inconsistent. To be consistent, and to that extent rational, we must either treat the humans the same way we now treat the non-human animals or treat the non-human animals the same way we now treat the humans.

F. And there does not seem to be a morally relevant characteristic that distinguishes all humans from all other animals. Sentience, rationality and so forth all fail. The assertion that the difference lies in the *potential* to develop interests analogous to those of normal adult humans should also be dismissed. After all, it is easily shown that some humans – whom we nonetheless refuse to treat as non-human animals – lack the relevant potential. In short, the standard candidates for a morally relevant differentiating characteristic can be rejected.

G. The conclusion is, therefore, that we cannot give a reasoned justification for the differences in ordinary conduct towards some humans against some non-human animals (loosely based on Becker 1983).

In one sense, the point of AMC is to ask for a more responsible use of apparently harmless terms like 'all' and 'only'. Any morally relevant characteristic that is possessed *only* by human beings will not be possessed by *all* human beings. To try to escape from the ramifications of this observation by claiming, as many philosophers do, that all humans deserve moral respect because they *are* human, is clearly to beg the question. Exactly what morally relevant property is it that all humans, but only humans, possess that non-human animals do not possess?

I should note here my willingness to adjust any language I have used in this section that might be offensive. For example, to speak as I have of the 'mental impairment' of some human beings is in one sense quite accurate, I think (other things being equal, we would wish our children to have brains and/or mental lives that function well), but it could be interpreted by some to imply a rational essence to humanity. Along with Whitehead, however, I am a critic of essentialism. Or again, to refer to the argument in question as that from 'marginal cases' is a concession to standard usage among philosophers and it is not meant to imply that those who are different should be pushed to the margins. Actually, my obvious intent is quite the opposite. The point is that *if* we committed the mistake of making rationality the criterion for moral patiency status, then many human beings *would* be marginalised. Perhaps 'argument for moral consistency' or 'argument from species overlap' might be better.

Reflective Equilibrium, Again

A defence of AMC does not have to be based on the idea that there are independently existing facts out there that dictate our morality, as in some versions of natural law theory. Rather, our values and obligations can legitimately be derived from facts if the facts to which they refer are intelligibly seen as the relevant ones, and if the values derived from these facts are defensible ones. Or again, a defender of AMC need not commit to the naive view that facts wear their relevance on their face and that values can be immediately derived from them. That is, AMC is indeed an *argument* that gives reasons for the defensibility of the claims that non-human animals have basic rights due to their sentiency and that species membership is irrelevant when considering moral patiency status itself.

By way of contrast, critics of AMC like Elizabeth Anderson and Cora Diamond seem to move illegitimately from the claim that human decision making is a necessary condition for there being rights to the claim that it constitutes a sufficient condition for there being rights. Another way to put the point is to say that Anderson's and Diamond's views are overly nominalistic when they hold that beings acquire status as moral patients (entirely?) because *we* say that they deserve such status. Human beings on this view have the Orpheus-like and Wittgenstein-inspired ability to bring moral patiency status to life merely by saying that it should be so. The remedy to such an approach does not run to the other extreme, where it is assumed that moral patiency status is a fact 'out there' waiting to be discovered. Rather, human beings are the measurers of nature, but not necessarily the measure; they are the primary beholders of value in nature, but not necessarily the only holders of such value (to use Holmes Rolston's helpful language).

In is quite understandable why some people are sensitive to the possibility that others might exhibit insensitivity regarding marginal cases of humanity. This is because marginal cases of humanity have been treated deplorably in the past and because, for example, a United Nations statement declaring the rights of intellectually impaired beings did not occur until the 1970s, with many other historically marginalised groups receiving attention years before.

But as philosophers we must be on the alert to continue the Aristotelian project of treating similar cases alike and varying cases differently in proportion to their variances. James Rachels is on the mark in regard to AMC in stating that:

> Aristotle knew that like cases should be treated alike, and different cases should be treated differently; so when he defended slavery he felt it necessary to explain why slaves are 'different'. Therefore, if the doctrine of [anthropocentrism] was to be maintained, it was necessary to identify the differences between humans and other animals that justified the difference in moral status . . . [AMC is] . . . nothing but the consistent application of the principle of equality to decisions about what should be done . . . about our relation to the other creatures that inhabit the earth. (Rachels 1990: 196–7)

My defence of AMC, along with the amplification of this argument by Whitehead, is compatible with the method of reflective equilibrium made famous by Rawls regarding theory of justice, and which is of use in ethics generally. We have seen that the idea is that we should first carefully examine all of the relevant intuitions that we have and the judgements that we make, asking which are the most basic intuitions or which are the considered judgements.

Then we should investigate different theories that claim to organ-
ise these intuitions and judgements. Nothing is held to be fixed.
The goal is to seek consistency and fit among both intuitions/
judgements and theory when all are taken together as a whole. Or
again, AMC follows the pattern of many contemporary arguments
in applied philosophy in that it starts with considered opinion
among reflective people, then moves to relatively unconsidered
consequences. Thus, it makes sense to think that AMC could also
be called the argument for moral consistency.

It is crucial in this method that we be able to revise our considered
judgements, and even our intuitions, if such revision is required by
a powerful theory. It is also possible that we might revise, or even
reject, a theory in the face of considered judgements or intuitions.
Neither component is fixed in advance. It is my hope that some
small, yet real, contribution to ethics can be made by AMC. As a
result of this theoretical argument, which has as its aim the familiar
goal of logical consistency, closer attention should be paid to our
common sympathetic politically liberal intuitions in the face of: the
suffering of non-human animals and the marginal cases of humanity, the basic rights of all human beings, as well as the special moral
patiency status of rational beings. Both Anderson and Diamond
should be seen by animal rightists as dialectical partners rather than
as antagonists in the pursuit of this goal. That is, animal rightists can
deliberate together with them, as derived from the Latin *deliberare*:
to weigh in mind, to ponder, to thoroughly consider.

Whiteheadian Contributions

In order to see the contributions that a Whiteheadian could make
to the debate regarding non-human animal rights, a preliminary
distinction is required between two sorts of sentiency. S1 refers to
the microscopic sentiency that lies behind Whiteheadian defences
of panexperientialism, whereas S2 refers to sentiency per se as found
in human beings and other animals with central nervous systems. It
is this latter sort of sentiency that is seen as the criterion for moral
patiency status in AMC. Brian Henning has done exemplary work
in articulating the sort of aesthetic concern (Whitehead would say,
Quaker concern) S1 requires of us in that not even microscopic

organisms are machines incapable of internal relations or mattering. But this is a type of 'mattering' that is quite different (in degree if not in kind) from the moral respect that is due to S2 organisms who can experience pain intensely, indeed whose premature or violent loss is tragic. No *moral rights* are claimed by, or for, S1 organisms (see Dombrowski 1988).

Regarding the argument from sentiency, a Whiteheadian could emphasise that higher animals with central nervous systems have an enhanced mental pole and do not thoughtlessly or mechanically adjust to causal factors affecting them. Life, in general, is the 'clutch at vivid immediacy', an immediacy that is especially noteworthy from an ethical point of view when it involves unnecessary or gratuitous infliction of pain or suffering. Although feeling of some minimal sort is spread throughout the universe (S1), in a Whiteheadian view, it is only with non-human animal sense perception that the Rubicon of sentiency per se (S2 in contrast to S1 microscopic sentiency) is crossed. Further, non-human animal minds are temporally ordered; indeed, according to Whitehead, they are *personally* ordered societies in which the events of a non-human animal's life are connected to the past through memory and thrown towards the future through expectation. For these and other reasons, non-human animals rightly claim our 'love and tenderness' in return. As before, there is some 'holiness' or 'sacredness' in their beauty that civilised beings like ourselves cannot fail to notice (Whitehead 1968: 120). This emphasis on what we *civilised* beings should notice (as Whitehead problematically uses this term in that it could play into the hands of a dualistic contrast with the savage) indicates that a Whiteheadian approach to non-human animals is as much a virtue approach as a rights-oriented one. However, as a political liberal Whitehead was not skittish regarding the language of rights.

Whitehead also helps us to understand the implications of AMC. There are no airtight boundaries (whether scientific or ethical) between species in that different modes of existence shade off into each other. Specifically, there is no absolute boundary between non-human animals and human beings at the very least because human beings *are* animals. Whitehead defends both hierarchy in nature *and* continuity and shades of difference between each hierarchical level: we live *within* nature, as do non-human animals.

Further, we have seen that there is something hyperbolic in claiming that human beings *are* rational. Rather, some of them are rational some of the time and others (the marginal cases of humanity) are rarely or never rational. And some non-human animals exhibit remarkable mentality, such that we are tempted to think that they are either rational or are on the cusp of rationality. AMC makes it clear that there are ethical implications to the continuity (and overlap) thesis that Whitehead defends.

Some Whiteheadians resist the conclusions to the arguments from sentiency and marginal cases because a chicken, they allege, does not have a mental life that is very high and its momentary suffering just before its death is outweighed by all of the pleasurable moments it could have had in its life before the point of death; a life, by the way, that probably would not have come into being were it not for the practice of meat-eating (see Dombrowski 2001b regarding the contrasting positions of John Cobb, Timothy Menta and Clare Palmer).

But even if a non-human animal is killed painlessly, the loss involved is grievable on Whiteheadian grounds. The reason for this is that such a killing denies the non-human animal all of the future momentary experiences it would have had in *its* life (not ours). It should be remembered that it is young, vibrant non-human animals that are killed for the table, such that even if they are killed painlessly we should (and many do) grieve for the *unnecessary* loss of the rest of *their* lives. As in the argument from sentiency stated above, the words 'unnecessary' or 'gratuitous' are crucial. We should note once again that Whitehead thinks that not only do non-human animals try to avoid pain, but they also engage in *self-preservation*, which seems to presuppose a sort of stable identity, albeit short of a substantial self, that is nonetheless stronger than that found in the view that there really is no enduring self whatsoever to be preserved. A process view of a self changing through time is nonetheless compatible with a genetic relatedness among the events in a temporal series that constitutes the same self; in fact, a personal society is one that *sustains a character* (Whitehead 1978: 34–5, 176).

We should take Whitehead's example seriously where, in the Garden of Eden, Adam saw non-human animals before he named them; whereas children today can name non-human animals before they ever see them (Whitehead 1967b: 198). Granted, in this context Whitehead is discussing education, in general, but it is not too much of a stretch to apply his poetic performance of the Garden of Eden example to the education of real human beings regarding equally real non-human animals, in particular. That is, by extension, justifications of meat-eating are often very abstract, armchair (or better, dining room table) sorts of affairs that unthinkingly involve preaching what Whitehead calls the 'Gospel of Force' (Whitehead 1967b: 206) rather than that of persuasion. Actually seeing what goes on in slaughterhouses moment by moment is an educational, albeit gruesome, affair that causes nothing short of grief, as almost anyone who takes the time to do so will quickly learn. As more people become aware of non-human animal sentiency (S2) and mentality, we can hope with Whitehead that 'if mankind can rise to the occasion, there lies in front a golden age of beneficent creativeness' (Whitehead 1967b: 205). Or again:

There is something in the ready use of force which defeats its own object. Its main defect is that it bars cooperation. Every organism requires an environment of friends, partly to shield it from violent changes, and partly to supply it with its wants. The Gospel of Force is incompatible with a social life. (Whitehead 1967b: 206)

One practical advantage of Whitehead's metaphysics is that it could enable us to give a more accurate analysis than has been given historically of quite ordinary propositions like (to use Whitehead's own example): 'There is beef for dinner today' (Whitehead 1978: 11). The process analysis would insist that 'the point to be emphasised is the insistent particularity of things experienced and of the act of experiencing', in contrast to a very abstract description of the act of meat-eating wherein the point at which the cow suffers intensely is left out of the picture and hence is not grievable; that is, the cow appears only later in a creation *ex nihilo* wrapped in cellophane at the grocery store (see Whitehead 1978: 43).

Whitehead notes that for a living organism to survive it needs food, even if there is no absolute distinction between living and 'non-living' organisms, as we have seen. The foods that are eaten are themselves societies of some sort. Whitehead's term for what is required in order for living organisms to survive is 'robbery'. The question is whether the robbery is to be a mere petty theft or a major heist. As he puts the point, 'life is robbery. It is at this point that . . . morals become acute. The robber requires justification' (Whitehead 1978: 105–6). It is noteworthy that in the paragraphs immediately following this passage Whitehead speaks of divine tenderness directed towards each actual occasion as it arrives in the evocation of intensities of experience.

It is commonly acknowledged that there is a Romantic compo-nent to Whitehead's thought, wherein the Wordsworthian dictum that 'we murder to dissect' is taken quite seriously. Whitehead's philosophy (or better, the philosophy of organism), as he sees it, is explicitly an attempt to *enlarge ethical discourse* so as to include con-sideration of the non-human animals whom we rob or murder. No hyperbole is committed here on a Whiteheadian view. The goal should be to foster intensities of experience that are positive 'adver-sions' or contributions to reticulative beauty rather than negative, painful 'aversions' to gratuitous killing of beings whose lives are grievable. Moral responsibility consists in owning up to the ways in which we use our power of self-motion to determine the course of events (Whitehead 1978: 140, 204, 254–5; 1967b: ch. 5).

A non-human animal body is a nexus of many cellular events that can be treated as though it were one whole actuality. This one actuality when considered in reference to the publicity of things is a 'superject'; but in reference to its own privacy it is a subject, a moment in the genesis of its own self-enjoyment. As Whitehead famously suggests, God is the 'fellow-sufferer who understands' such self-enjoyment (Whitehead 1978: 351). To put the point in different Whiteheadian terms, intense self-enjoyment has value for itself, for others, and for the whole. The key thing to notice in the present context is that human experience is but one, albeit espe-cially exalted, sort of higher experience (S2), given the doctrine of evolution that Whitehead supports (Whitehead 1978: 287, 298, 351; 1968: 111–12).

It may very well be the case, however, that the greatest contri-bution a Whiteheadian could make to the current debate regard-ing non-human animal entitlements would involve the emphasis

Whitehead placed on what I have called reflective equilibrium. All of us, or almost all of us, recoil emotionally at the thought of (more so at the sight of!) a cow having its carotid artery slit. This emotional reaction needs to be reconciled with the justification we give for our eating practices (or robberies). The meat-eater, at the very least, is in a state of disequilibrium between *emotional* response and *rational* justification (Whitehead 1978: 16). Granted, some momentary incoherence or disequilibrium or contrast is needed in order for novelty to emerge, but this is a far cry from leaving the tension between emotional response and rational justification in a permanent state of disequilibrium that tends towards dualism. Why exactly is it that beer drinkers like to visit breweries and bread-lovers like to visit bakeries, but meat-eaters (like the rest of us) would never take a vacation to view a slaughterhouse?

No doubt some Whiteheadians (e.g. Cobb – see Dombrowski 2001b) will reach a different conclusion. They will say that because human eating invariably involves robbery, we can eat what we wish as long as we do so 'mindfully', by recognising the loss in intrinsic value that occurs when we eat non-human animals. Two comments are in order by way of response. (1) It is crucial that we not commit the fallacy of misplaced concreteness by thinking that it is the Platonic forms of Cowhood or Chickenness that suffer and die. It is individual cows and chickens, here and now, who are the loci of value in a Whiteheadian universe and it is their loss that is (or should be) grieved (see Dombrowski 1988). (2) When these individuals are killed for food, their suffering and death are *unnecessary*, given the healthiness of a vegetarian diet, and hence the robbery involved is, as implied above, a major heist rather than a petty theft. Granted, all of the pleasures the non-human animal experienced up until the point of death are not negated, in that they are preserved in the divine life, but neither are its sufferings negated, nor is the loss of *its* life (not ours) forgotten. It is unclear, to say the least, whether these meat-eating 'contributions' (to use Hartshorne's terminology) to the divine life are the sorts that we would like to make when seen from the perspective of the adventure of ideas that spreads across the generations. That is, speciesism may very well eventually go the way of racism, sexism, classism and heterosexism.

Granted, 'moral obligation' is not a characteristic way of speaking in Whitehead and he apparently felt some distaste for overly zealous approaches to righteousness. But he is insistent that morality has to do with increasing generality of outlook and with concern for the longer rather than the more limited future. Further, he thinks that this generality of outlook requires a disinterested assessment of all available knowledge so as to fairly consider intrinsic value wherever it is found (see Whitehead 1967a: 346, 371, 375–6; 1978: 15; and Cobb 2007: 54, 64, 71–4).

Rawls and Animals

It will be helpful at this point to show how the Whiteheadian character of the two arguments that I have presented in favour of non-human animal rights relate to Rawls's complicated view. Rawls is clear in *A Theory of Justice* that the basis of equality does not extend to non-human animals. This is because they are not moral persons with the two basic moral powers: the ability to develop a conception of the good and a sense of justice or the right. Strictly speaking, equal justice applies only to those with these two powers. Hence non-human animals are left out of Rawls's famous social contract experiment. Another way to put the point is to say that it is those who can give justice who are owed justice (Rawls 1999c: 15, 441–9; also 1999b: 92, 171).

In an earlier piece, 'The Sense of Justice' (1963), Rawls asked the question, 'who is owed justice?' His response was that the capacity to be just was a necessary and sufficient condition for receiving justice. He admits that establishing that the capacity to be just is a necessary condition for receiving justice is much more difficult than it is to establish that the capacity to be just is a sufficient condition for receiving justice. (In *A Theory of Justice* Rawls is not explicit that the two moral powers are necessary for being owed justice, only that they are sufficient for being owed justice, although the necessary condition may be implied in *A Theory of Justice*.) Nonetheless he concludes that we have no duty of justice to non-human animals, as there might be in utilitarianism where possession of sentiency seems to be a sufficient condition for being a full subject of rights (Rawls 1999a: 112–16).

Rawls is aware of the fact that high-level criteria for being owed justice, like the aforementioned two moral powers, have implications not only for non-human animals, but for some human beings as well. Once a certain minimum level of the two moral powers is met, citizens are entitled to equal justice, Rawls thinks. In *A Theory of Justice* he does not examine those who do not meet this minimum level, but he does say that the vast majority of human beings have the capacity for, if not the actual ability to enact, the two moral powers. Thus, for practical purposes, he thinks, 'all' humans 'originally' possess moral personality. And the capacity for love and affection are universal among human beings. Once again, he chooses not to examine those who have lost these capacities through congenital defect or illness or accident (Rawls 1999c: 441–9; 1999a: 112–16).

Although non-human animals are not owed justice, and this because they do not have a moral status equal to human beings with the two moral powers, they should be afforded some protection. Because they are capable of feeling pleasure and pain, Rawls holds that we have duties of compassion and humanity towards them and thus we ought not to be cruel to them. And destruction of a whole non-human animal species is a great evil. But Rawls thinks that the protections that we ought to give to non-human animals are not the result of a duty of justice on our part. Rather, a conception of justice is only one part of an overall moral theory and there are moral virtues besides justice. That is, the principle of humanity is more inclusive than justice (Rawls 1999c: 441–9; 1999a: 112–16).

In *Political Liberalism* Rawls expands on the relatively narrow concerns of *A Theory of Justice* by treating four problems of extension, three of which are amenable to resolution, he thinks (by extending the principles of justice to future generations, by expanding them so as to include the international law of peoples, and by covering the health care needs of citizens). But concerning the fourth problem of extension, he doubts if non-human animals can be brought within justice as fairness as a *political* conception. He admits that this may be due to a lack of ingenuity. If we start with full persons in adult society with the two moral powers, he cannot see how non-human animals can be included in the social contract (Rawls 1996: 21, 244–6). The ambiguity in *A Theory of Justice* is removed in *Political Liberalism*: the two moral powers are necessary (not only sufficient) to be owed justice (Rawls 1996: 302). He does not consider the efforts by Donald VanDeVeer and others to develop a revised original position where 'marginal' human beings and non-human animals, although not moral agents, are nonetheless seen as moral patients who are the beneficiaries of decisions made in the original position. The revised original position requires that behind a veil of ignorance we be ignorant not only of our race, sex and so on, but also of our species membership. That is, regardless of what Rawls himself thought, VanDeVeer makes it clear that there is a strong Rawls*ian* argument in favour of non-human animal rights.

Also in *Political Liberalism* he treats two contrasting views that have implications for non-human animals. The traditional Christian view, on his interpretation, sees non-human animals as subject to our use, as in the biological and medical knowledge that they make possible. By way of contrast, the view of natural religion (which is either a separate comprehensive doctrine from the traditional Christian view or a countercultural tendency within that view) is one wherein non-human animals are seen as the loci of rights and are hence brought within the scope of justice. But this view, Rawls claims, cannot direct us towards a constitutional essential in that it is like opposition to abortion on strictly religious grounds. That is, the values cherished by the natural religionist are non-political. Rawls does not state explicitly that the traditional view of non-human animals is also non-political, leading some to wonder whether this was the view he endorsed at a political level (Rawls 1996: 244–66). This is reminiscent of the open question in *A Theory of Justice* regarding how to fit justice as fairness within a metaphysical system that explains humanity's place within the natural world (Rawls 1999c: 448–9).

Rawls admits, relying on evidence provided by ethologists, that non-human animals resemble human beings in their desire for self-realisation. In a way the Aristotelian Principle of self-realisation also applies to them, as is borne out by the facts of everyday life and which can be given an evolutionary explanation. In effect, natural selection, he thinks, would have favoured non-human animals concerning whom the Aristotelian Principle would have applied (Rawls 1999c: 378–9).

The undergraduate Rawls saw a wide gap between human beings

and other animals in that he opposed what he saw as the superficial modern view that human beings were merely biological animals. Human beings, he thought, were not so much biological animals as they were persons (Rawls 2009: 217–18). This view is continuous with his later Kantian view that we are not dignified as animals, but as personal beings with the two moral powers.

Wild Animals

If I am correct that the case for non-human animal rights is a strong one in Whiteheadian thinking – and in Rawls*ian* thinking, if not in Rawls himself – as evidenced in the interplay between these philosophies and the arguments from sentiency and marginal cases, then I am in an advantageous position from which to sketch the 'to the environment' part of my thesis. Indeed, this will only be a sketch of what could be said regarding environmental ethics on the basis of process thought. This sketch will be facilitated by an attempt to be clear regarding the distinction between domestic and wild animals.

Consider initially a stunning example provided quite ironically by Leopold, who ceased killing wolves for the National Forest Service when he came upon a wolf he had shot, but who had not yet died:

> We reached the old wolf in time to watch a fierce green fire dying in her eyes. I realised then, and have known ever since, that there was something new in me in those eyes – something known only to her . . . I was young then, and full of trigger-itch; I thought that because fewer wolves meant more deer, that no wolves would mean hunters' paradise. But after seeing the green fire die, I sensed that . . . the wolf [did not agree] with such a view. (Leopold 1987: 130)

Although we have been formed in habits of violence, our norms are iterable and in process and hence are, at least in principle and in the long run, subject to change. This provides hope for the Whiteheadian and Rawlsian non-human animal rightist. If the generalised condition of precariousness and interdependency is made more visible, and is framed more carefully for us so that we may really see vulnerability, a more non-violent, a fairer, world is possible. Further, a Whiteheadian list of virtues would have compassion towards the top of the list. The stage could be set for the realisation that non-violence is a result of the apprehension of equality in the midst of precariousness.

It is crucial at this point to notice the difference between our moral obligations to domestic animals and those to wild animals, such as the wolf described above by Leopold. Focusing on this difference provides a bridge from moral obligations to individual animals to a Whiteheadian environmental ethics, in general, as developed by several excellent scholars, especially Cobb and Henning. Although process thinkers have contributed significantly to environmental ethics, this bridge is a much needed new one. In this regard I will rely heavily and positively on a recent book by Palmer, who is familiar to process thinkers because of her first (largely critical) book on process environmental ethics. That is, process thinkers who were turned off by Palmer's first book should think again about the contribution she could make to a defensible process environmental ethics as a result of her second book.

Debates in philosophy regarding animal ethics have understandably centred around the question of *harm*: do non-human animals have rights not to be harmed? Do human beings have duties not to harm non-human animals? Along with Palmer it makes sense to focus as well on questions regarding when we may *assist* non-human animals: when is it permissible to assist non-human animals? Are we ever duty-bound to assist non-human animals? The distinction between domesticated and wild animals looms large in how we should respond to these questions. It makes sense to claim that we have a prima facie duty not to harm domesticated animals, but because we have bred them to be docile and vulnerable to us, we also have a prima facie duty to assist them when they are in trouble. By contrast, although we have a prima facie duty not to harm wild animals (as in the wolf mentioned by Leopold), we do not generally have a duty to assist them when they are in trouble. This lack of a duty to assist wild animals Palmer calls the laissez faire intuition (LFI).

However, there are at least three different versions of LFI: strong, weak and relational. In strong LFI we should neither harm nor assist wild animals because by assisting them we might be reconstituting them in our own anthropocentric image and hence be stripping them of their wildness. In weak LFI we should not harm wild animals, but it might be *permissible* to assist them if we could alleviate their pain while allowing them to be who they are. In relational LFI we should not harm wild animals, but there might also be *duties* to assist them generated by our causing the destruction of their habitat. Relational LFI is especially congenial to the process-relational stance found in a Whiteheadian view. Further, Whitehead's and Palmer's relational approach is close to the rights-based approach of Regan in his defence of AMC. This view is relational in the sense that the permissibility of assistance, or even the duty to assist, depends on what sort of relationship we have to the wild animal in question (e.g. whether we are the ones who have caused the trouble the wild animal is in).

Consider several examples: coyotes displaced by a new suburban subdivision, the endangered status of polar bears, the question of assistance to neighbourhood squirrels, possible duties to restrain house cats when birds are attacked, possible duties to rescue dumpster kittens, the status of massive numbers of wildebeests who die in migration, the question as to whether one should intervene with respect to preventable disease in mountain goats, and so on. From a process theistic point of view, the way to put the possible tension between non-human animal rights and environmental ethics is to say that an omnibenevolent God must not only love *each* sentient being but *all* of them.

I will not attempt to deal with these examples, which are ably treated by Palmer. But I would like to note that an adequate treatment of these examples would require awareness of both perpetrator and beneficiary versions of reparations theory in the effort to understand the concept of past harms to non-human animals, harms that bear directly on whether we have duties to assist. Even if we are not the ones who deprived the coyotes of their habitat, if we benefit from such deprivation we may have a duty to assist. Or again, recent work on agent-centredness by virtue ethicians can be used profitably to understand agent-relatedness, which is crucial in the effort to understand when one has a duty to assist. In this regard one wonders about what sort of person could remain indifferent to the plight of a polar bear who has to swim hundreds of miles in order to find safe haven for her cubs. The effort to bridge whatever gap there might be between non-human animal rights and environmental ethics is much facilitated by relational LFI as defended by Palmer, which I think should also be the view of process-relational thinkers. That is, the permissibility of assistance, or perhaps even the duty to assist, cannot be determined in abstraction from a consideration of the relations human beings have with non-human animals. If we have domesticated them, then we have a duty to assist them. However, if they are almost entirely unrelated to us, as in the case of almost fully wild animals, then we have no duty to assist; in some cases, it might not even be permissible to assist. In between are an increasing number of non-human animals who are in the 'contact zone'. Our acquired relations to non-human animals who enter into, or who are pushed into, the contact zone entail acquired duties.

Sketches of an Environmental Ethic

In an influential article written a generation ago, J. Baird Callicott called attention to what he called 'a triangular affair'. That is, the conceptual battle is not merely between anthropocentrists and environmentalists, but also includes politically liberal animal rightists, who are neither anthropocentric nor unqualified supporters of the ecoholism that is assumed by many to be required in a defensible environmental ethics. Callicott himself modified his view somewhat so as to facilitate rapprochement between environmental ethics and non-human animal rights. I would like to push further so as to claim that a reticulative vision of the non-human animal rights stance *is itself* a defensible environmental ethics. Although I will not offer a detailed defence of this claim here, I will indicate three points that should indicate to the reader what such a defence would look like. These three points will deal with three different sorts of sentiency: S1, S2 and S3.

First, there is a certain primacy to the interests of those who are sentient per se (S2) because they can experience intense pain and can be harmed. Pain *hurts*. In one sense this point is obvious; but in another sense ethical theory is still trying to catch up with this insight.

This means that a defensible version of environmental ethics would have to take seriously the conditions necessary for the flourishing of sentient and rational human beings, with their only partial transcendence of animality. In the legitimate move away from anthropo*centrism* we should not forget that one of the reasons why we want a defensible environmental ethics is to enable human beings, including myriads of future generations of them, to flourish. More colloquially, we ought not throw away the (potentially rational) baby with the dirty anthropocentric bathwater (to borrow a metaphor from Evelyn Pluhar). There is nothing shallow about this concern for human beings, especially when it is realised in a Whiteheadian way that in the quest for a beautiful world we need to be concerned not only with the greatest unity in the midst of the greatest diversity, but *also* with (rather than instead of) high-grade intensity of experience (see Dombrowski 2004a). Sentient and rational human beings add something significant to the aesthetic value of the world, hence we ought to try to ensure that they continue to do so.

But a defensible environmental ethics would also have to take seriously the conditions necessary for the flourishing of domesticated animals. The two arguments stated above regarding non-human animal rights indicate the significant changes that would have to occur in order to approximate reflective equilibrium with respect to domesticated animals. Further, these two arguments have consequences far beyond those that involve domesticated animals themselves. If our duties to domesticated animals were more widely acknowledged and protected by law, radical environmental changes for the good would be evidenced. For example, when it is considered that it takes between fifteen and twenty pounds of grain to produce one pound of meat in the beef industry, one realises how wasteful it is environmentally to eat beef. Analogous arguments could be developed regarding pork and poultry. It is a commonplace among animal rightists, but still curiously ignored by others, that switching to a vegetarian diet is more environmentally efficacious than switching from a gas-powered car to a hybrid or electric vehicle.

A more defensible treatment of domesticated animals would also have a positive effect on wild animals. If the United States became a vegetarian nation, for instance, there would be far less land needed in cultivation such that vast stretches of the Midwest and elsewhere could be turned into national parks and national forests and national grasslands. Here the great numbers of domesticated animals would gradually go down in that there would be less of a need to breed them, but there would be a gradual increase in wild or semi-wild animals who could roam freely. Or again, it is widely noted that deforestation is a problem worldwide, especially deforestation of tropical rainforests in Brazil and Indonesia and elsewhere. It is not widely noted, however, that such deforestation largely occurs so as to make room for cattle ranchers.

In short, all of the major environmental problems (deforestation, climate change, aquifer depletion, desertification, etc.) are connected to, indeed are made worse by, the institution of meat-eating. By carefully attending to the conditions required for S2 animals (of whatever species) to flourish, we would be responding positively to the demands of well informed and morally reflective environmentalists. The thesis of the present chapter is thus very much in conformity with the Thoreauvian dictum that in wildness is to be found the preservation of the world (see Dombrowski 1986).

Of course the non-human animal rights approach cannot do all of the work of environmental ethics. For example, this work is enormously facilitated by widespread commitment to children's health and women's rights. This is because when parents, especially mothers, are confident that their children will survive, they have fewer of them. And when women attain political autonomy and economic security, they do not perceive the need to bear a large number of children. That is, although the solution to environmental problems hinges on slowing human population, it is crucial to do so in ways that are compatible with justice. An asymptotic approach to justice in enhanced when we note the conceptual link between sexism and speciesism in that both tend to rely on the (mistaken) assumption that rationality is the criterion for moral patiency status, with women (incredibly) seen as failing to meet the proposed criterion in some way.

It is to be hoped that what I have said thus far in this section is sufficient to dispel any suspicion that the environmentalism I am defending lacks depth. As we move from respect for sentient and rational human beings to sentient domesticated animals, the range of our duties gets wider and the depth of such concern grows because, as a result of including domesticated animals within the scope of moral concern, it becomes clear that environmental issues are vitally important not because their resolution would be conducive to the flourishing of disembodied Cartesian cogitos (if such were to exist), but rather because they would enhance the flourishing of sentient animals, including ourselves *as animals*. Likewise, the range and depth of our environmental ethics grows still further when we attend to the needs of not only human beings and domesticated animals, but also to the needs of wild animals. This is because by attending to the necessary conditions for the flourishing of wild animals – polar bears and halibut and Western meadowlarks – we are: (1) led to think globally if not cosmically; and (2) led to consider carefully the quality of air, water, soil, temperature, climate and so on, as these impact the flourishing of animals, in general, whether human or non-human (both domestic and wild).

In the Whiteheadian transition from mechanism to organism, there is an abandonment of both the Cartesian idea that non-human animals are mere machines and the related idea that the only intrinsic values to be found in nature are located in human beings. As before, there is both intrinsic value in us *and* continuity in nature. Of course, there is also conflict among the values in nature, as becomes especially evident when the phenomenon of predation is considered. Although I will not treat this complex issue in any detail, I would like to make two brief points: first, because lions are not rational enough to be moral agents, their killing of a gazelle is of a different moral quality than the human killing of a sentient animal at the abattoir; and second, in the Whiteheadian quest for a more beautiful world it should be clear that the beautiful should not be equated with the pretty. That is, prettiness is only one sort of beauty, as is sublimity (see Dombrowski 2004a).

There are at least two sorts of aesthetic disvalue or evil, on a Whiteheadian view, both of which lead to a world that is uglier than it need be. One sort involves destruction or violence and the other sort is anaesthesia, wherein one settles for a lesser value when a higher one was easily available. Non-human animal rights on a Whiteheadian basis are obviously key components in the effort to block the former. But it is not often noticed that by avoiding unnecessary or gratuitous violence we also counteract anaesthesia. There always was something suspect about attempts to exalt humanity via violence inflicted on non-human animals. In fact, the reverse seems to be the case. By humbling ourselves to take stock of our own sentient animality, we are exalted (see 2 Corinthians 12:9). Or again, Jesus reminds us that God cares even for the fall of a sparrow (Matthew 10:28), a claim that was not lost on Hamlet (Act 5, Scene 2), as we have seen.

Second, on a Whiteheadian basis animal rights environmentalism can avoid the familiar charge that although the animal rights stance avoids anthropocentrism, it is nonetheless 'sentient-centric'. This avoidance is due to the fact that minimal sentiency (S1), if not morally considerable sentiency in the sense of acutely experienced gratuitous pain (S2), pervades nature. Indeed, we should be attentive to, exhibit (Quaker) concern for, the ubiquity of S1 value in nature as part of the aesthetic drive to contribute to the beauty of the world, with 'beauty' referring to both high-grade intensity of experience *and* unity-in-the-midst-of-diversity in a panexperientialist world wherein minimal experience is pervasive.

Henning is surely correct to emphasise that Whitehead's widely noted critique of *ontological* dualism is integrally connected to his less widely known critique of *axiological* dualism. In effect, process panexperientialism includes the claim that there is a continuum of *value* in nature. Although there are debates among process thinkers regarding how microscopic experience and hence value in nature is aggregated or compounded, it seems clear that all process thinkers have to steer clear of two extremes. If one leans too hard in the direction of giving a Whiteheadian society a unity proper to itself, one runs the risk of moving too close to the classical concept of substance; however, if one offers a strictly reductionist description of a Whiteheadian society, such that it is constituted *solely* in terms of the interplay of its constituents, then one runs the risk of making a whole nothing but an aggregate that is the mere sum of its parts (see Bracken 2013).

As I see things, both poles in this tension (not contradiction) need to be acknowledged and preserved. Hence, I think that, despite the obvious advantages of ecoholism, it is a view that should be defended with a grain of salt. As we have seen, a tree, even a glorious redwood, is a democracy in Whitehead (e.g. Whitehead 1967a: 205–6) in that its principle of unity is not nearly as real as the principle of unity found in an animal (of whatever species) with a central nervous system. That is, sentient animals have a level of coordination of diverse parts that is quite remarkable (indeed, it is Rubicon-crossing!) in contrast to the level of coordination found in a plant, say, at one end, and in the level of coordination found in an ecosystem, on the other. But the ubiquity of S1 in nature means that it is inaccurate to say that the rest of nature is meant merely to serve the interests of S2 beings. Rather, *all* concrete singulars have value not only for others and for the whole, but also to some extent *for themselves*.

And third, the value for the whole mentioned by Whitehead is called 'contributionism' by Hartshorne, which is a label that can easily cause confusion, especially if it is assumed that the goal of process theists is to give over everything to God, hence leaving us and the rest of the natural world impoverished. Theological fascism fuelled by a belief in divine omnipotence, after all, would be just as bothersome as environmental (or political) fascism. We have seen in a previous chapter that at one point Whitehead is alleged to have compared the classical theistic omnipotent God with Hitler (Whitehead 1954: 174–6, 189, 198). Hartshorne's language regarding God as a Platonic World Soul is particularly helpful here in that, if we conceive of God as the mind or soul not for this or that particular body, but for the body of the entire universe, then we and other animals are by analogy cells in the divine life. We can refer to the World Soul in terms of divine sentiency or S3. The advantage of this interpretation of value for the whole is that healthy cells are good in themselves and do not lose their individual worth when they contribute to the entire body, in this case to the cosmic divine body. That is, what we can contribute to God is our own happiness, our own refusal to settle for anaesthesia, and our own dogged attempt to live non-violently.

To use Henning's helpful language that he has adopted from Whitehead, the obligation to contribute to the greatest possible universe of beauty (importance) is at odds with neither the obligation to maximize intensity and harmony among one's own experiences (self-respect) nor the obligation to facilitate the same in others (love). These goals, in turn, require the avoidance of wanton destruction of natural value (peace) and the expansion of the breadth and depth of aesthetic horizons (education).

More needs to be said here about the relationship between an animal rights stance and environmental ethics. My overall view is like Dale Jamieson's in claiming that an animal rights view *is* an environmental ethic (Jamieson 1998). There is nonetheless a tension (once again, not a contradiction) between my defence of moral patiency status in S2 beings and my defence of the Whiteheadian idea that all concrete singulars have value of some sort, however minimal (S1). This tension is best dealt with in terms of the claim that the continuity of value in nature that goes all the way down is nonetheless compatible with the existence of certain thresholds that are crossed that lead to qualitative changes. An analogy for the S2 threshold provided by a functioning central nervous system can be found in water being gradually heated (or cooled) until a qualitative change occurs at 212 degrees Fahrenheit (or 32 degrees Fahrenheit). A Whiteheadian can see value of some sort as ubiquitous yet reject Heideggerian biotic egalitarianism.

One way to finesse this point would be to say that only S2 organisms are subjects-of-a-life who deserve rights, whereas S1 organisms, although they are to be seen as objects of concern, are not possessors of rights. Another way to finesse it would be to say that moral patiency status pervades nature, but S2 organisms have it to a qualitatively higher degree than S1 organisms. I find the latter way of speaking somewhat cumbersome in that it puts our emotions into disequilibrium with our rational understanding. To repeat an odd, yet instructive, example: bread lovers enjoy visiting bakeries, yet I have never met a meat-eater who enjoyed going to slaughterhouses. Cutting down wheat shafts in their prime just does not bother us emotionally, whereas cutting down cows does. Clearly, there is a qualitative difference between S2 organisms and S1 organisms even when this difference is seen against the backdrop of the continuity thesis and of the escape from dualism. Hartshorne and others are surely correct, however, to emphasise that because of the defensibility of panexperientialism and of the continuity thesis there will always be something rough about the S2/S1 distinction, hence such a distinction ought not to degenerate into an absolute bifurcation.

Conclusion

The difficulty involved in pinning down exactly what process ethics can contribute to ethical (including political) theory can actually be seen as one of its strengths. Once one becomes convinced of the need for a sort of moral eclecticism (see Fleischacker 2011), process ethics looks more appealing because of its systematic (yet fallible) attempt to bring all of the relevant theoretical considerations to bear in the effort to achieve reflective equilibrium. The emphasis in process ethics on education has led several scholars to emphasise connections with virtue ethics; its prominent place for the maximisation of value of all sorts has led Palmer and others to see its similarities to utilitarianism; and the important place in it for the irreplaceability of individuals capable of high-grade experience leads us to consider seriously its close connection to deontology. Although Henning is rightly sceptical of any claim to the *absoluteness* of deontology in process ethics, this scepticism is perfectly compatible with deontological considerations being necessary if not sufficient conditions for a defensible environmental ethics from a politically liberal process perspective. These deontological considerations are directed towards sentient individuals, both human and non-human. Further, Palmer was surely correct in noting that my own version of process ethics is deontology-heavy, but the stance I am taking is nonetheless amenable to rapprochement not only with Palmer but also with an appropriately qualified ecoholism.

If intrinsic value is on a continuum, as process thinkers hold, then we should not be surprised to learn that continuum-thinking is nonetheless compatible with there being morally relevant thresholds that make a significant difference. That is, continuum-thinking is not at all at odds with threshold-thinking. As before, think of water gradually being heated to 212 degrees Fahrenheit, when a qualitative change occurs as it evaporates into air; likewise regarding water being gradually cooled to 32 degrees when it turns to ice. It is hard for me to imagine how to reach reflective equilibrium in a sort of biocentric egalitarianism that is, at the very least, vulnerable to compelling *in extremis* cases. It is clear that some beings are more morally significant than others. Who really doubts that one should swat the tsetse fly that is about to bite one's granddaughter? The two most significant threshold points, as I have treated them above, are the rise of the central nervous system and hence sentiency (S2) and hence moral patiency status, on the one hand, along with the rise of rationality and hence moral agency status, on the other. We ignore these thresholds at our (reflective equilibrium) peril.

Bibliography

Anderson, Elizabeth (2004), 'Animal rights and the value of nonhuman life', in Cass Sunstein and Martha Nussbaum (eds), *Animal Rights: Current Debates and New Directions*, New York: Oxford University Press.

Arendt, Hannah (1958), *The Human Condition*, Chicago: University of Chicago Press.

Arendt, Hannah [1951] (1966), *The Origins of Totalitarianism*, New York: Harcourt, Brace, and World.

Armstrong, Susan (1976), 'The rights of nonhuman beings: a Whiteheadian study', PhD dissertation, Bryn Mawr College.

Baily, Tom, and Valentina Gentile (eds) (2015), *Rawls and Religion*, New York: Columbia University Press.

Balzac, Honoré de [1835] (1991), *Old Goriot*, trans. Ellen Marriage, New York: Knopf.

Becker, Lawrence (1983), 'The priority of human interests', in Harlan Miller and W. Williams (eds), *Ethics and Animals*, Clifton, NJ: Humana.

Beiner, Ronald (2018), *Dangerous Minds: Nietzsche, Heidegger, and the Return of the Far Right*, Philadelphia: University of Pennsylvania Press.

Bodin, Jean (1975), *Colloquium of the Seven about Secrets of the Sublime*, trans. M. L. D. Kuntz, Princeton: Princeton University Press.

Bok, Sissela (1999), *Lying: Moral Choice in Public and Private Life*, New York: Vintage Books.

Bookchin, Murray (1988), 'A reply to my critics', *Green Synthesis*, 29: 5–7.

Bracken, Joseph (2013), 'Actual entities and societies, gene mutations and cell development', *Process Studies*, 42: 64–76.

Brink, David (1987), 'Rawlsian constructivism in moral theory', *Canadian Journal of Philosophy*, 17: 71–90.

Bromwell, Anna (1989), *Ecology in the Twentieth Century*, New Haven: Yale University Press.

Callicott, J. Baird (1989), *In Defense of the Land Ethic*, Albany: State University of New York Press.

Caputo, John (1993), 'Heidegger and theology', in Charles Guignon (ed.), *The Cambridge Companion to Heidegger*, New York: Cambridge University Press.

Carcieri, Martin (2015), *Applying Rawls in the Twenty-First Century*, New York: Palgrave Macmillan.

Clayton, Philip, and Justin Heinzekehr (2014), *Organic Marxism: An Alternative to Capitalism and Ecological Catastrophe*, Claremont: Process Century Press.

Clayton, Philip, and Justin Heinzekehr (eds) (2017), *Socialism in Process*, Claremont: Process Century Press.

Cobb, John (1989), 'Review of Daniel Dombrowski, *Hartshorne and the Metaphysics of Animal Rights*', *Environmental Ethics*, 11: 373–6.

Cobb, John (2004), 'Palmer on Whitehead', *Process Studies*, 33: 4–23.

Cobb, John (2005), 'Another response to Clare Palmer', *Process Studies*, 34: 132–5.

Cobb, John (2007), *A Christian Natural Theology: Based on the Thought of Alfred North Whitehead*, 2nd edn, Louisville: Westminster John Knox Press.

Cobb, John (2014), 'Foreword', in Philip Clayton and Justin Heinzekehr, *Organic Marxism*, Claremont: Process Century Press.

Cobb, John, and Charles Birch (1981), *The Liberation of Life*, New York: Cambridge University Press.

Cobb, John, and Herman Daly (1994), *For the Common Good*, Boston: Beacon Press.

Collins, James (1972), *Interpreting Modern Philosophy*, Princeton: Princeton University Press.

Dahlstrom, Daniel (1994), *Heidegger's Concept of Truth*, New York: Cambridge University Press.

Daniels, Norman (1979), 'Wide reflective equilibrium and theory acceptance in ethics', *Journal of Philosophy*, 76: 256–82.

Daniels, Norman (1996), *Justice and Justification: Reflective Equilibrium in Theory and Practice*, New York: Cambridge University Press.

Daniels, Norman (2003), 'Democratic equality: Rawls's complex egalitarianism', in Samuel Freeman (ed.), *The Cambridge Companion to Rawls*, New York: Cambridge University Press.

Daniels, Norman (2015), 'Reflective equilibrium', in Jon Mandle and David Reidy (eds), *The Cambridge Rawls Lexicon*, New York: Cambridge University Press.

Daniels, Norman (2017), 'Reflective equilibrium', *Stanford Encyclopedia of Philosophy*. Online.

Davidson, Arnold (1989), 'Questions concerning Heidegger: opening the debate', *Critical Inquiry*, 15: 407–26.

Defoe, Daniel [1719] (1983), *Robinson Crusoe*, New York: Scribner.

DePaul, Michael (1988), 'The problem of the criterion and coherence methods in ethics', *Canadian Journal of Philosophy*, 18: 67–86.

Diamond, Cora (2004), 'Eating meat and eating people', in Cass Sunstein and Martha Nussbaum (eds), *Animal Rights: Current Debates and New Directions*, New York: Oxford University Press.

Dikotter, Frank (2010), *Mao's Great Famine*, New York: Bloomsbury.

Dombrowski, Daniel (1986), 'Thoreau, sainthood, and vegetarianism', *American Transcendental Quarterly*, 60: 25–36.

Dombrowski, Daniel (1988), *Hartshorne and the Metaphysics of Animal Rights*, Albany: State University of New York Press.

Dombrowski, Daniel (1997a), *Babies and Beasts: The Argument from Marginal Cases*, Champaign: University of Illinois Press.

Dombrowski, Daniel (1997b), 'Plato's "noble" lie', *History of Political Thought*, 18: 565–78.

Dombrowski, Daniel (1997c), 'Process thought and the liberalism-communitarianism debate', *Process Studies*, 26: 15–32.

Dombrowski, Daniel (2000), *A Brief, Liberal, Catholic Defense of Abortion*, Champaign: University of Illinois Press.

Dombrowski, Daniel (2001a), *Rawls and Religion: The Case for Political Liberalism*, Albany: State University of New York Press.

Dombrowski, Daniel (2001b), 'The replaceability argument', *Process Studies*, 30: 22–35.

Dombrowski, Daniel (2002), 'Rawls and war', *International Journal of Applied Philosophy*, 16: 185–200.

Dombrowski, Daniel (2004a), *Divine Beauty: The Aesthetics of Charles Hartshorne*, Nashville: Vanderbilt University Press.

Dombrowski, Daniel (2004b), 'On the alleged truth about lies in Plato's *Republic*', *Polis*, 21: 93–106.

Dombrowski, Daniel (2005), *A Platonic Philosophy of Religion: A Process Perspective*, Albany: State University of New York Press.

Dombrowski, Daniel (2006), *Rethinking the Ontological Argument: A Neoclassical Theistic Response*, New York: Cambridge University Press.

Dombrowski, Daniel (2009), *Contemporary Athletics and Ancient Greek Ideals*, Chicago: University of Chicago Press.

Dombrowski, Daniel (2011), *Rawlsian Explorations in Religion and Applied Philosophy*, University Park: Pennsylvania University Press.

Dombrowski, Daniel (2016), *A History of the Concept of God: A Process Approach*, Albany: State University of New York Press.

Dombrowski, Daniel (2017), *Whitehead's Religious Thought: From Mechanism to Organism, From Force to Persuasion*, Albany: State University of New York Press.

Dostoevsky, Fyodor [1866] (1964), *Crime and Punishment*, trans. Jessie Coulson, New York: Norton.

Dreben, Burton (2003), 'On Rawls and political liberalism', in Samuel Freeman (ed.), *The Cambridge Companion to Rawls*, New York: Cambridge University Press.

Dworkin, Ronald (1977), *Taking Rights Seriously*, Cambridge, MA: Harvard University Press.

Eberle, Christopher (2002), *Religious Conviction in Liberal Politics*, New York: Cambridge University Press.

Ebertz, Roger (1993), 'Is reflective equilibrium a coherentist model?', *Canadian Journal of Philosophy*, 23: 193–214.

Farias, Victor (1989), *Heidegger and Nazism*, Philadelphia: Temple University Press.

Farin, Ingo, and Jeff Malpas (eds) (2016), *Reading Heidegger's Black Notebooks: 1931–1941*, Cambridge, MA: MIT Press.

Feuerbach, Ludwig [1841] (1957), *The Essence of Christianity*, trans. George Eliot, New York: Harper Torchbooks.

Finnis, John (1980), *Natural Law and Natural Rights*, Oxford: Clarendon Press.

Fleischacker, Samuel (2011), 'The virtues of eclecticism', *Process Studies*, 40: 232–52.

Foot, Philippa (1961), 'Goodness and choice', *Proceedings of the Aristotelian Society*, supplemental vol. 35.

Freeman, Samuel (2007a), *Justice and the Social Contract: Essays on Rawlsian Political Philosophy*, New York: Oxford University Press.

Freeman, Samuel (2007b), *Rawls*, New York: Routledge.

Fukuyama, Francis (2006), *The End of History and the Last Man*, New York: Free Press.

Gadamer, Hans-Georg (1989), 'Back from Syracuse?', *Critical Inquiry*, 15: 427–30.

Gamwell, Franklin (1984), *Beyond Preference: Liberal Theories of Independent Associations*, Chicago: University of Chicago Press.

Gamwell, Franklin (1990), *The Divine Good: Modern Moral Theory and the Necessity of God*, New York: Harper Collins.

Gamwell, Franklin (1995), *The Meaning of Religious Freedom: Modern Politics and the Democratic Revolution*, Albany: State University of New York Press.

Gamwell, Franklin (2002), *Democracy on Purpose: Justice and the Reality of God*, Washington, DC: Georgetown University Press.

Gamwell, Franklin (2005), *Politics as a Christian Vocation: Faith and Democracy Today*, New York: Cambridge University Press.

Gamwell, Franklin (2011), *Existence and the Good: Metaphysical Necessity in Morals and Politics*, Albany: State University of New York Press.

Gamwell, Franklin (2015), *Religion among We the People*, Albany: State University of New York Press.

Gamwell, Franklin (forthcoming), *On Metaphysical Necessity: Essays on Existence, Subjectivity, and God*.

Gide, André (1962), *Travels in the Congo*, trans. Dorothy Bussy, Berkeley: University of California Press.

Glendon, Mary Ann (2001), *A World Made New: Eleanor Roosevelt and the Universal Declaration of Human Rights*, New York: Random House.

Graves, Robert (1934), *I, Claudius*, New York: Harrison Smith and Robert Haas.

Griffin, David Ray (2001), *Reenchantment without Supernaturalism: A Process Philosophy of Religion*, Ithaca: Cornell University Press.

Griffin, David Ray (2007), *Whitehead's Radically Different Postmodern Philosophy*, Albany: State University of New York Press.

Griffin, Donald (1976), *The Question of Animal Awareness*, New York: Rockefeller University Press.

Habermas, Jürgen (1987), *The Philosophical Discourse of Modernity*, trans. Fred Lawrence, Cambridge, MA: MIT Press.

Habermas, Jürgen (2002), *Religion and Rationality: Essays on Reason, God, and Modernity*, Cambridge, MA: MIT Press.

Hardie, W. F. R. (1968), *Aristotle's Ethical Theory*, Oxford: Clarendon Press.

Harries, Karston (1990), 'Introduction', in *Martin Heidegger and National Socialism*, New York: Paragon House.

Hartshorne, Charles (1934), *The Philosophy and Psychology of Sensation*, Chicago: University of Chicago Press.

Hartshorne, Charles (1935), 'An economic program for religious liberalism', *The Christian Century*, 5 June: 761–2.

Hartshorne, Charles (1937), *Beyond Humanism*, Chicago: Willet, Clark, and Co.

Hartshorne, Charles (1948), *The Divine Relativity*, New Haven: Yale University Press.

Hartshorne, Charles (1953a), *Philosophers Speak of God*, Chicago: University of Chicago Press.

Hartshorne, Charles (1953b), *Reality as Social Process*, New York: Free Press.

Hartshorne, Charles (1962), *The Logic of Perfection*, LaSalle: Open Court.

Hartshorne, Charles (1970), *Creative Synthesis and Philosophic Method*, LaSalle: Open Court.

Hartshorne, Charles (1983), *Insights and Oversights of Great Thinkers*, Albany: State University of New York Press.

Hartshorne, Charles (1984a), *Creativity in American Philosophy*, Albany: State University of New York Press.

Hartshorne, Charles (1984b), *Existence and Actuality*, Chicago: University of Chicago Press.

Hartshorne, Charles (1984c), *Omnipotence and Other Theological Mistakes*, Albany: State University of New York Press.

Hartshorne, Charles (1987), *Wisdom as Moderation*, Albany: State University of New York Press.

Hartshorne, Charles (1990), *The Darkness and the Light*, Albany: State University of New York Press.

Hartshorne, Charles (1997), *The Zero Fallacy and Other Essays in Neoclassical Philosophy*, LaSalle: Open Court.

Hartshorne, Charles (2001), *Hartshorne and Brightman on God, Process, and Persons*, ed. Randall Auxier and Mark Davies, Nashville: Vanderbilt University Press.

Hartshorne, Charles (2011), *Creative Experiencing*, ed. Donald Viney and Jincheol O, Albany: State University of New York Press.

Haslett, D. W. (2013), 'Is inheritance justified?', in William Shaw and Vincent Barry (eds), *Moral Issues in Business*, 12th edn, Belmont: Wadsworth.

Heidegger, Martin [1935] (1961), *An Introduction to Metaphysics*, trans. Ralph Manheim, Garden City, NY: Anchor Books.

Heidegger, Martin [1927] (1962), *Being and Time*, trans. John Macquarrie and Edward Robinson, New York: Harper & Row.

Heidegger, Martin (1971), *Poetry, Language, Thought*, trans. Albert Hofstadter, New York: Harper & Row.

Heidegger, Martin (1976), 'Only a God can save us: *Der Spiegel*'s interview with Martin Heidegger', *Philosophy Today*, 20: 267–84.

Heidegger, Martin (1977), *Basic Writings*, trans. David Krell, New York: Harper & Row.

Heidegger, Martin [1942] (1992), *Parmenides*, trans. A. Schuwer and R. Rojcewicz, Bloomington: Indiana University Press.

Heilbron, John (1986), *The Dilemmas of an Upright Man: Max Planck*, Berkeley: University of California Press.

Henning, Brian (2005), *The Ethics of Creativity: Beauty, Morality, and Nature in a Processive Cosmos*, Pittsburgh: University of Pittsburgh Press.

Hersh, Seymour (2003), 'Selective intelligence', *The New Yorker* (12 May).

James, William [1902] (1985), *The Varieties of Religious Experience*, Cambridge, MA: Harvard University Press.

Jamieson, Dale (1998), 'Animal liberation is an environmental ethic', *Environmental Values*, 7: 41–57.

Junker-Kenny, Maureen (2014), *Religion and Public Reason*, Boston: DeGruyter.

Kearns, Madeleine (2018), 'Sir Roger Scruton on what it means to be a conservative', *National Review* (18 July).

Lacy, Allen (1989), 'Comfortable with Hitler', *New York Times Book Review* (17 December).

Lang, Berel (2002), 'Misinterpretation as the author's responsibility', in Jacob Golomb and Robert Ristrich (eds), *Nietzsche, Godfather of Fascism?*, Princeton: Princeton University Press.

Latour, Bruno (2014), 'What is the style of matters of concern?', in Nicholas Gaskill and A. J. Nocek (eds), *The Lure of Whitehead*, Minneapolis: University of Minnesota Press.

Lehning, Percy (2009), *John Rawls: An Introduction*, New York: Cambridge University Press.

Leopold, Aldo [1949] (1987), *A Sand County Almanac*, New York: Oxford University Press.

Levinas, Emmanuel (1989), 'As if consenting to horror', *Critical Inquiry*, 15: 485–8.

Lilla, Mark (1990), 'What Heidegger wrought', *Commentary* (1 January).

Locke, John [1689] (1983), *A Letter Concerning Toleration*, Indianapolis: Hackett.

Loomer, Bernard (2013), 'The size of the everlasting God', *Process Studies Supplements*, 18: 1–45.

Lucas, George (1989), *The Rehabilitation of Whitehead*, Albany: State University of New York Press.

Malone-France, Derek (2012), *Faith, Fallibility, and the Virtue of Anxiety*, New York: Palgrave Macmillan.

Mandle, Jon (2009), *Rawls's 'A Theory of Justice': An Introduction*, New York: Cambridge University Press.

Maritain, Jacques (1951), *Man and the State*, Chicago: University of Chicago Press.

Marsh, James (1999), *Process, Praxis, and Transcendence*, Albany: State University of New York Press.

Marx, Karl [1844] (1964), *The Economic and Philosophic Manuscripts of 1844*, trans. Martin Milligan, New York: International Publishers.

Marx, Karl [1843] (1970), *Critique of Hegel's Philosophy of Right*, trans.

Joseph O'Malley and Annette Jolin, Cambridge: Cambridge University Press.

Marx, Karl (1977), *Selected Writings*, trans. David McLellan, New York: Oxford University Press.

Menta, Timothy (2004), 'Clare Palmer's environmental ethics and process thinking', *Process Studies*, 33: 24–45.

Miłosz, Czeław [1996] (2005), *Legends of Modernity*, trans. Madeline Levine, New York: Farrar, Straus, and Giroux.

Milton, John [1644] (1911), *Of Education, Aeropagitica, the Commonwealth*, ed. Laura Lockwood, Boston: Houghton Mifflin.

Morris, Randall (1991), *Process Philosophy and Political Ideology*, Albany: State University of New York Press.

Moynihan, Daniel Patrick (1996), *Miles to Go: A Personal History of Social Policy*, Cambridge, MA: Harvard University Press.

Murray, John Courtney (1960), *We Hold These Truths: Catholic Reflections on the American Proposition*, New York: Sheed and Ward.

Nagel, Thomas (2003), 'Rawls and liberalism', in Samuel Freeman (ed.), *The Cambridge Companion to Rawls*, New York: Cambridge University Press.

Nozick, Robert (1974), *Anarchy, State, and Utopia*, New York: Basic Books.

Nussbaum, Martha (2006), *Frontiers of Justice: Disability, Nationality, Species Membership*, Cambridge, MA: Harvard University Press.

Ott, Hugo (1993), *Martin Heidegger: A Political Life*, trans. Allan Blunden, New York: Harper Collins.

Page, Carl (1991), 'The truth about lies in Plato's *Republic*', *Ancient Philosophy*, 11–33.

Palmer, Clare (1998), *Environmental Ethics and Process Thinking*, Oxford: Clarendon Press.

Palmer, Clare (2004), 'Response to Cobb and Menta', *Process Studies*, 33: 46–70.

Palmer, Clare (2010), *Animal Ethics in Context*, New York: Columbia University Press.

Pinker, Steven (2011), *The Better Angels of Our Nature: Why Violence Has Declined*, New York: Viking.

Pluhar, Evelyn (1995), *Beyond Prejudice: The Moral Significance of*

Human and Nonhuman Animals, Durham, NC: Duke University Press.

Pogge, Thomas (2007), *John Rawls: His Life and Theory of Justice*, Oxford: Oxford University Press.

Pöggeler, Otto (1997), *The Paths of Heidegger's Life and Thought*, Atlantic Highlands, NJ: Humanities Press.

Pomeroy, Anne Fairchild (2004), *Marx and Whitehead: Process, Dialectics, and the Critique of Capitalism*, Albany: State University of New York Press.

Rachels, James (1990), *Created from Animals: The Moral Implications of Darwinism*, New York: Oxford University Press.

Rawls, John [1993] (1996), *Political Liberalism*, New York: Columbia University Press.

Rawls, John (1999a), *Collected Papers*, ed. Samuel Freeman, Cambridge, MA: Harvard University Press.

Rawls, John (1999b), *The Law of Peoples*, Cambridge, MA: Harvard University Press.

Rawls, John [1971] (1999c), *A Theory of Justice*, revised edn, Cambridge, MA: Harvard University Press.

Rawls, John (2000), *Lectures on the History of Moral Philosophy*, ed. Barbara Herman, Cambridge, MA: Harvard University Press.

Rawls, John (2001), *Justice as Fairness: A Restatement*, ed. Erin Kelly, Cambridge, MA: Harvard University Press.

Rawls, John (2007), *Lectures on the History of Political Philosophy*, ed. Samuel Freeman, Cambridge, MA: Harvard University Press.

Rawls, John [1942] [1997] (2009), *A Brief Inquiry into the Meaning of Sin and Faith with 'On My Religion'*, ed. Thomas Nagel, Cambridge, MA: Harvard University Press.

Regan, Tom (1983), *The Case for Animal Rights*, Berkeley: University of California Press.

Rockmore, Tom (2002), *Marx after Marxism*, Oxford: Blackwell.

Rolston, Holmes (1988), *Environmental Ethics*, Philadelphia: Temple University Press.

Rorty, Richard (1999), *Philosophy and Social Hope*, New York: Penguin.

Rorty, Richard (2008), *An Ethics for Today*, New York: Columbia University Press.

Russell, Bertrand (1956), *Portraits from Memory*, New York: Simon and Schuster.

Sapontzis, Steve (1987), *Morals, Reason, and Animals*, Philadelphia: Temple University Press.

Scanlon, Thomas (2003), 'Rawls on justification', in Samuel Freeman (ed.), *The Cambridge Companion to Rawls*, New York: Cambridge University Press.

Scheler, Max (1961), *Ressentiment*, trans. Lewis Coser, New York: Free Press.

Schirmacher, Wolfgang (1983), *Technik und Gellasenheit*, Freiburg: Verlag Carl Alber.

Schweitzer, Albert (1992), *Reverence for Life*, trans. Reginald Fuller, Cooper Station, NY: Irvington Publishers.

Sheehan, Thomas (1988), 'Heidegger and the Nazis', *New York Review of Books* (16 June).

Smith, Adam [1776] (1976), *An Inquiry into the Nature and Causes of the Wealth of Nations*, Chicago: University of Chicago Press.

Smith, Adam [1759] (2002), *The Theory of Moral Sentiments*, Cambridge: Cambridge University Press.

Snyder, Timothy (2006), 'Review of *Legends of Modernity*', *The Nation* (9 January), pp. 26–9.

Snyder, Timothy (2010), *Bloodlands: Europe between Hitler and Stalin*, New York: Basic Books.

Snyder, Timothy (2017), 'Hitler's American dream', *Slate Magazine* (9 March). Online.

Stendhal (1961), *The Red and the Black*, trans. Charles Tergie, New York: Collier.

Strauss, Leo (1964), *The City and Man*, Chicago: University of Chicago Press.

Strauss, Leo [1963] (1972), *History of Political Philosophy*, Chicago: University of Chicago Press.

Strauss, Leo (1983), *Studies in Platonic Political Philosophy*, Chicago: University of Chicago Press.

Sturm, Douglas (1979), 'Process thought and political theory', *Review of Politics*, 41.3: 375–401.

Tebbe, Nelson (2017), *Religious Freedom in an Egalitarian Age*, Cambridge, MA: Harvard University Press.

Tocqueville, Alexis de [1835] (1988), *Democracy in America*, New York: Perennial Library.

Tolstoy, Leo [1869] (2008), *War and Peace*, trans. Richard Pevear and Larissa Volokhonsky, New York: Vintage.

VanDeVeer, Donald (1979), 'Of Beasts, Persons, and the Original Position', *Monist*, 62: 368–77.

Walzer, Michael [1977] (2006), *Just and Unjust Wars*, 4th edn, New York: Basic Books.

Weinberger, David (1984), 'Earth, World, and Fourfold', *Tulane Studies in Philosophy*, 32: 103–9.

Weithman, Paul (2002), *Religion and the Obligations of Citizenship*, New York: Cambridge University Press.

Weithman, Paul (2011), *Why Political Liberalism?*, New York: Oxford University Press.

Weitzman, Martin (1984), *The Share Economy*, Cambridge, MA: Harvard University Press.

Whitehead, Alfred North (1941), 'Autobiographical notes', in P. A. Schilpp (ed.), *The Philosophy of Alfred North Whitehead*, LaSalle: Open Court.

Whitehead, Alfred North (1947), *Essays on Science and Philosophy*, New York: Philosophical Library.

Whitehead, Alfred North (1954), *Dialogues of Alfred North Whitehead*, ed. Lucien Price, New York: Mentor Books.

Whitehead, Alfred North [1933] (1967a), *Adventures of Ideas*, New York: Free Press.

Whitehead, Alfred North [1925] (1967b), *Science and the Modern World*, New York: Free Press.

Whitehead, Alfred North [1938] (1968), *Modes of Thought*, New York: Free Press.

Whitehead, Alfred North [1929] (1978), *Process and Reality*, ed. David Ray Griffin and Donald Sherburne, New York: Free Press.

Whitehead, Alfred North [1927] (1985), *Symbolism*, New York: Fordham University Press.

Whitehead, Alfred North [1926] (1996), *Religion in the Making*, New York: Fordham University Press.

Wolin, Richard (1990), *The Politics of Being*, New York: Columbia University Press.

Wolterstorff, Nicholas (2008), *Justice: Rights and Wrongs*, Princeton: Princeton University Press.

Wolterstorff, Nicholas, and Robert Audi (1997), *Religion in the Public Square*, Lanham, MD: Rowman and Littlefield.

Wynne-Tyson, Jon (1985), *The Extended Circle*, London: Centaur Press.

Young, Julian (1997), *Heidegger, Philosophy, Nazism*, New York: Cambridge University Press.

Zimmerman, Michael E. (1975), 'Heidegger on nihilism and technique', *Man and World*, 8: 394–414.

Zimmerman, Michael E. (1977), 'Beyond humanism: Heidegger's understanding of technology', *Listening*, 12: 74–83.

Zimmerman, Michael E. (1979), 'Marx and Heidegger on the technological domination of nature', *Philosophy Today*, 23: 99–112.

Zimmerman, Michael E. (1983), 'Toward a Heideggerian *ethos* for radical environmentalism', *Environmental Ethics*, 5: 99–131.

Zimmerman, Michael E. (1985), 'The critique of natural rights and the search for a non-anthropocentric basis for moral behavior', *Journal of Value Inquiry*, 19: 43–53.

Zimmerman, Michael E. (1986), 'Implications of Heidegger's thought for deep ecology', *Modern Schoolman*, 64: 19–43.

Zimmerman, Michael E. (1987), 'Feminism, deep ecology, and environmental ethics', *Environmental Ethics*, 9: 21–43.

Zimmerman, Michael E. (1989), 'The thorn in Heidegger's side: the question of National Socialism', *Philosophical Forum*, 20: 326–65.

Zimmerman, Michael E. (1990), *Heidegger's Confrontation with Modernity*, Bloomington: Indiana University Press.

Zimmerman, Michael E. (1993), 'Rethinking the Heidegger–deep ecology relationship', *Environmental Ethics*, 15: 195–224.

Zimmerman, Michael E. (1994), *Contesting Earth's Future: Radical Ecology and Postmodernity*, Berkeley: University of California Press.

Žižek, Slavoj (2003), *The Puppet and the Dwarf: The Perverse Core of Christianity*, Cambridge, MA: MIT Press.

Žižek, Slavoj (2008), *In Defense of Lost Causes*, London: Verso.

Zuckert, Michael (2002), *Launching Liberalism: On Lockean Political Philosophy*, Lawrence: University Press of Kansas.

Index

EU representative:
Easy Access System Europe
Mustamäe tee 50, 10621 Tallinn, Estonia
Gpsr.requests@easproject.com

www.ingramcontent.com/pod-product-compliance
Lightning Source LLC
Chambersburg PA
CBHW071020280326
41935CB00011B/1431